TEACHING THE PRIMARY CURRICULUM

TEACHING THE PRIMARY CURRICULUM

Edited by
**Jane Johnston, Mark Chater
and Derek Bell**

Open University Press
Buckingham · Philadelphia

Open University Press
Celtic Court
22 Ballmoor
Buckingham
MK18 1XW

email: enquiries@openup.co.uk
world wide web: www.openup.co.uk

and
325 Chestnut Street
Philadelphia, PA 19106, USA

First Published 2002

A catalogue record of this book is available from the British Library

ISBN   0 335 20772 3 (pbk)   0 335 20773 1 (hbk)

Library of Congress Cataloging-in-Publication Data
Teaching the primary curriculum / [edited by] Jane Johnston,
Mark Chater, and Derek Bell.
     p. cm.
  Includes bibliographical references and index.
  ISBN 0-335-20773-1 – ISBN 0-335-20772-3 (pbk.)
     1. Education, Elementary–Great Britain–Curricula.   2. Elementary school teaching–Great Britain.   I. Johnston, Jane, 1954–   II. Chater, Mark, 1956–
III. Bell, Derek, 1950–
LB1564.G7 T435 2001
372.19′0941–dc21   2001033923

The authors have made every effort to trace the copyright holder and to obtain permission to use the cover photograph. Any claim brought to our attention will be forwarded to the authors.

Typeset by Graphicraft Limited, Hong Kong
Printed in Great Britain by St Edmundsbury Press Limited,
Bury St Edmunds, Suffolk

Contents

List of contributors

David Banks was a primary headteacher for 15 years and is now Head of the Design and Technology Centre at Bishop Grosseteste College. He is an Ofsted inspector and a member of the Schools Advisory Council of the Independent Television Commission. He has written educational material for Channel 4 Schools and the National Council for Educational Technology, and has worked on the use of television in mathematics teaching. He has been a consultant for the World Bank and UNICEF, and is presently a key consultant with the British Council responsible for a primary education project in Jordan.

Derek Bell is Vice-Principal at Bishop Grosseteste College and has extensive experience in teaching and teacher education. Throughout his career he has maintained a strong interest in the enhancement of teaching and learning, and approaches to helping children develop their understanding of the world around them. His current research interests include teaching and learning in primary schools with particular reference to children's understanding in science, and the roles of subject leaders. He has published widely in primary science and is joint author of *Towards Effective Subject Leadership in the Primary School* published by Open University Press in 1999.

Keith Bennett trained as a teacher at Goldsmith's College and has taught in both primary and secondary schools before working in initial teacher training. He joined the staff at Bishop Grosseteste College as a sociologist and has extensive experience of team work, leadership and partnership with primary schools. His specialist areas are sociology, history and science education. He has worked with the Open University as a consultant for an area health authority and is the team leader of the college's training consultancy for primary teachers in Bosnia-Herzegovina.

Sally Bentley is the subject leader for English QTS and programme leader for the BA (Hons) English literature degree at Bishop Grosseteste College, where she has worked for the past seven years. Her MA at Sheffield University was in modern literature, while her more recent MPhil from Hull University is in children's literature. She has taught English in secondary schools and has trained markers for Key Stage 1 and 2 SATs in English, mathematics and science for the NEAB.

Mark Chater is Senior Lecturer and course leader of the secondary PGCE course at Bishop Grosseteste College. Formerly he was the subject leader in religious studies and has been involved in curriculum development in primary and secondary religious education. He wrote support materials for the Scottish 5–14 programme in religious and moral education and for the MA in church school education. He has published several articles on children's and teachers' spirituality, citizenship and ethical dimensions of educational management. He is a member of the International Seminar on Religious Education and Values, and an associate editor of the *International Journal of Children's Spirituality*.

Ashley Compton is a senior lecturer at Bishop Grosseteste College, primarily on the three-year BA in primary education. Although she has a BSc in chemistry, music has always been a large part of her life and her MEd research focused on children's musical listening preferences. She trained in Canada, but most of her teaching career has occurred in Lincoln, where she has taught Years 1 through to 6 and been subject coordinator for music, ICT and mathematics. Before joining the college, Ashley worked as a mathematics advisory teacher for Lincolnshire County Council and spread the joys of numeracy across the county.

Peter Crowther is Head of Science at Bishop Grosseteste College, where he lectures in virtually all aspects of science up to degree level. Prior to this, he was an industrial chemist before becoming a teacher. For almost 20 years he gained experience in teaching science to children of all ages. He has been involved in the 'Interactive Learning in Physics Project' in the former Yugoslavian republic of Macedonia and a similar project in Bosnia-Herzegovina. His interests are centered around developing strategies for the understanding of some of the more difficult conceptual areas in science and in making scientific knowledge and understanding more available to the non-specialist.

David Fox has been involved in the development of information technology since it was first introduced into primary schools and is a member of the Lincolnshire ICT executive. His research interests, as a teacher researcher and an academic researcher, include consideration of effective teaching methods and approaches to school management that support the development of teachers' skills through the application of shared values and goals. After various posts in middle schools, he moved into higher education at Bishop Grosseteste College. In 2001 he took up an appointment as a headteacher of a primary school in Bradford.

John Halocha is currently a senior lecturer in primary education at Bishop Grosseteste College. He taught in primary and middle schools for 17 years and was deputy headteacher in two schools. He began work in initial teacher education at Westminster College, Oxford before moving to the University of Durham School of Education. His area of curriculum specialism is in the field of geographical education in primary schools. John has a broad publishing record in this field. His current research interests include investigations into the use of ICT to develop pupils' understanding of people and places.

Peter Harrod is a senior lecturer in teaching studies at Bishop Grosseteste College, where he has been a tutor for more than 30 years. He began his career as a primary school teacher, and has always been particularly interested in children's language development. He holds an MPhil from the University of Nottingham, and an MEd (with distinction) from Sheffield University. He has research interests in children's speaking and listening skills and, during his career at the college, has taught on undergraduate, PGCE, MA and MEd courses. He also served as an associate lecturer with the Open University for 22 years.

Jane Johnston is a senior lecturer in primary education at Bishop Grosseteste College. Formerly she was a primary classroom teacher with experience throughout Key Stages 1 and 2. Her particular interests in education are in primary science and early years education with research interests in the development of attitudes to science, the role of parents in educational development and values education. She is the author of several books and chapters on early years and science education, including *Early Explorations in Science* and *Enriching Early Scientific Learning*, both published by Open University Press in 1996 and 1999 respectively.

Judith Laurie has worked at the college for five years and teaches English on both undergraduate and postgraduate courses as well as leading English in-service courses for teachers. Judith has also contributed material to the National Literacy Strategy for training in shared writing for teachers and trainees. Before joining the college she had taught all ages from nursery to Key Stage 2, and from 1989 to 1991 was an advisory teacher for English in Humberside. In the two years before leaving the LEA she helped coordinate a county reading initiative designed to raise standards in reading.

Jean MacIntyre is a design historian and primary history specialist, with teaching experience in every phase from nursery to higher education. She was previously employed as a primary education coordinator for the Design Council, working with educational instititions nationwide. She has produced training programmes, educational resources and exhibitions for teachers and children and been involved in education projects for museums, galleries and organizations such as English Heritage. She has a particular interest in museums education, her MA being conducted at the Victoria and Albert Museum and the Royal College of Art. Her current research interest is in the design of interactive projects.

Harriet Marland taught in secondary, middle and primary schools before joining Bishop Grosseteste College as a senior lecturer in primary education. She has worked extensively with the Mathematical Association and contributed to a number of publications including *Sharing Mathematics with Parents* (1987), *Develop your Teaching* (1991), *The Teachers' Challenge* (1991) and *A First Resort: Mental Methods in Mathematics* (1992).

Sally Newton is a senior lecturer in teaching studies at Bishop Grosseteste College and specializes in physical education. She has worked as a primary teacher, humanities coordinator, PE coordinator and a lecturer in further education, where she taught A level National Diploma and Higher National Diploma, specializing in the sociological, psychological and biological aspects of sport. Before joining Bishop Grosseteste College, Sally was an advisory teacher in outdoor education, where she worked as part of the PSHE section of the advisory service. She has interests in outdoor education and is studying an MA in international sport law.

Ruth Sayers is a senior lecturer in drama and a programme leader for the BA (Hons) Drama in the Community course at Bishop Grosseteste College. She has previously been head of an arts faculty in a large comprehensive and has worked for the dance and drama support service in Nottinghamshire. Ruth has been a youth theatre leader, an

A level examiner and has served on the Executive Committee of National Drama.

Kathleen Taylor is a qualified infant teacher working in initial teacher education where she is leader of the three-year BA in Primary Education at Bishop Grosseteste College. Her master's dissertation was on narrative and the young child. Her published works include design and technology materials written in collaboration with industry and a series of literacy hours and literacy homework hours. She has recently co-written, for the Teacher Training Agency, kite-marked materials for English. She has undertaken educational consultancies in the former Yugoslavian republic of Macedonia, Pakistan and Bosnia-Herzegovina.

Christine Watson has taught in primary, secondary and special schools. Prior to working at Bishop Grosseteste College, she was an LEA adviser having responsibility for special needs and the more able. At Bishop Grosseteste College she was a principal lecturer in education, course leader for the four-year ITT course and course director for the certificate/diploma in special educational needs. She is currently working as a curriculum innovation and learning manager on a New Deal for Communities project in the city of Hull. Her main areas of interest are behaviour management and self-esteem and she is involved in the European 'Erasmus' project looking at how to train the inclusive teacher.

Foreword

To say that the last two decades have seen significant change in English (and Scottish, Welsh and Irish, but chiefly English) primary education is to invite a hollow laugh at the extent of the understatement. Teachers, those who educate and train them and above all pupils and their parents, inhabit a radically different educational environment from that of the early 1980s. This book is a response to this change.

Since before the introduction of the UK's first National Curriculum in 1988 and during the welter of debate, disagreement, correspondence, conferences and training which preceded and followed it, primary practitioners have been involved in creating and responding to a revolution. Implementing new educational initiatives has become a way of life. At the same time a crisis has been developing in teacher morale and there has been a decline in their status and influence. The restoration of both depends on teachers' dedicated pursuit of pupils' educational entitlement and policy makers' recognition of teachers' expert contribution to progress and high standards. Everyone involved bears a responsibility for what happens next.

Responsibility is the unifying theme of this book, and is evident in advice on the implementation of the National Literacy and Numeracy Strategies, in the explicit treatment of spirituality and morality in secular education and in many other ways besides. The editors' responsibilities have included compiling a compendium which addresses the subject areas identified by the National Curriculum, but the contributions range far beyond this in their exploration of what constitutes sound, sustainable learning and teaching in the fundamental phase of formal education.

Teachers have achieved a great deal since 1980 and most are committed to achieving more. The motivation for this volume is the sharing of experience and expertise in that highest of aspirations – the fulfilment of the potential of the young.

Professor Eileen Baker
Principal
Bishop Grosseteste College

Acknowledgements

The editors would like to thank current and former colleagues, students and teachers in schools, whose interactions with us have facilitated reflection on primary education practice and policy. Particular thanks go to all the contributors (named and unnamed) who have been involved in this publication.

List of abbreviations

AD/HD	attention deficit/hyperactivity disorder
DATA	Design and Technology Association
HMI	Her Majesty's Inspectorate of Schools
ICT	information and communication technology
ITT	initial teacher training
LEA	local education authority
NCC	National Curriculum Council
NEAB	Northern Examination and Assessment Board
NFER	National Foundation for Educational Research
NGfL	National Grid for Learning
NLS	National Literacy Strategy
NNS	National Numeracy Strategy
NQT	newly-qualified teacher
Ofsted	Office for Standards in Education
PE	physical education
PGCE	Postgraduate Certificate of Education
PSHE	personal, social and health education
QCA	Qualifications and Curriculum Authority
QTS	qualified teacher status
RE	religious education
SACRE	standing advisory council on religious education
SAT	Standard Assessment Task
SCAA	Schools Council and Assessment Authority
SEN	special educational needs
SMSCD	spiritual, moral, social and cultural development
UNICEF	United Nations Children's Fund

Part 1

Contexts and current issues

The changing face of teaching and learning

Jane Johnston

This chapter provides an overview of the recent history of primary education, looking particularly at the changes in primary education over the past ten years. These include:

- the introduction of and subsequent changes to the National Curriculum;
- changes in expectations and emphasis within the curriculum (e.g. literacy and numeracy);
- challenges to existing teaching methodologies and practice.

The chapter also provides a brief introduction to the book, with rationale, aims and suggestions for use by schools and teachers.

The end of the last century saw some significant developments in primary education. Some of these were due to legislative changes within the educational system, while others were due to changes in public and professional opinion, or were the effect of legislation. The 1988 Education Reform Act began the process of educational development with the introduction of the National Curriculum for all children of compulsory school age. Subsequent changes to the National Curriculum, the introduction and development of a curriculum for early years children, and the introduction of the National Literacy Strategy (NLS) and National Numeracy Strategy (NNS) (DfEE 1998, 1999a) have all had an effect on the curriculum. National testing at the end of each key stage, appraisal of teachers and the inspection of schools have all had an effect on teaching. All these changes together with greater understanding of children and how they learn have had an effect on the learning of children.

Curricular changes have raised the educational profile nationally and encouraged the expectation that all children of compulsory school age should have equal access to a quality curriculum. The National Curriculum, with all its changes, placed (and still places) an emphasis on knowledge. The role of understanding, skills, attitudes and the application of knowledge and skills in real life situations can be lost when we are overwhelmed by the amount of knowledge in the National Curriculum (DfEE 1999b). On the positive side, a focus on learning objectives has helped teachers be more explicit about what they want children to learn, and better assessment has led to better understanding of how children learn and how we can support learning and raise standards.

Assessment has become a very important part of the education process, and again emphasizes knowledge. End of key stage assessments do not formally assess attitudes, skills or, in many cases, even understanding, and so knowledge is considered to be the main learning objective. In a content-heavy curriculum, it is easy to understand why a teacher teaches knowledge in a methodical way without consideration of the development of other aspects of learning. The development of the National Curriculum can be thought to belittle generic learning and social skills such as observation, analysis and working together. These skills are not assessed, but their development can have a profound effect on learning. In the same way, moral, social, emotional and cultural development have an impact on learning. It is interesting to note that details of moral and ethical issues were removed from the science curriculum in 1995, possibly in an attempt to cut down the curriculum content. This did not go uncontested (Johnston 1995), but some years later we were told that education lacked a moral and ethical dimension and the theme of citizenship was added to the curriculum. This change is illustrative of a curriculum-focused education system, rather than a child-centered education system.

Traditionally, a child-centered approach has been felt to be the distinctive element – the heart – of primary education in the UK. It is, however, also thought to be at the root of criticism levelled at teachers and learning in primary schools (Cullingford 1997). It is this criticism, in part, which has led to a curriculum, rather than a child-focused system. Many groups and individuals outside and within education have been suspicious of the model of teaching and learning which puts the child at its centre (Alexander *et al.* 1992). Other groups, mainly from within education, have kept the focus on the child with a particular emphasis on how the child learns. As our education system becomes more curriculum focused, the emphasis moves increasingly to how teachers teach and how children are taught. There are potential problems with both perspectives. It is possible that, whereas a curriculum-centred approach is seen as inflexible, a more child-centred approach is seen as so flexible that it is in fact unworkable! We can ask ourselves whether we have moved too far towards the curriculum-centred approach and need to refocus the child in the middle of the educational debate, while still retaining the emphasis on teaching as well as learning.

The introduction of the NLS and NNS (DfEE 1998, 1999a) has led to whole-class teaching becoming more common in some subjects than group and individual work. Success in literacy and numeracy appears to support opinions that thematic teaching is not effective (Alexander *et al.* 1992), but an alternative explanation could be that teaching through topic work is less successful as the result of the increasingly diverse, and for many children, irrelevant curriculum. Another effect of whole-class Literacy and Numeracy Hours is that other curricular subjects are time-tabled later in the day (when children are not at their most receptive) and have reduced hours spent on them. A national survey on the effect of the NLS on the teaching of science (ASE 1999) brought about media coverage (*TES* 1999) which claimed that science had been 'sacrificed on the alter of literacy'.

If large parts of the school morning are used in whole-class literacy and numeracy lessons, school facilities such as the hall may not be effectively utilized, and specialized equipment, such as the overhead projector, may be in great demand. Practical subjects, such as design technology, science and art are all difficult to teach as a whole class and the result can be transmission of knowledge which is quickly forgotten, rather than experiential development of skills which can be used in later life. In such a situation how much actual learning takes place? Consider a whole-class art lesson involving 30 Year 1 children on mixing paints. The lesson began for the teacher throughout the lunch hour when the resources were prepared. When the children arrived a whole-class introduction took place which involved discussion about colour mixing. This took approximately 30 minutes. Then the rather restless children moved on to the practical part of the lesson. Within 15 minutes, there was a mess and a great deal of noise and children were walking around the classroom with painted paper, hands, etc. The remainder of the lesson (45 minutes) was spent clearing up and in looking at the results of the practical work as a whole class plenary. How much time was spent on 'real' learning?

This example can also be used to explore the role of the teacher and the learner. In this case learning about mixing colours was viewed mainly as the acquisition of factual knowledge. Teaching involved a methodology to ensure learning, a methodology given to teachers as part of training in the NLS. There was a whole-class introduction, then some individual work, and finally a whole-class plenary session to share experiences. This methodology suggests that the role of the teacher is to impart knowledge or to 'train'. This is a view which is emphasized in recent curricular changes and is in contrast to the child-centered education of the 1960s and 1970s. The view of a teacher as an imparter of knowledge implies that teachers are actually *able* to impart knowledge. The contrasting view is that learning is concerned with the construction of understandings, skills and attitudes; it is a meeting or interaction of cognition, conation and affectation (Johnston 1996). In this view, teaching is a flexible process which considers the learner's previous understandings and attempts to develop, modify or challenge understandings, skills or attitudes. In this view the role of the teacher is also considerably different; teachers are viewed as facilitators of learning – as educators. Education is concerned with providing 'learners with the basis for understanding why and how new knowledge is related to what they already know and give[ing] them the affective assurance that they have the capability to use this knowledge in new contexts' (Novak and Gowin 1984: xi).

The role of the teacher can also be said to be part of a learning partnership between the child, other children, the teacher and other adults involved with the learning process. This partnership is one where all parties are actively engaged in learning and interaction. Interaction is the key word: interaction between pupil and teacher, pupil and other pupils, pupil and other adults, with learners constructing ideas as a result of experiences (Von Glaserfeld 1995). In this model the role of the teacher is a complex one involving interaction with the individuals involved in the learning partnership and with the cognitive, conative and affective dimensions. However, this view of teaching and learning is not always supported by our education system and particularly not by assessment methods of learning.

Another effect of the National Curriculum has been on educational and curricular diversity across the UK. Since the introduction of key stages and testing at the end of them, school organization has changed, for curricular rather than educational reasons. Vertical grouping of children, where more than one year group is placed in one class, has become rarer, as has the first, middle and upper school system. Horizontal groupings, where classes are grouped according to year groups are now the norm. In the primary school, this has put a strain on teachers of Year 2 and Year 6 classes as they abandon progressive learning for understanding so as to focus on revision of knowledge to improve test results.

Once the educational system moved away from the child towards the curriculum, it became easier to make significant changes to teaching and learning for fiscal and pragmatic reasons, rather than educational reasons. Many educational changes have been dictated by financial concerns. These have been exacerbated since the early 1990s. Class sizes have increased and small schools have closed or merged as educationalists attempt to run schools as profit-making businesses rather than services. The move away from vertical grouping of children and integrated teaching of the curriculum towards horizontal grouping of children and subject teaching of the curriculum is an example of apparent change for both pragmatic and educational reasons. Vertical grouping was a common feature in many Key Stage 1 and some Key Stage 2 classrooms and was seen as a sound educational policy, enabling children to progress within the security of one class. At the present time, it is often seen as a historical oddity, occurring only where class numbers dictate. This change occurred mainly because it was pragmatically difficult to organize a rigid curriculum for a year group and end of key stage assessments with a vertically grouped class. Educationally, single year groups are more viable and help to facilitate teaching and learning in literacy and numeracy. The other side of the educational argument is that children have been taught successfully in vertically grouped classes for many years. This system has nurtured the individual child rather than expecting children to conform to a supposed norm of maturity and achievement.

Rigid, subject-curricular assessment and inspection of subject teaching discourages an integrated approach, and yet there are good educational and pragmatic reasons why such an approach might be considered. Educationally, integrating subject teaching can help children to relate subjects to real life and to each other, seeing the relevance of learning to everyday life. It is essential that learning objectives in each subject are clearly identified and their achievement planned, but this is essential in subject and integrated teaching alike. Pragmatically, an integrated approach will support the coverage of subject areas. For example, in making a musical instrument which produces a range of notes, children can be developing learning in design technology, science and music. In technology, children will be engaged in the design, production and evaluation of the instrument. In science, they can be developing understanding of how to change the pitch of vibrating objects. In music, they can be developing performing skills, controlling sounds through playing their instrument.

There are changes in teaching and learning that appear to have resulted from both pragmatic and educational reasoning. The 'setting' of primary-school children, common at the present time throughout primary education, supports the differentiation of learning and planning to meet children's needs and abilities. Care does have to be taken that the criteria for setting are identified for subject reasons, so that setting in history or science is not made on the basis of ability in literacy. In a modern primary school, teachers may teach to their strengths and plan and teach collaboratively. This can be a positive trend, encouraging staff development and the sharing of expertise and workload. But whatever the reason for change, the overall effect has been to increase the complexity of teaching and learning. In addition, public and professional opinions are increasingly important in a society that expects quality outcomes and demands accountability. The media, politicians and parents are all vocal in identifying curricular needs and expected learning outcomes. The increasing accountability of teachers and the increased role of society in the management of schools is a double-edged sword; it involves society fully in the important task of educating itself, but it appears to devalue professional educators and can lead to teacher vulnerability and stress. In part, the stress is caused by the move away from education as a service towards education as a quality product in a consumers' world.

The intervention, initiatives and accountability described above, create some confusion as to what our purpose in education is. Are we attempting to develop well-rounded individuals who can take an informed place in society, or are we improving the average levels of attainment in tests of knowledge? As Cullingford (1997: 12) says, 'children go on learning and teachers teaching, but the sense we are left with is that this is increasingly in spite of, not because of, outside interference'. It may well be that the emphasis on raising standards in education is not a result of falling standards, but of *changing* standards – or as Mortimore (2000) has suggested, a result of standards not being *good enough* for today's world. The confusion develops further as emphases change. Just as the emphasis on morals and ethics changed over a short period of time, from 1995 to 2000, so too has the emphasis on play as a factor supporting learning and development. The early years of curricular change saw play, both structured and unstructured, become less frequently observed. Inspection (Ofsted 2000) focused on specific areas of learning has identified a lack of variety in teaching and learning methods and has set targets relating to the development of a more structured learning environment for the under 5s. This may be because the outcome of play is difficult to ascertain (as is work without a written or drawn product), and can therefore be undervalued. At the same time, the introduction of the Foundation Stage of learning (DfEE/QCA 2000) appears to contradict inspection advice by placing an emphasis on play, stressing its importance in the development of learning in the early years.

There are many factors and issues which play a part in discussion or writing on primary education today. In focusing on teaching and learning in this book, we need to keep the educational context in mind. The following chapters have all been written by teachers who have considerable experience in primary education. They have a depth of understanding of young children and their development, as well as curriculum knowledge and expertise. Their collective educational philosophy is one which emphasizes the importance of high-quality teaching and learning, characterized by challenging and enjoyable experiences.

Throughout this volume the aim is to identify the features of good teaching and learning and to provide support for teachers. The focus will be on proven effectiveness and good practice, through case study exemplars of effective methodologies in action to support the raising of educational standards in primary education.

Throughout the book there are a number of key emphases. The importance of *interaction* in developing understanding has been stressed for some time (Rowland 1981; DfEE 1998) and is the basis of many teaching methodologies. The authors of this book believe that effective learning does not occur through a transmission model of teaching but through an interactive model, where the teacher facilitates learning and the child constructs meaning from experiences. Interaction involves all those included in the partnership of learning: children, teachers, teaching assistants, parents, family members and the wider community – all of whom share the experiences of teaching and learning. Interaction is therefore an important feature of this book and the chapters describe different types of quality interaction, providing examples of effective practice in the primary classroom.

Preferred and effective teaching and learning styles differ between individual learners and teachers. It is important to be aware of differing *preferences* (Johnston 1996) and to broaden these so that children are able to learn in a variety of contexts and in a variety of ways. Throughout this book the changing role of the teacher in different teaching contexts will be examined and opportunities for cooperation, collaboration and creativity identified. The importance of the teacher as a critical reflective practitioner will also be emphasized. The book also focuses on the *child* as the central, pivotal point of teaching and learning. The authors feel strongly that the learning interests of the child should be at the forefront of educational debate.

The structure is designed to take the reader through the primary curriculum, looking at permeating issues and themes affecting the whole curriculum, before focusing more directly on the core and foundation curriculum areas. Readers may wish to focus on specific chapters or look at the book as a whole. There is a collective philosophy underpinning the book, but each chapter reflects the individual nature of the subject and the authors.

References

Alexander, R., Rose, J. and Woodhead C. (1992) *Curriculum Organisation and Classroom Practice in Primary Schools: A Discussion Paper*. London: DES.

ASE (Association for Science Education) (1999) *ASE Survey on the Effect of the National Literacy Strategy on the Teaching of Science.* Hatfield: ASE.

Cullingford, C. (1997) Changes in primary education, in C. Cullingford (ed.) *The Politics of Primary Education.* Buckingham: Open University Press.

DfEE (Department for Education and Employment) (1998) *The National Literacy Strategy.* London: DfEE.

DfEE (Department for Education and Employment) (1999a) *The National Numeracy Strategy.* London: DfEE.

DfEE (Department for Education and Employment) (1999b) *The National Curriculum: Handbook for Primary Teachers in England.* London: QCA.

DfEE/QCA (Department for Education and Employment/Qualifications and Curriculum Authority) (2000) *Curriculum Guidance for the Foundation Stage.* London: DfEE.

Johnston, C. (1996) *Unlocking the Will to Learn.* London: Sage.

Johnston, J. (1995) Morals and ethics in science education: where have they gone? *Education in Science,* 163: 20–1.

Mortimore, P. (2000) Does educational research matter?, *British Educational Research Journal,* 26(1): 5–24.

Novak, J.D. and Gowin, D.B. (1984) *Learning How to Learn.* Cambridge: Cambridge University Press.

Ofsted (Office for Standards in Education) (2000) *The Annual Report of Her Majesty's Chief Inspector of Schools.* London: DfEE.

Rowland, S. (1981) *The Enquiring Classroom: An Approach to Understanding Children's Learning.* London: Falmer Press.

TES (*Times Educational Supplement*) (1999) Science sacrificed on the altar of literacy, *Times Educational Supplement,* 25 June.

Von Glaserfeld, E. (1995) *Radical Constructivism: A Way of Knowing and Learning.* London: Falmer Press.

2

Curriculum entitlement and individual differences

Christine Watson

Introduction

A key question frequently raised by teachers is 'How do we provide access to the curriculum for children with a wide range of individual needs?' This question becomes even more important in a context of rapid curriculum change. Teachers often respond with the magic word 'differentiation', but the theory is not always easily translated into action. With the requirement for inclusion, the question of curriculum access for all is constantly to the fore. In this chapter, consideration will be given to what 'inclusion' means in practical terms and to what can be done in the primary classroom to ensure access to all areas of the curriculum for all children. The individual needs considered will cover the wide spectrum of differences brought together under the umbrella title of special educational needs (SEN), as identified within legislation. In addition, more able children will also be considered because their individual needs, while not being acknowledged as 'special' in legislative terms, raise significant questions in relation to curriculum entitlement.

The road to inclusion

To understand the significance of the idea of inclusion we must refer back to the Warnock Report (DES 1978) and the subsequent Education Act of 1981 (DES 1981). The recognition of and response to individual differences triggered a move away from categories of disability (e.g. blind, deaf, educationally subnormal, etc.) towards making educational provision based on a child's individual needs, with the expectation that wherever possible all children should be educated within the mainstream provision. In addition, staged procedures were introduced to ensure that individual needs were recognized and assessed as early as possible, and appropriate provision was made to meet these individual needs. This vision of integration was widely supported but practical implementation was varied (Hegarty *et al.* 1982; Booth and Potts 1983; Fish 1985; Dessent 1987), and remains so today. One important factor frequently impeding successful integration was the fact that the curriculum offered in segregated provision was often more developmental in style, addressing personal and social skills before any subject area coverage. To make provision more consistent in quality, the advisory *Code of Practice* (DfE 1994) formed the basis from which all special needs provision has since been maintained.

In 1998 the government introduced a programme of action in response to its consultative document *Excellence for all Children: Meeting Special Educational Needs* (DfEE 1997a). The document was an extension of the government White Paper *Excellence in Schools* (DfEE 1997b), identifying expectations and strategies for school improvement particularly in relation to raising standards in literacy and numeracy. It was in the programme of action that the term 'inclusion' came to be used in place of the earlier term of 'integration'. The reasoning behind the change in terminology was that 'integration' implied that children with specific individual needs had to 'fit into' an existing provision, whereas with 'inclusion' the expectation would be that planning and overall provision would take into account all the possible individual needs that children might present.

The programme of action has further influenced practice and policy. At the time of writing the revised *Code of Practice*, which takes into account the intentions of the programme of action, is out for consultation. In addition, a new advisory document *SEN Thresholds: Good Practice Guidance in Decision-making on Identification and Provision for Pupils with Special Educational Needs* (DfEE 2000a) is being considered. This suggests action at various levels of need and identifies possible aspects of differentiation that can be deployed. Case studies are provided to exemplify some of the suggestions in practice.

A question of curriculum

The Education Reform Act of 1988 and the introduction of the National Curriculum were the key to addressing the curricular variance when considering integration, with the Act clearly stating that all children were entitled to receive a broad and balanced curriculum whether they were receiving segregated or integrated provision. While there was general support for the underlying philosophy of the intentions, there were several issues that emerged initially:

- How appropriate was the content of the National Curriculum for all children, particularly for those with more severe and complex needs?
- Where would there be time within the demands of the National Curriculum for the developmental aspects of the curriculum required by many pupils with SEN?
- If integration became more widespread as a result of the common curriculum, how would mainstream teachers be supported to provide access to the curriculum for the wider range of individual needs present in the classroom?

Options were included in the Act to address the first two issues including the use of 'disapplication' where individual children could be exempt from parts of the National Curriculum. However, this was viewed by many teachers as contrary to the spirit of entitlement and the emphasis moved onto how access to all parts of the curriculum could be made possible for all children whatever their individual needs. A review of the National Curriculum in 1993, led by Sir Ron Dearing (1993), resulted in additional advice being added to the revised documentation, encouraging teachers to pay particular attention to providing access to the curriculum for pupils with SEN. Teachers were also given the discretion to teach pupils material from earlier stages in the curriculum (or later in the case of more able pupils) without having to undertake formal modification or disapplication procedures.

Many researchers considered the issue of access to the curriculum (e.g. Booth *et al.* 1992; Bovair *et al.* 1992; Rose *et al.* 1994) and concerns were well expressed by Norwich (1989: 94), when he stated:

> There must be many, who like me, are watching the gradual implementation of the Education Reform Act with increasing bewilderment and wondering how it will work. How will the principle that there should be maximum participation in the National Curriculum by all children, and minimal use of the statutory exceptions be reconciled with the practical realities of operating a new curricular framework?

Recent curriculum development in relation to the National Literacy Strategy (NLS) and National Numeracy Strategy (NNS) has continued to raise concerns for teachers as to how access can be ensured for the pupils with increasingly complex SEN who are being included within the mainstream classroom.

How can entitlement and access be ensured?

Although specific reference has so far been made to pupils with *special* educational needs, my experience has led me to believe that the most effective way of addressing provision is to consider *all* children as having *individual* needs and to match teaching to learning ability accordingly. In simplest terms this can be seen as a working definition of that 'magic' solution *differentiation*, but I feel it is worth considering the underlying principles that should be addressed in relation to curriculum access for all children before specific examples of provision for pupils with SEN are considered.

Sebba *et al.* (1993) consider the importance of the 'whole' curriculum for pupils with SEN. They propose that effective learning experiences for pupils with identified difficulties should combine achievement in the National Curriculum with progress in relation to personal and social development. Byers (1994) supports this, but goes further by identifying what he describes as 'established and familiar strategies employed by staff in schools for pupils with learning difficulties' (p. 108) in order to bring about an appropriate balance of learning within the whole curriculum.

The strategies identified are:

- pupils are involved;
- pupils are cued into the activity;
- the whole pupil is engaged;
- any performance criteria are shared;
- tasks are relevant to the context in which they occur;
- the learning experience is coherent, relevant, purposeful and meaningful;
- tasks are clearly identified;
- planning takes account of existing skills, interests, aptitudes and experiences;
- learning is interactive – there is dialogue;
- there is pupil initiation, exploration and problem solving;
- learning activities are intrinsically motivating;
- there is pupil self-evaluation.

It would seem from this that the approaches employed by experienced SEN teachers are no different from the strategies used by most teachers in relation to accessing learning for all children. This suggests that there should be no difficulty in ensuring access for pupils with SEN in the mainstream classroom. I can almost hear the cries of 'If only it were that simple!!', but it has to be accepted that the majority of pupils with a wide range of complex needs are being educated successfully within mainstream classrooms. They are receiving full entitlement to a broad and balanced curriculum, as demanded by the 1988 Education Act, and teachers are being imaginative and skilful in ensuring access for all children. The question is, how are they doing it? The following sections discuss some examples relating to differing types of disability and consequent special needs.

Physical and sensory impairment

One particularly successful aspect of curriculum access is that of address-ing the needs of pupils with physical and sensory disabilities, particu-larly when the pupils do not have associated learning difficulties. Access to the curriculum for pupils with visual impairment usually involves the adaptation of materials or classroom organization. For children who are partially sighted this can include such strategies as:

- consideration of seating position;
- appropriate lighting conditions (this does not always mean *more* light – for example, children with albinism need *protection* from light);
- the use of bold, clear text, particularly in the shared text work of the Literacy Hour;
- adapted print (not always enlarged, as children with tunnel vision often require reduced-size print);
- use of appropriate background colours, chalk, marker pens, etc. for clarity;
- use of low-vision aids (magnifying glasses);
- use of raised desks/workboards;
- use of information and communication technology (ICT) facilities;
- vocalizing when writing information on the board;
- recognizing that non-verbal communication may not be picked up.

For children who are designated as blind:

- reading material will need to be tactile (e.g. Braille) and illustrations will need to be raised;
- other tactile resources will need to be available (e.g. globes, rulers, etc.);
- in the Literacy Hour, 'real' objects will help to illustrate the story;
- there may be teaching assistant support available;

- ICT facilities can be used (e.g. talking programs; tape recorders; Braille and print machines attached to the computer);
- tactile display can be used.

One primary school I visited, where there were a significant number of pupils with visual impairment, had created a completely tactile display down the length of the corridor related to literacy work involving the story *The Very Hungry Caterpillar* (Carle 1970). Using such resources as tissue paper, newspaper, ping-pong balls and cut-out sponges, the story was told in three dimensions and all labels were in both printed text and Braille, enabling access for both sighted and non-sighted pupils.

A range of strategies can be deployed with children with hearing impairment, depending on the severity of the impairment:

- improve the acoustics (e.g. use curtains, carpets, enclosed areas);
- consider seating arrangements;
- check hearing-aids regularly (more cunning children can switch them off!);
- use visual signals to cue attention;
- try to write on the board from the side rather than with your back to the class;
- use symbolic representation to indicate meaning (this could be linked to signing if total communication is in use).

One strategy I saw used with a Year 2 class was to have the desks arranged in a horseshoe shape. Each child had been given a small flag (the sort you use to put in sandcastles). When a child began to speak, they waved their flag to draw the deaf child's attention.

Initial considerations of access for pupils with physical impairment can often involve adaptations to the actual structure of the building. In relation to the curriculum, access can frequently involve ICT usage. Various pieces of hardware (e.g. touch screens, pointers attached to mobile parts of the body, speech units) can be employed and, depending on the severity of the disability, teaching assistants can be used to aid mobility. Activities such as field trips need to be planned to ensure arrangements take mobility needs into account. It can be easy to over-compensate for physical disability. In my Year 6 class, I had a pupil who was a wheelchair user. We had a visit from a former Yorkshire cricketer, to encourage the pupils to take part in short cricket. Despite frantic non-verbal signals from me, he let the pupil bat first. Half an hour later she was still 'at the crease' and intending to stay there. Our visitor soon realized that it is very difficult to bowl somebody out with a wheelchair in front of the stumps!

Safety aspects related to curriculum areas such as physical education (PE), science and design technology are usually overcome through the appropriate use of additional classroom support, or by pairing/grouping children for support.

Children with learning and behavioural difficulties

These two categories of special need combine to present the greatest issues for the mainstream primary teacher in relation to curriculum access. One key difficulty is the 'chicken and egg' syndrome where it is often problematic to identify whether it is a behavioural difficulty that is impeding the learning process or a learning difficulty that is causing a behavioural difficulty.

Within their short-term planning, most teachers are regularly differentiating to take into account the range of ability in their class, identifying additional support or extension for individuals at the extremes of the range. One of the issues related to this aspect of differentiation is that consideration is predominantly given to the teaching perspective rather than the learning perspective. This is often led by the teacher's perceived need to fit children into the curriculum that has to be delivered (this being a particular issue in relation to the prescribed, structured approach of the Literacy Hour), rather than responding to the individual needs of any pupil. A particular example of this is where the content of direct instruction during the initial whole-class input is at a level way above the learning ability of some individual children. Where teachers feel unable to offer alternative approaches (such as withdrawal to work with additional support) many of these children effectively lose valuable learning time. Work by Hart (1996), based on research in the mainstream classroom, has considered an analytical framework for matching teaching approaches to pupils' learning needs. Tilstone *et al.* (1998) describe Hart's approach as advocating positive intervention so that teachers look for, and address, any deficiencies in a pupil's functioning, any elements missed through prior experiences, or any restricting factors in the learning environment. As Tilstone *et al.* (1998: 35) report, Hart's approach has been triggered by her concerns that: 'The substitution of different and less demanding tasks which appear to have pupil occupation as a primary objective, and remove him or her from the activities being undertaken by others in the class, denies the pupil a right of access to the curriculum'.

In the light of Hart's concerns it is interesting to look at the range of approaches being employed, particularly in relation to the Literacy Hour. Some of the strategies I have observed during my time in schools include:

- mixed-age pupils in the same Literacy Hour grouped according to ability (often referred to as 'setting');
- children withdrawn on an individual basis for various parts of the Literacy Hour and supported by a range of additional classroom helpers or external support services;
- children with SEN having a parallel Literacy Hour to the rest of the class with content pitched at an appropriate ability level rather than the prescribed content within the Literacy Strategy.

The frequently occurring strategy of setting has been considered in the training pack *Supporting Pupils with Special Educational Needs in the Literacy Hour* (DfEE 2000b). Sheet M2, Handout 7, summarizes findings from research by the Office for Standards in Education (Ofsted) (1998) and Sukhnandon and Lee (1998) for the National Foundation for Educational Research (NFER). While the Ofsted findings identified the fact that teachers believe setting to be good in its support of the lowest achievers, the NFER research suggested that setting might reinforce existing social divisions and further reinforce the lack of self-esteem felt by pupils with learning difficulties.

In practical terms, a large number of books and publications, including journals such as *Special Children* and *Special* regularly include a range of well-produced classroom resources. The DfEE training pack identified in the previous paragraph contains a valuable appendix identifying further suggestions for strategies to include pupils with SEN in the Literacy Hour. It would appear, however, to be important that teachers view all suggested strategies and approaches to supporting pupils with special needs with Hart's research findings in mind so that the intentions of 'inclusion' and 'entitlement' can be maintained.

There has been an increasing number of children identified as having specific learning difficulties, raising issues of access across all curriculum areas. These difficulties are often referred to as 'dyslexia' when related to language, this being based on the literal interpretation of the Greek '*dys*' meaning 'difficulty with' and '*lexis*' meaning 'words'. Much work, in relation to the identification of specific learning difficulties in the classroom and in terms of curriculum access, has been effectively carried out by researchers such as Miles and Miles (1990), Pumphrey and Reason (1991) and Pollock and Waller (1994). One key strategy that is regularly promoted is that employing a multi-sensory approach such as *The Hickey Multi-Sensory Language Course* (Augur and Briggs 1992) or the *Alpha to Omega* programme as developed by Hornsby and Shear (1977). Specific work by Chinn and Ashcroft (1993) has particularly considered curriculum access in relation to mathematics and it has been identified that the multi-sensory approach employed in response to language difficulties can also be successful when used to address specific learning difficulties related to number. Pollock and Waller (1994: 6) demonstrate a realistic understanding when they state, 'Class teachers and subject teachers cannot be expected to give enough individual attention to any one pupil experiencing difficulties, but recognition of the learning difficulty and support in the form of learning strategies can do much for the confidence of a dyslexic child in class'.

The issues related to curriculum access for pupils with behavioural difficulties and associated emotional problems are growing, with increasing numbers of pupils identified as being on the autistic spectrum or as having attention deficit/hyperactivity disorder (AD/HD) being included in the mainstream classroom. While supervising students on a recent school placement in one local education authority (LEA), over half of the classes I visited contained pupils identified as having autistic tendencies or AD/HD. Curriculum access in these cases depended on effective classroom management and particularly the use of additional classroom support. Individuals were frequently removed when disruptive behaviour occurred and these personal observations reinforce the concerns stated by Hart (1996) in relation to curriculum entitlement. Research identified in the DfEE training pack mentioned earlier raised a pertinent point in warning the teacher against the temptation of putting all the pupils identified as having special educational needs in the bottom set regardless of their actual needs.

Schools employ a wide range of strategies to manage the behaviour of pupils in order that curriculum access and entitlement can be maintained. Many schools describe their approach as 'assertive discipline', an idea promoted by Bill Rogers (1994) and by Lee Canter (1992).

More able children

Meeting the needs of more able pupils has been an area of educational concern for many years. One key difficulty lies in the fact that there is very little legislation related to provision for these pupils and, as indicated at the start of the chapter, they are not considered as having SEN. The DfE (1993) did recognize that children with exceptional abilities need to be catered for in the National Curriculum. There are more able individuals in all primary classrooms and the majority can be well provided for through the usual extension strategies planned for within differentiation. The pupils who seem to miss out are those often referred to as 'gifted'. The definition I frequently use to identify the gifted child is one presented by Belle Wallace (1983: 11) when she describes the individual concerned as 'a child who has outstanding potential or ability in any one area or in several areas so that s/he needs more than the teacher usually provides in the way of extension activities and resources'. It is her reference to 'more than the teacher usually provides' that I feel clearly places the gifted child within the area of special need provision.

There have been three main approaches to supporting more able pupils. As with special needs provision, one of the options has been 'segregation' where pupils have been educated in separate schools, particularly where the gifted area has been related to the performing arts. Given the emphasis on inclusion it could be argued that, as with children with special needs, this sort of provision is no longer viewed positively. A second approach has been 'acceleration' where the child is educated alongside others with a similar mental ability rather than with peers of the same age (e.g. class jumping). This system has only proved successful when early entry is facilitated at all phases although, even then, the question could be raised as to how a child's social needs can be met. There have been cases where young children have entered university and I sometimes wonder what these individuals do when the other students are in the Union bar! The third approach, that of 'enrichment', would appear to be the one that would support the commitment to inclusion. In this approach, the child would remain in their own classroom for the majority of the time and undertake individual study at their own level, being supported by appropriate resources and teaching.

In one particular school I was involved in providing support for a 6-year-old pupil who had a reading age of over 14 and had successfully completed all the Key Stage 2 Standard Assessment Tasks (SATs) at Levels 5 and 6. The school was in the middle of a large urban estate and the parents were reluctant to have their son 'singled out' for additional support. In this particular case an enrichment programme was put in place where the pupil was set individual tasks based on the same content area being covered by the class but with a focus on investigation and personal study. For two afternoons each week he worked with the Year 6 children on project work, where he was given a range of specific responsibilities within his group, reporting back his findings, thus providing the discussion opportunities not available when working with his chronological equals. Despite this pupil's above-average ability he did not like producing extended pieces of imaginative writing, seeing this as unnecessary, as only 'facts' were important to him, and particular opportunities had to be developed using ICT resources to encourage the development of this specific area of the curriculum. As the pupil moved into Key Stage 2, links with the local secondary school were planned to enable opportunities for extended learning experiences at the appropriate ability level, while maintaining the social development within the appropriate chronological group.

As stated earlier in the chapter, more able pupils are not identified in legislative terms as having SEN. However, with the recent emphasis on raising standards, the government has begun to acknowledge the individual learning needs of pupils demonstrating higher levels of ability and LEAs are now providing advisory support for the more able.

Conclusion

When considering all the changes made within education over the past decade there will always be heated debate as to the benefits or otherwise of any new initiative. Implications of change, specifically in relation to pupils with SEN, have not always been considered thoroughly enough prior to the implementation of the change and it has frequently been left to the classroom teacher to find strategies and approaches that enable all pupils to receive appropriate education. The recent drive for a more inclusive education system is founded within the recognition that all pupils should be entitled to the same opportunities and access to learning whether, at one extreme, they have profound and complex needs or, at the other end of the continuum, they are gifted in some area of ability or skill. If this entitlement is to be realized, further consideration and development will have to continue in order that classroom teachers can be supported in providing access to a broad and balanced curriculum for all children.

Useful reading

In addition to the texts identified in the references, the following four journals provide valuable background reading on both theoretical and practical issues related to provision for pupils' individual needs.

British Journal of Special Education. Tamworth: The National Association for Special Educational Needs (NASEN).
Special. Tamworth: The National Association for Special Educational Needs (NASEN).
Special Children. Birmingham: Questions Publishing.
Support For Learning. Tamworth: The National Association for Special Educational Needs (NASEN).

References

Augur, J. and Briggs, S. (1992) *The Hickey Multi-Sensory Language Course*. London: Whurr.

Booth, T. and Potts, P. (eds) (1983) *Integrating Special Education*. Oxford: Blackwell.

Booth, T., Swann, W., Masterton, M. and Potts, P. (1992) *Curricula for Diversity in Education*. London: Routledge.

Bovair, K., Carpenter, B. and Upton, G. (1992) *Special Curricula Needs*. London: David Fulton.

Byers, R. (1994) Providing opportunities for effective learning, in R. Rose, A. Fergusson, C. Coles, R. Byers and D. Banes (eds) *Implementing the Whole Curriculum for Pupils with Learning Difficulties*. London: David Fulton.

Canter, L. (1992) *Assertive Discipline*. Santa Monica, CA: Lee Canter Associates.

Carle, E. (1970) *The Very Hungry Caterpillar*. Harmondsworth: Penguin.

Chinn, S. and Ashcroft, R. (1993) *Dyslexia and Mathematics: A Teaching Handbook*. London: Whurr.

Dearing, R. (1993) *The National Curriculum and its Assessment: An Interim Report* (the Dearing Report). York: NCC.

DES (Department of Education and Science) (1978) *Special Educational Needs* (the Warnock Report). London: HMSO.

DES (Department of Education and Science) (1981) *Education Act*. London: HMSO.

Dessent, T. (1987) *Making the Ordinary School Special*. London: Falmer Press.

DfE (Department for Education) (1993) *Exceptionally Able Children: Report of Conferences, October 1993*. London: DfE.

DfE (Department for Education) (1994) *Code of Practice on the Identification and Assessment of Special Educational Needs*. London: DfEE.

DfEE (Department for Education and Employment) (1997a) *Excellence for all Children: Meeting Special Educational Needs*. London: DfEE.

DfEE (Department for Education and Employment) (1997b) *Excellence in Schools*. London: DfEE.

DfEE (Department for Education and Employment) (2000a) *SEN Thresholds: Good Practice Guidance in Decision-Making on Identification and Provision for Pupils with Special Educational Needs*. London: DfEE.

DfEE (Department for Education and Employment) (2000b) *The National Literacy Strategy: Supporting Pupils with Special Educational Needs in the Literacy Hour*. London: DfEE.

Fish, J. (1985) *Educational Opportunities for All*. London: ILEA.

Hart, S. (1996) *Beyond Special Needs*. London: Paul Chapman.

Hegarty, S., Pocklington, K. and Lucas, D. (1982) *Integration in Action: Case Studies in the Integration of Pupils with Special Educational Needs*. Slough: NFER.

Hornsby, B. and Shear, F. (1977) *Alpha to Omega*. Oxford: Heinemann Educational.

Miles, T.R. and Miles, E. (1990) *Dyslexia a Hundred Years On*. Buckingham: Open University Press.

Norwich, B. (1989) How should we define exceptions?, *British Journal of Special Education*, 16(3): 94–7.

Ofsted (Office for Standards in Education) (1998) *Setting in Primary Schools*. London: Ofsted.

Pollock, J. and Waller, E. (1994) *Day-to-Day Dyslexia in the Classroom*. London: Routledge.

Pumphrey, P. and Reason, R. (1991) *Specific Learning Difficulties (Dyslexia)*. London: Routledge.

Rogers, B. (1994) Teaching positive behaviour to behaviourally disordered students in primary schools, *Support for Learning*, 9(4): 166–70.

Rose, R., Fergusson, A., Coles, C., Byers, R. and Banes, D. (1994) *Implementing the Whole Curriculum for Pupils with Learning Difficulties*. London: David Fulton.

Sebba, J., Byers, R. and Rose, R. (1993) *Redefining the Whole Curriculum for Pupils with Learning Difficulties*. London: David Fulton.

Sukhnandon, L. and Lee, B. (1998) *Streaming, Setting and Grouping by Ability: A Review of the Literature*. London: NFER.

Tilstone, C., Florian, L. and Rose, R. (1998) *Promoting Inclusive Practice*. London: Routledge.

Wallace, B. (1983) *Teaching the Very Able Child*. London: Ward Lock.

3

Teaching and learning in the early years

Jane Johnston

Introduction

Early years experiences are the important first step to future development. These experiences can be formal or informal, preschool or within compulsory education, at home or in an educational context. Informal experiences begin in the womb, as the foetus experiences sound, movement and emotion. Learning about the world continues from birth, with sights, sounds, movements, feelings and rudimentary belief. Babies soon know that if they cry someone responds. They learn that smiling and laughing elicit pleasurable responses. They learn to mimic facial expressions or language. As they develop they learn about the wider world: that mimicking a word produces a positive response; that moving their limbs in the bath makes splashes; or that a toy dropped from a cot or high chair falls to the ground. These experiential play activities can support cognitive, conative and affective development and lay the foundations for future learning experiences. As children explore the world around them, they develop knowledge about how the world works. The wider their informal experiences, the broader and deeper will be their understandings. They may watch the sun cast shadows while playing and begin to develop understandings about light and how shadows are made. They may experience sound in an echoing tunnel or room and develop some understandings of sound and echoes. They may be taken to the park, the zoo, a farm or have a patch of soil to dig in the garden, or have pets, all of which will provide them with understandings about plants and animals.

In discussing early years teaching and learning, we need to identify what we mean by the term 'early years'. This term has been used within formal education in the UK to mean those children of playgroup and nursery age, the Foundation Stage of learning between 3 and 5 years of age (DfEE/QCA 2000). In many countries formal education begins later than in the UK and so from a global perspective 'early years' can be said to mean any child in education under the age of 7. Both definitions can also be said to be deficient because they only refer to formal education. In this chapter we have a wider definition of the term 'early years' to mean children from *birth* to 7 years of age, thus including both the Foundation Stage of learning and Key Stage 1 of the National Curriculum (DFEE/QCA 1999).

It is during the early years that children make rapid growth emotionally, physically, socially and intellectually through both formal and informal experiences. Our policy and practice in the early years has changed considerably in recent times and this has left many teachers and the general public confused as to what is essential or desirable educational provision for our young children.

Good early learning involves children in play

Well-planned play, both indoors and outdoors, is a key way in which young children learn with enjoyment and challenge.

(DfEE/QCA 2000: 25)

At one time, formal experiences for the very young would have taken place in the home and the family would have had full responsibility for early learning. Some children may have had some physical, social and emotional needs cared for in a nursery but development and learning was often incidental rather than planned. Prior to the National Curriculum, education from 5 to 7 was influenced by the work of educators such as Froebel (1826), Montessori (1912) and Piaget (1962). Friedrich Froebel was the originator of kindergarten education, which advocated the natural growth of children from 3 to 7 years of age through play. Maria Montessori's methods of teaching and learning supported the development of initiative and intrinsic learning by encouraging and supporting children to learn from their own interests and at a rate that was appropriate to them, that is, more structured and supported learning through play. Jean Piaget's theories of learning continue to influence education and his arguments that play can facilitate cognitive development are central to the ethos of formal early learning establishments. Playgroups, nurseries and early years classrooms took heed of these ideas and many parents and carers sought to take advantage of the opportunities early education provided.

During the 1990s, early years policy and practice was influenced by individuals and groups with little or no knowledge of how young children learn, who thought play 'a frivolous and low status activity' (Anning 1994: 67). This resulted in 'play in early years classrooms being limited in frequency, duration and quality' (Bennett *et al.* 1997), despite support for learning through play coming from leading researchers in the field (Moyles 1989, 1994; Anning 1991; Bennett *et al.* 1997). The emphasis on more didactic learning was increasingly evident. At Key Stage 1, children would often learn without the support of the concrete experiences which develop understanding, skills and attitudes, and play resources were left untouched, especially as class sizes increased to numbers which made practical, exploratory learning more difficult to organize. These changes resulted in practice that appeared to ignore the research and experience of educationalists, psychologists and teachers, which demonstrated that practical, relevant experiences are essential in learning.

I observed a group of children playing with a selection of electrical and magnetic toys. After they had played with the toys for about ten minutes, they began to look at how they worked:

Child 1: Look at this, it moves.
Teacher: What do you think makes it move?
Child 1: Electric, it's electric.
Child 2: Can't be, there's no wires.
Child 1: Wires inside.
Teacher: Let's look inside and see.

They went on to explore the toys and look for similarities and differences between them, sorting them into ones that used electricity and ones that used magnetism (Johnston and Gray 1999). In this example the unstructured play experience led on to more structured learning experiences, supported by the teacher. However, it would not have been as effective a learning experience without the initial free play.

Effective early years learning involves development of understanding, skills and attitudes

The Education Reform Act of 1988 and the introduction of the National Curriculum for all children of compulsory school age, led to assessment of knowledge which appeared to devalue understanding, skills and attitudes. As a result, it is easy to forget that learning involves

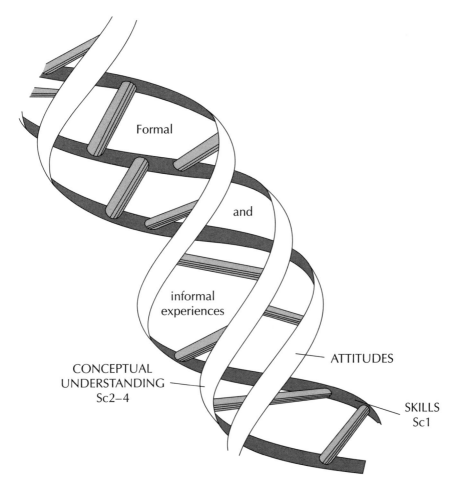

Figure 3.1 The development of conceptual understanding, skills and attitudes
Source: Johnston (1998).

an interrelationship between understandings, skills and attitudes which develop together throughout life (Johnston 1996, 1998) (see Figure 3.1).

Children playing with bubble mixture in a water trough or a large tank can be seen to be developing in all three areas. They are exploring the world around them through play and developing understanding of the shape, size and colours of bubbles. They are developing observational skills as well as an interest in and curiosity about the world. Children described by the Schools Council and Assessment Authority (SCAA) (1997: 53–5) who were playing with bubbles were developing both knowledge and understanding of the world and their own creativity:

> *Teacher:* What is a bubble?
> *Claire:* Soap that has been blown up full of air.
> *Josh:* I know. It is air surrounded by water!
> *Hugh [looking into his bubble-blower]:* I can see a rainbow!
> *Teacher:* What colours can you see?
> *Hugh:* White, black spots, yellow, purple.

While making bubbles, an early years child once asked me, 'Why can I see myself the right and wrong way up in the bubble?' She had observed the reflective and transparent properties of the bubble and we began to look for other things which were both 'like mirrors and see-through' (windows, some plastic) and for things in which we could see our reflection 'the right and wrong way up'.

This kind of play supports development of understandings, skills and attitudes when:

- there are clear learning objectives which identify what knowledge and understanding is involved. When playing with bubbles this is knowledge and understanding of light, colour and change;
- it is exploratory in nature, enabling the children to develop skills – in bubble-blowing the key skills would be observation and raising questions, but there are also social skills in playing with other children;
- it is a motivating experience, enabling the children to enjoy learning and develop positive attitudes to school.

Interaction is a key to effective early learning

> *Above all, effective learning and development for young children requires high-quality care and education by practitioners.*
> (DfEE/QCA 2000: 12)

Experiential play, which involves opportunities for the development of understandings, skills and attitudes, will be less successful without good interaction. It is essential that quality interaction occurs throughout children's learning, and interaction can take a number of different forms. Children should be interacting with the world around them, with phenomena, with motivating resources and with well-planned experiences. Well thought-out activities which enable children to develop in a number of directions and which motivate children are an essential ingredient of good early years learning. Stimulating experiences alone are not enough. Children need also to interact with each other during experiences, because 'effective learning involves interaction with each other and with adults' (DfEE/QCA 2000: 82). It is through interaction with each other that children develop important social skills. Peer interaction also provides opportunities for children to see different ways of interpreting their experiences and that different people may have different ideas.

Playing in a water trough, a small group of nursery children were looking at what containers they could fill using a full jug.

John [predicted]: I think it will fill all these.
Chloe [felt differently]: No, this one's too big.
Teacher: Let's fill them and see.
*John [fills a long thin container and finds it takes nearly all the
        water]:* This one's thin but it takes a lot. It won't fill all
        these up now.

In this short interaction, John and Chloe made different predictions about the capacity of the jug and other containers of different shapes and sizes. John revised his prediction based on his interaction with Chloe, the teacher and the experience.

Of crucial importance is the interaction of adults in learning. These adults can be the teachers who plan and set up the experience, nursery nurses and classroom assistants who support planning and preparation, and/or parents or carers. The importance of this adult interaction cannot be underestimated. Children may, and do, learn from informal experiences and from the experiences we set up for them, but that learning is greater, more focused and longer-lasting with quality adult interaction. As Heaslip (1994: 102) says, 'the adult's role is neither passive nor active. It should be proactive'.

There are two main ways that adults affect learning through interaction. First, the adult is an important role model for the children and can show them by example. Adults should 'model a range of positive behaviours' (DfEE/QCA 2000: 22) showing children how they, as adults, work together, how enthusiastic they are to learn, how to observe, how ask questions. They can do this by interacting with the children while they are involved in learning and by learning *with* them. It is important that children do not see adults as having a complete set of knowledge, understandings and skills. Learning is lifelong. Adult interaction can help children to see this – to see that we all have learning opportunities and that learning can be fun for all. The interaction between John, Chloe and the teacher above is an example of teacher interaction to support learning. The interaction continued with the teacher saying: 'I did not expect that. I thought the jug would fill more'. Chloe responded by asking the teacher: 'How may cups do you think it would take to fill the bucket?' The exchange then went:

> *Teacher:* Let me think, I think it might be five. What do you think?
> *Chloe:* I think it will be ten.
> *John:* Mmm, I think five like you.
> *Teacher:* Shall we try it and see?

The second way that adults affect learning through interaction is by focusing the children's attention and by questioning them. If children are playing in a water trough and the main learning objective is to begin to develop an initial understanding of capacity, then a few questions can help to focus the children's attention on this concept. For example: 'Can you find me the biggest container'?; 'How many cups do you think it will take to fill this bucket?'; 'Did you think this would hold more water?' With activities such as this, which are intended to focus on the early stages of development, it is also important that the children are only comparing two containers at a time (Cook *et al.* 1997). In this way the teacher can help the children to manage the possible complexity of an exploration, ensuring that they do not focus on too many different containers. By interacting with children in the water trough and asking questions of them, the teacher was helping the children in exploring and developing an understanding of capacity. They were observing, predicting, counting and communicating. For other ideas about mathematical development in the area of capacity see Cook *et al.* (1997: 47–9).

A learning partnership supports effective teaching and learning in the early years

> *Parents and practitioners should work together in an atmosphere of mutual respect within which children can have security and confidence.*
>
> (DfEE/QCA 2000: 11)

Learning is a partnership which involves a number of different individuals and bodies. There are two levels of partnership: one involving those in daily contact with the children and one which influences that contact and subsequent learning. These levels are illustrated in Figure 3.2.

All partners in the learning partnership have important roles to play. Within the second level, the government makes decisions about early years education – for example, whether to fund more preschool provision. They are influenced by public opinion, but are to a large extent

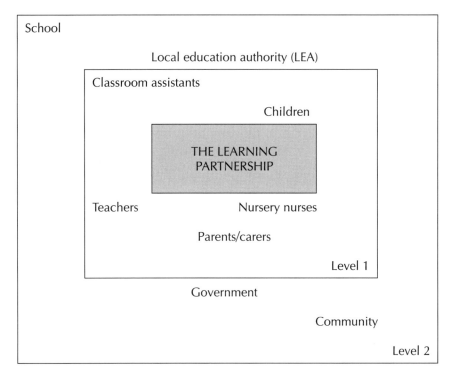

Figure 3.2   The learning partnership

fiscally rather than educationally driven; the public want better education and more early years places, but not at the cost of higher taxes. Government officials, such as the Chief Inspector of Schools and Office for Standards in Education (Ofsted) inspectors, will be influenced by the government, public opinion and personal expertise and experience, which may not include first-hand early years expertise. Hopefully, they seek and listen to public opinion. Their views and decisions influence the nature of early years policy and practice, which from the beginning of the 1990s became more formal and focused towards key language and mathematical skills. New guidelines (DfEE/QCA 2000) have reemphasized what is good about early years education and redressed the imbalance between formal teaching and experiential learning.

The local education authority (LEA) is similarly influenced by government and government advisers and gives advice to schools and supports early provision through in-service training for school staff inspection and advisory services. The school will be made up of teachers with a variety of expertise and experiences. Some will be trained to teach the later years, some may be early years specialists, and all (hopefully) will have had some early years theoretical and practical input in initial teacher education and in-service education. If the early years part of the school is large, then early years provision is likely to be well represented, although in some schools a Key Stage 2 trained teacher will be endeavouring to develop early years provision in isolation.

Most communities are very supportive of early years education and not only influence provision but can be very useful in extending learning. Many within the community have expertise which the teacher cannot replicate. Many local shops, industry and services are happy to support visits to workplaces or visit the class and support learning. The community policeman once came to my class and did some fingerprinting with the children, and a local electrician brought a giant electrical plug and socket (used in electrical training) to school so that children could practise wiring a plug. Both of these were experiences I could not have given the children without support.

The first level of partnership is one with a daily effect on learning. Within this partnership are those working directly with children in the classroom and at home: the teachers, nursery nurses, classroom assistants, parents and carers. In any partnership, the roles and responsibilities may be different but the prime aim should be the same. Sometimes the aim of developing children in the early years can be adversely affected by confusion about roles and responsibilities, or because relationships within the partnership are not strong. In all partnerships there must be trust. In a sexual partnership you need to trust the fidelity of your partner. In a dancing partnership you need to trust that your partner will not make the wrong move. Similarly, you must have a high level of trust in a climbing or diving partner. In an educational partnership we must trust in the abilities and expertise of our partners and learn to value their role in children's learning.

I have found that it is difficult for newly-qualified teachers (NQTs) to demonstrate these high levels of trust in the parental partnership. A few years ago, I asked a group of early years postgraduate students, at the start of their course, how they valued the role of parents and carers in education. Many of the students were parents themselves and all pro-claimed the importance of the parental role and identified how parents could support learning in the class and at home in a wide variety of creative ways. At the end of the course I asked the same question and a significant number of students had revised their initial ideas. All saw the value of parental support for learning, but few felt ready to involve parents in their classrooms. This was of real concern to me, but in many ways it was understandable. At an early stage of their career these teachers did not feel confident enough in their own teaching to share their successes and failures with other adults, particularly with those who may appear more confident, expert and critical. However, in excluding parent involvement, even for a few years, they were denying children valuable opportunities, for as the DfEE/QCA (2000: 85) say, we should use 'parents' knowledge to extend children's experiences of the world'.

Early years practitioners should be well qualified and knowledgeable

> *Effective education requires both a relevant curriculum and practitioners who*
> *understand and are able to implement the curriculum requirements.*
>
> (DfEE/QCA 2000: 13)

All those involved in early years education need to be well qualified and able to work together in the learning partnership. If each partner has different expertise, roles and responsibilities, it is essential that we are clear about what they are. Teachers in the early years should have some knowledge of early years development. They will be able to determine appropriate learning objectives in line with the curriculum and match the children's needs and abilities. They will have skills in planning learning so that children can progress through the planned curriculum. Nursery nurses and many classroom assistants will be able to bring to the partnership in-depth knowledge of child care and child development. They have skills in preparing for learning and in supporting learning. Parents and carers have particular knowledge of their children which can be invaluable in planning for learning and assessing learning. They can also support learning both inside and outside school. Many parents/carers will be able to support their developing children; many will be grateful for support and advice. Parental information sessions, family learning workshops, newsletters and individual guidance or advice are all examples of home/school support. It is important, however, to remember that home/school support is a two-way process. Many parents have expertise and qualities from which the learning partnership will benefit. All will have knowledge of their children, most will be willing to support their children's learning and some will be eager to play a more active role in the partnership. The key to the learning partnership is for all to value the different roles. Teachers have a responsibility to plan for the partnership, to coordinate roles within the partnership, to inform those supporting learning of learning objectives and to accept and seek advice. An important task in planning is to plan for time to liaise with other adults, to share planning and learning objectives, so that they can undertake their role in supporting learning from an informed position.

Young children learn best in a motivating learning environment in which they can develop understandings in a relevant cross-curricular approach

> *For children to have rich and stimulating experiences, the learning environment should be well planned and well organised.*
>
> (DfEE/QCA 2000: 12)

In the early years, children have a love of learning. They are curious, enthusiastic and eager to please. We have a duty to promote this interest in learning and to create a safe, motivating and stimulating environment in which they can learn. Motivating, practical experiences such as blowing bubbles, making pancakes, making mud pies or collecting leaves help children to develop positive attitudes to learning. This can be further developed by positive adult interaction and adult role-modelling. An example of children exploring funny fruit and vegetables (Johnston and Gray 1999) illustrates this. The children were sorting fruit and vegetables according to certain criteria. Each child and adult was given a fruit or vegetable and we described them in our own words:

'It's heavy.'
'Round.'
'Mine's smooth.'
'It's squidgy.'
'It smells nice.'

The children were motivated because they had their own fruit or vegetable and they even became rather attached to them! My role was important in:

- motivating them;
- showing them by example by describing my fruit;
- challenging them by asking questions;
- encouraging them to describe their fruit or vegetable;
- helping to create an environment in which the children wanted and felt able to participate.

Together all these aspects helped to create a motivating learning environment.

Young children are not aware of the different curriculum areas. Neither are they aware of the differentiation between work and play. Early learning should not create artificial division in learning. However, teachers will need to be aware of the learning objectives in different areas. 'Exploring Fruit and Vegetables' is a good example of a cross-curricular approach, and my initial planning for this session is shown in detail in Figure 3.3.

Key learning objectives

Whole class introduction

- Communication, language and literacy. Describing using their own words and extending their vocabulary.
- Knowledge and understanding of the world. Exploring fruit and vegetables by using all their senses as appropriate.
- Personal, social and emotional. Develop curiosity and motivation.

Fruit matching game

- Mathematical development. Shape and colour matching.
- Personal, social and emotional. Cooperating with others as they play the game.

Making banana sandwiches

- Communication, language and literacy. Using language in play.
- Knowledge and understanding of the world. Using their senses in their play.
- Personal, social and emotional. Cooperating with others as they play. Maintain interest and motivation.

Sorting and classifying fruit and vegetables

- Communication, language and literacy. Describing using their own words and extending their vocabulary.
- Knowledge and understanding of the world. Using their senses to sort fruit and vegetables.
- Personal, social and emotional. Develop curiosity and motivation.

Printing with fruit and vegetables

- Knowledge and understanding of the world. Looking at similarities, differences, patterns and change with different fruit and vegetables.
- Creative development. Exploring colour, texture and shape.
- Personal, social and emotional. Develop curiosity and motivation.

Story

- Communication, language and literacy. Retelling story in words and play.
- Personal, social and emotional. Cooperating with others as they play. Maintain interest and motivation.

Key teaching points

- The fruits and vegetables have different properties which can be described in different ways.
- Fruits and vegetables have many properties in common.
- Patterns occur in nature and can be created.

Figure 3.3 Initial planning for 'Exploring Fruit and Vegetables'

Activities

Whole class introduction
Observing and describing a collection of fruit and vegetables using own words. Vocabulary extended as appropriate (e.g. fruit, vegetable, size, colour, soft, hard, rough seed, skin, heavy, light, round, etc.).

Group/individual activities
No more than six children are involved in each activity. They can move to another activity if there is room for them to do so.

Sorting and classifying fruit and vegetables
Children sort fruit and vegetables into groups according to observable features (size, colour, texture, weight, etc.). They can be encouraged to re-sort the fruit and vegetables and to extend the criteria for sorting as appropriate).

Fruit matching game
Children turn over top and bottom half of apple and banana cards and if the colours/shapes match they can keep the pair.

Printing with fruit and vegetables
Children make contact print pictures using pieces/slices of fruit or vegetables.

Making banana sandwiches
Children can role-play preparing banana sandwiches for tea.

Story
The Very Hungry Caterpillar by Eric Carle (1970). (This could be followed up by children playing with a toy caterpillar and reenacting the story.)

Figure 3.3   (*Cont'd*)

References

Anning, A. (1991) *The First Years at School*. Buckingham: Open University Press.

Anning, A. (1994) Play and legislated curriculum: back to basics, an alternative view, in J. Moyles (ed.) (1994) *The Excellence of Play*. Buckingham: Open University Press.

Bennett, N., Wood, L. and Rogers, S. (1997) *Teaching Through Play: Teachers' Thinking and Classroom Practice*. Buckingham: Open University Press.

Carle, E. (1970) *The Very Hungry Caterpillar*. Harmondsworth: Penguin.

Cook, G., Jones, L., Murphy, C. and Thumpston, G. (1997) *Enriching Early Mathematical Learning*. Buckingham: Open University Press.

DfEE/QCA (Department for Education and Employment/Qualifications and Curriculum Authority) (1999) *The National Curriculum: Handbook for Primary Teachers in England.* London: QCA.

DfEE/QCA (Department for Education and Employment/Qualifications and Curriculum Authority) (2000) *Curriculum Guidance for the Foundation Stage.* London: DfEE.

Froebel, F. (1826) *The Education of Man.* New York: Appleton.

Heaslip, P. (1994) Making play work in the classroom, in J. Moyles (ed.) *The Excellence of Play*, pp. 99–109. Buckingham: Open University Press.

Johnston, J. (1996) *Early Explorations in Science.* Buckingham: Open University Press.

Johnston, J. (1998) Learning science in the early years, in R. Sherrington (ed.) *ASE Guide to Primary Science Education.* Cheltenham: Stanley Thornes.

Johnston, J. and Gray, A. (1999) *Enriching Early Scientific Learning.* Buckingham: Open University Press.

Montessori, M. (1912) *The Montessori Method of Education.* London: Heinemann.

Moyles, J. (1989) *Just Playing? The Role and Status of Play in Early Childhood Education.* Buckingham: Open University Press.

Moyles, J. (ed.) (1994) *The Excellence of Play.* Buckingham: Open University Press.

Piaget, J. (1962) *Play, Dreams and Imitation.* New York: Norton.

SCAA (Schools Council and Assessment Authority) (1997) *Looking at Children's Learning: Desirable Outcomes for Children's Learning on Entering Compulsory Education.* London: SCAA.

4

The child as spiritual citizen, the school as moral society

Mark Chater

It is nonsense to say that there are only ten subjects.

(Brighouse, quoted in DfEE 1999: 67)

Introduction

This chapter will deal with features of education which address the child's growth into personal identity and which do not fit into subjects or curricular areas. Included here are concerns for the child's spiritual, moral, social and cultural development (SMSCD), for personal, social and health education (PSHE) and for citizenship education. These aspects have several features in common:

- they are defined, usually by law, as a part of the teacher's or a school's overall responsibility for the child;
- they are often described as elements of or dimensions to the curriculum, reaching across several or all subjects, existing in the ethos or life of the school, and in the school's dealings with its local community;
- they refuse to be confined to processes of knowledge or skill acquisition, instead addressing the child more deeply in terms of their personal identity, sense of purpose, feelings about self and others, ability to deal with life in practical and ideal terms, and sense of belonging and participation;
- they each have a distinctive role to play in the child's overall development, yet they relate closely to each other and overlap at several points (we shall see examples of this);
- they are widely accepted by primary teachers as important, even central, to their role, yet there is a need to build up confidence and success in this area.

After the initial section entitled 'Just a list of adjectives?', the PSHE and citizenship guidelines will be critically discussed. This will lead us on to an exploration of the SMSCD dimensions which raise many questions for PSHE and citizenship teachers. The reader may wish to refer to the curriculum guidelines, and to other recent official documents, in order to gain a fuller picture.

Meanwhile, day-to-day life in school must go on. Two short sections with a necessarily limited selection of practical suggestions for staff teams and for teachers individually in classrooms follow on.

Just a list of adjectives?

The 1996 Education Act (Section 351) proclaims that education is about promoting the spiritual, moral, cultural, mental and physical development of pupils at the school, and of society. The list of adjectives was inherited from the Education Acts of 1944 and 1988 but its inclusion was by no means token. The 1990s witnessed much public discussion on spiritual and moral education, including the publication of a series of official documents (Ofsted 1994; SCAA 1996) which, despite their faults, demonstrated a seriousness of purpose in this difficult area.

Opening the revised *National Curriculum Handbook for Primary Teachers in England* (QCA 1999: 10), we see an initial statement on the curriculum's values, aims and purposes in which the list of adjectives is extended to include the social development of pupils and their wellbeing. Not only the individual, but the community and society should benefit from education: 'Education is . . . a route to equality of opportunity for all, a healthy and just democracy, a productive economy, and sustainable development' (QCA 1999: 10).

Behind the social and economic benefits lies a moral purpose: 'Education should reaffirm our commitment to the virtues of truth, justice, honesty, trust and a sense of duty' (QCA 1999: 10). It may be comforting, and also instructive, to realize that this cluster of personal, moral and social concerns in the curriculum is not new. It has been variously expressed by Socrates, Augustine, Henry Newman, John Dewey and Maria Montessori. The overwhelming majority of primary teachers would agree.

An educational theme may have history on its side and still lack the power to spark the present. There is a vagueness, perhaps a lack of coherence, about the emphasis on the personal element in education. The talk of spiritual, moral, social, cultural and (more recently) personal, social, health and citizenship education, presents us with a list of adjectives which sit awkwardly with each other, are hard to rattle off in one convenient phrase, and contain some interesting tensions. The adjectives have sometimes been brought together under the umbrella word 'whole'. Thus, educators speak of teaching the whole child, and of ensuring that knowledge is a united whole, not a fragmented set of parcels. It has been suggested that this interest in 'wholism' indicates a feeling that the child, or the curriculum, or perhaps the world, are broken and need integrating. To speak of the 'whole' may be to wish to cure or repair that which has been divided (Best 1996). Such discourse may also reveal a desire to reach towards that which is complete and integrated in the individual child and in the universe of knowledge.

Howard Gardner's theory of multiple intelligences (1983) is a major contemporary theoretical expression of the idea of the whole child moving through a whole body of knowledge. Gardner's six intelligences – linguistic, musical, logical-mathematical, spatial, bodily-kinesthetic and personal – offer a comprehensive picture of the rounded being. While much of our matter will fall naturally into the 'personal' category, significant aspects of social, cultural and citizenship education have connections to all six intelligences.

Personal intelligence includes the capacity to 'access one's own feeling life' (Gardner 1983: 240); or, as others have put it, to know one's self, with all this implies in terms of self-acceptance, esteem and social and emotional competence. It also means noticing and understanding the emotions, motivations and intentions of others. Gardner believes this capacity to be highly developed in religious and political leaders. These two forms of personal intelligence are intimately related, each having its own direction opposed to the other, yet in practice intermingled. Children develop these intelligences in a particular cultural context which offers them frequent clues as to how to understand both themselves and others. And the culture will convey these clues in ways which are linguistic, musical, spatial and bodily. Once again we see the overlap between these areas, and neat classifications evade us.

Previous attempts at a framework for the personal element of education recognized the interconnectedness and built on it. Richard Pring's work held that personal development included intellectual, moral, social, practical and, in its broadest sense, political traits (Pring 1984).

We see, then, that the present National Curriculum's interest in the spiritual, moral and other aspects of education has a long-established tradition. We learn that the list of adjectives is not, as it might first seem, a clumsy series of adjuncts to an already overloaded curriculum. They are in fact an attempt to reach towards some mysterious, yet essential, element – an education which addresses the whole child on all levels of their being. This is alchemy: to transform the drudgery of training into the gold of education.

PSHE and citizenship: a critical review

The non-statutory guidelines in the National Curriculum lead with a section on PSHE combined with citizenship (QCA 1999: 137–8). It is expected that pupils will be: 'Developing confidence and responsibility and making the most of their abilities'; 'Preparing to play an active role as citizens'; 'Developing a healthy, safer lifestyle'; 'Developing good relationships and respecting the differences between people'. Under these four areas, specific targets are given for the two key stages. These include items such as taking part in a discussion, being taught to maintain personal hygiene, recognizing how behaviour affects others, recognizing personal worth, understanding why and how rules and laws exist, understanding about peer pressure and puberty, and realizing the nature and consequences of prejudice. There are link opportunities with several core and foundation subjects. Sections entitled 'Breadth of opportunities' (QCA 1999: 138–41) give an idea of some of the active learning contexts in which the learning could take place – school environment projects, befriending, school council participation and meeting representatives of international aid agencies are just a few. The guidelines are brief, broad in scope, and likely to elicit considerable agreement. Much of what they recommend (though not all) will be happening already in many primary schools.

It is interesting to note the many strands woven into the PSHE and citizenship guidelines. They include the social education, community service and citizenship programmes of the 1970s and 1980s (Schools Council 1974). Sex education is visible in the present focus on hygiene, appropriate behaviour and relationships; drugs education is likewise visible, implicitly in Key Stage 1 through self-worth and relationships, and explicitly in Key Stage 2. Multicultural education (Swann 1985) is visible, but its partner, antiracist education, is excluded. Moral education forms a substantial part; yet there is a failure to examine what kind of moral education works, and what we could learn from previous debates (Straughan 1982; Bottery 1989). The recent work on SMSCD (Ofsted 1994; SCAA 1996) is very much a part of the targets, as well as being visible in the statement of values appearing at the back of the curriculum guidelines (QCA 1999). Each one of these strands was the fruit of dedicated work and each represented deep divergences of theory and approach. These interesting variations in the strands have become flattened out in the brevity of the targets.

Equally interesting, but giving cause for concern, are the areas of educational research and practical work which have not been adequately represented in the PSHE guidelines. These are like strands which should connect but which have been snapped off and left aside. Oddly enough, the first of these omissions is that of the Crick Commission itself, whose 1998 report (Crick/QCA 1998) restarted the debate on citizenship education. The Crick Report's emphasis on political literacy, its strong concern about the need to encourage active participation, and its focus on areas (such as democracy and autocracy, human rights, power and authority) are muted in the primary PSHE guidelines. It is true that the list of targets uses concepts such as 'fair', 'unfair', 'needs', 'responsibilities', 'communities' and 'democracy' (QCA 1999: 137–9), but it does so flatly, as if the meanings were obvious to all. The interesting multidimensional realities of life in all groups, by which these moral absolutes are interpreted and lived out with endless variety, seems to have passed the writers by. Little of Crick's urgent passion for active, critical participation can be sensed here.

If we seek democracy in education, one natural place to look is the free schools, Steiner schools and other alternatives. Yet they are scarcely ever acknowledged by curriculum writers and education managers in the UK. However, their existence on a small scale and in small numbers *is* important. Generally, and with variations, their ethos includes a commitment to non-compulsion, a curriculum driven by the children's interest and enquiry, a democratic decision making structure and a discipline forum in which pupils and staff have an equal voice. In some cases there is an additional commitment to communal living expressed in a sharing of household tasks (Harber 1996). Advocates of the free schools point to this ethos as a means to producing better adjusted citizens. By several measures, such as the quality of personal relationships, the incidence of disruptive behaviour and the reality (as distinct from the rhetoric) of participation, these schools are held up as more effective (Harber 1996). While the PSHE guidelines make much of the language of pupil choice and responsibility, especially in the 'breadth of opportunities' (QCA 1999: 138, 141) there is no sense in which they envisage this extending to the power of choice over curricular content or timetabling. The gap between the rhetoric of responsibility and the reality of a highly controlled and tightly policed curriculum will create difficulties for the flourishing of an effective citizenship programme.

Race as an issue is underplayed in the PSHE guidelines. Previous official reporting exposed both a cause for deep concern and a variety of responses. The 1985 Swann Report, *Education for All*, was an uneasy compromise between two strategies. On the one hand, multicultural education focused on the fostering of good relations in the school and the classroom, while antiracist education took a wider and more political perspective. Swann argued that the (often latent) background assumptions of an essentially racist culture must be exposed and challenged, otherwise multiculturalism would be ineffective (Leicester and Taylor

1992). In the PSHE guidelines, neither the multicultural nor the antiracist analysis is in evidence. Two targets mention racism, both at Key Stage 2 (QCA 1999). In both cases, the focus is on behaviour and consequences. There is no mention of history or culture. In the light of the ongoing evidence of persistent racism, it is disappointing to see no explicit mention of the moral and civic necessity of tackling racism and no exemplification of the varied analyses and methods of the recent past.

Pacifist and internationalist education usually assumes a radical critique of world trade relations, especially the arms trade (CEWC 1986). The 1990s evolved some of these concerns into a European dimension to education which contributed an understanding of global trade patterns, awareness of cultural context, an aim to overcome historical prejudices and a moral commitment to harmony (Bell 1991). The PSHE guidelines do deal frequently with differences and similarities, likes and dislikes, and respect, tolerance and open discussion as alternatives to violence, all on personal levels (QCA 1999). There is presumably a belief that creating a peaceful and just world in the classroom will be the beginning of real social change. It has not happened yet, and internationalist education believes in enhancing this approach with more explicit teaching.

Cultural awareness and development were emphasized in the report of the National Advisory Committee on Creative and Cultural Education (DfEE 1999) which pointed out the creative opportunities not only in artistic and imaginative subjects but also in science, the humanities, the realm of beliefs and values and the school's general everyday life. The drawing out of every pupil's creativity contributes to self-esteem and their appreciation of diversity. Cultural and creative dimensions do feature in limited ways in the PSHE guidelines, for instance in taking opportunities to make choices about what to watch on television and the appreciation of ethnic identities (QCA 1999: 138–9).

Finally, there is the contemporary interest in emotional literacy and emotional intelligence. The PSHE guidelines do mention self-worth and the understanding of other people's feelings (QCA 1999: 137ff.) but these concerns need to become more mainstream in order to be widely implemented. Goleman (1996) has established a physiological as well as a sociological basis for believing in a connection between emotional state and intellectual performance. The ability to understand and to manage one's own emotions thus becomes not only an important personal skill in itself, but also a key to learning in the rest of the curriculum – and a key to effective citizenship. The quality circle time materials are a good example of this in practice. One teacher using the materials reports, 'It gives all children a chance to participate on an equal footing with both their peers and the teacher and raises their self-esteem when they realize that everyone's ideas are valid' (Mosley 1993: 17). This field of concern has staked a claim for recognition in the curriculum through the campaigning work of organizations like Antidote, the campaign for emotional literacy.

On realizing these gaps and tensions in the PSHE guidelines, one has an impression that certain crucial points of principle in the recent educational past are now closed, settled and simple, and that alternative approaches, which bring awkward questions to populist certainties and the systematic exposure of social forces, are not worthy of mention. One wonders why.

When the PSHE guidelines raise so many moral questions, it is appropriate to explore the idea of moral development and moral education.

Moral development and education

Do young people develop morally by being told what is right and wrong, or by discovering pleasure, meaning and intellectual and emotional satisfaction in doing right, or through being encouraged to discover (and, to some extent, to redefine) right and wrong for themselves? Or would moral development happen anyway, regardless of adult intervention? Western education has, at different times, placed its faith in all three and been disappointed. This has left behind a vast body of theoretical literature, but a useful summary discussion can be found in Straughan (1982). The most obvious difficulty lies in deciding what right and wrong are. How can the education system do anything effective towards moral education if there is so much disagreement? Must it resort to lowest common denominator values such as tolerance, fairness and honesty? And if it does, won't it run the risk of levelling down children's moral aims? Or if it becomes too specific, for instance on family life, might it not run an equal risk of excluding some children and implying their moral inadequacy? Is a moral development programme possible, or even desirable, in a pluralist liberal democracy?

The boldest answer lies in the statement of values (QCA 1999), a summary of the work of the National Forum for Values in Education and the Community. Its author, Marianne Talbot, has argued that a statement of values can work because of an underlying consensus across religions and lifestyles. Her work was based on research in schools and, it is argued, essentially expresses widely-held beliefs 'from the bottom up'. Its democratic and inclusive nature is stressed by exponents. The statement offers positions in relation to four cluster areas: valuing the self (self-esteem, health); valuing others (property, toleration, respect); valuing society (participation); and valuing the environment. This is a notable, systematic and laudable attempt at a moral education framework for a liberal pluralist democracy. But such statements do not necessarily answer the problems outlined above. Listing values such as truth, human rights and the environment meets with all but universal support until we realize the difficulty when the values clash with each other, as they inevitably must: for instance, when being honest, truthful and open clashes with being concerned and respectful for other people's feelings or safety; or when, in situations of political oppression and injustice, honouring justice and fair play may get an oppressed group precisely nowhere. When the clash comes, which values are more important and which go to the wall? Such lists of values rarely, if ever, acknowledge that life and moral choices are complex and messy. Yet it is at these real moments of clash and choice that moral development gets interesting.

A reflective teacher needs to be mindful of the theoretical difficulties. As is so often the case, what seems to work best is a pragmatic approach, mixing old and new strategies: formal teaching, personal example and positive experiences of action. Lickona's 'five Es' are a useful summary: moral learning happens through a combination of example, exhortation ('it is good to . . .'), explanation ('I want you to do this because . . .'), experience, and an environment providing stability and love (Lickona 1999). Behaviour expectations and the quality of relationships will be crucial. For instance, a school which decides to prioritize care of the environment for a term might combine good examples discovered in geography and science with discussion of moral aspects in religious education (RE) and collective worship. This will be reinforced for the children by the pleasurable experience of seeing their own physical work making a difference.

The claimed consensus values outlined in the guidelines form a start – at the very least something to react to. But let's remember that Socrates claimed not to know what virtue was, let alone to be able to explain how the young learn it. The values statement leaves quite unanswered the questions of why people might need to develop morally, why we should wish to act morally (especially if, as in the great moral dilemmas, it is against our interests) and above all why we so often fail to act morally according to our own standards. These considerations spur us on to spiritual issues.

Spiritual development

Spiritual education, even more than moral education, raises questions of definition. Spirituality, depending on whom you ask, may mean anything from the rituals of a particular religious community through to the 9-year-old's feelings of joy, incommunicable mystery and unity at watching the sun come up over the mountains. Both may be healthy and valid, but how does one unite all forms of spirituality in a coherent definition? As with moral development, how does one avoid the twin dangers of loose vagueness and over-prescriptive exclusivity? The late Rabbi Hugo Gryn illustrated this with his (attributed) remark that 'spirituality is like a bird: if you hold it too tightly, it chokes; if you hold it too loosely, it flies away' (Brown and Furlong 1996: 3).

Both the School Curriculum and Assessment Authority (SCAA) (1996) and the Office for Standards in Education (Ofsted) (1994) assume spirituality to be something naturally human, shared by more or less all children and adults: in this they reflect reliable research findings (Hay 1998). Both organizations allude, in their definitions, to awareness of the other, of things beyond the immediate and material, and to recognition and valuing of a non-material dimension to life. But does it make sense to define the spiritual as non-material? For many Christian writers on spirituality, the spiritual is that which stands for the whole person, not one isolated part. It has been poetically described as 'a fall through ordinary life into the depths of life' (Butler and Butler 1996: 2). It is, therefore, not divorced from the material, social, cultural or any other aspects of human existence, to make that divorce is what theologians call 'dualism'. Spirituality embraces the material, but points beyond it. A broad consensus of educators in and out of Christianity supports this point (Best 2000). In this respect, the SCAA and the Ofsted definitions are misleading.

The two documents stop short of being more specific on the nature of spirituality because, as with morality, to point to particular forms of spirituality might imply exclusion of others. But is it possible to talk meaningfully about spirituality without reference to a particular spiritual tradition? How do I meditate without a guru or a set of beliefs about one's existence? Or to whom do I pray, and what do I believe about the God who hears me? To be real and earthed, spirituality must surely be connected to doctrine and practice, whether Franciscan or Sufi. At root, the documents are (for good multi-faith reasons) silent on the nature of spirituality. Into this silence, cynics have poured their contempt for tired phrases such as 'awe and wonder' and 'empathy'.

Another difficulty is in the documents' assumption that spirituality resides in the individual alone. Should there not be a recognition that spirituality exists between people, and that spiritual development usually happens in communities? To see spirituality as 'inner life' or personal 'quest' seems in some ways an extension of the damaging individualism of the 1980s. Some of the most admired spiritual leaders (for example,

Gandhi and King) have considered it their calling to bring to the surface profound and bitter conflicts in values.

These issues do not cancel out the importance and usefulness of the two documents. It is still a notable achievement in a secular pluralist democracy to have an official recognition of spirituality which is determinedly human-centred, and therefore potentially usable by educators of all faiths and of none. The weaknesses may do some good if they provoke the teacher to further reflection.

Suggestions for staff teams

It is the task of the school to bring these 'personal curriculum' elements together. Rather than receiving the parts already arranged into neat compartments, we must fit them together as interlocking and interpenetrating parts of an engine of our own making; or, better still, treat them as permeating oils in the engine – fluid, unpredictable, flowing and firing at different times and in different directions, yet indispensably serving the whole machine. Ofsted holds the view that this aspect should be visible in curriculum subjects and in the ethos of the school:

> The fairness, justice and respect for individuals which are evident in the daily conduct of a school and the way its rules are applied send powerful messages to pupils. Nevertheless, much is learned from a conscious development of knowledge, skills and understanding through the curriculum.
>
> (Trainor 1995: 9)

In this way the school becomes a small society in which the child learns how it is possible to be and to become a spiritual, moral citizen. Consider the following approaches:

- 'Think globally, act locally': create a just, peaceful, truthful community in the school, open to the world.
- Invite pupils and staff to be active citizens of this community.
- Review the National Curriculum documents in teams, or in small schools. Collaborate with the staff of neighbouring schools. Identify the PSHE, citizenship and SMSCD issues raised, and opportunities presented, by the content of the subjects.
- Use the cross-curricular links, and the affective and experiential possibilities in all subjects, to rebuild a sense of learning as a whole.
- Plan your provision, but be open to sudden opportunities, and be prepared to allow participating pupils the power to change those moments for themselves.

- Bring teaching teams together in in-service education to discuss their own attitudes, experiences and skills in creating and using opportunities for discussion of ultimate questions or setting up of projects.

Suggestions for teachers in classrooms

- Allow pupils to generate ideas. For instance, get them to nominate individuals in the school for a citizenship award. The challenge of thinking and explaining how and why individuals deserve the award brings to the fore many moral and spiritual qualities.
- Respond, with the pupils, to news events – environmental concerns, drugs in sport, tragedies, elections, new arrivals in family or neighbourhood.
- When appropriate, follow these events up with use of the Internet to expose a variety of viewpoints and types of argument.
- Use recent films to generate discussion on themes, which are both personal and social: *The Lion King* (self-identity, self-worth, duty); *The Hunchback of Notre Dame* (image, self-worth, prejudice, abuse of power); *The Prince of Egypt* (authority, loyalty, bullying, human rights, democracy).
- Organize project groups which take the pupils into the community (visiting the elderly) and bring the community into the school (local Christian Aid group).
- Buy the education packs of major world development agencies (for example, Burns and Lamont 1995; Oxfam, 1997). Take some staff development time to scan the contents pages and identify the practical activities – games, stories, thought-provoking reflections for assembly, and writing from other children. Make good use of the suggested progression charts. Plan their use in collective worship, circle time, geography, history, mathematics, English and RE.
- Always encourage discussion – in collective worship, classroom, corridor, lunchtime groups.
- Frequently encourage silence, as the embodiment of a human realization of the limits of our rationality, technology and activity.
- Use short excerpts from spiritual classics such as Psalm 8 to deepen awareness of self in a vast world and universe.
- Use artistic expression as a means to communicate the pupils' concerns for themselves, each other and the world.

References

Bell, G. (1991) *Developing a European Dimension in Primary Schools*. London: Fulton.
Best, R. (ed.) (1996) *Spirituality, Education and the Whole Child*. London: Cassell.

Best, R. (ed.) (2000) *Education for Spiritual, Moral, Social and Cultural Development.* London: Continuum.

Bottery, M. (1989) *The Morality of the School: The Theory and Practice of Values in Education.* London: Cassell.

Brown, A. and Furlong, J. (1996) *Spiritual Development in Schools: Invisible to the Eye.* London: National Society.

Burns, S. and Lamont, G. (1995) *Values and Visions: A Handbook for Spiritual Development and Global Awareness.* London: Christian Aid with the CAFOD and the Development Education Project.

Butler, T. and Butler, B. (1996) *Just Spirituality in a World of Faiths.* London: Mowbray.

CEWC (Council for Education in World Citizenship) (1986) *Citizens of the World.* London: Council for Education in World Citizenship.

Crick, B. (and QCA) (1998) *Education for Citizenship and the Teaching of Democracy in Schools* (Report of the Crick Commission). London: QCA.

DfEE (Department for Education and Employment) (with the Department of Culture, Media and Sport) (1999) *All Our Futures: Creativity, Culture and Education.* London: DfEE and DCMS.

Gardner, H. (1983) *Frames of Mind: The Theory of Multiple Intelligences.* London: Heinemann.

Goleman, D. (1996) *Emotional Intelligence.* London: Bloomsbury.

Harber, C. (1996) *Small Schools and Democratic Practice.* Nottingham: Educational Heretics Press.

Hay, D. (with Nye, R.) (1998) *The Spirit of the Child.* London: HarperCollins.

Leicester, M. and Taylor, M. (1992) *Ethics, Ethnicity and Education.* London: Kogan Page.

Lickona, T. (1999) *Educating for Character.* New York: Bantam Press.

Mosley, J. (1993) *Turn Your School Round.* Cambridge: LDA.

Ofsted (Office for Standards in Education) (1994) *Spiritual, Moral, Social and Cultural Development: A Discussion Paper.* London: Ofsted.

Oxfam (1997) *A Curriculum for Global Citizenship.* London: Oxfam.

Pring, R. (1984) *Personal and Social Education in the Curriculum.* London: Hodder & Stoughton.

QCA (Qualifications and Curriculum Authority) (1999) *The National Curriculum Handbook for Primary Teachers in England.* London: QCA.

SCAA (Schools Curriculum and Assessment Authority) (1996) *Education for Adult Life: The Spiritual and Moral Development of Young People.* London: SCAA.

Schools Council (1974) *Social Education.* London: Methuen Educational.

Straughan, R. (1982) *Can we Teach Children to be Good?* London: Allen & Unwin.

Swann, M. (1985) *Education for All: Report of the Committee of Inquiry into the Education of Children from Ethnic Minority Groups.* London: HMSO.

Trainor, D. (1995) The inspection of SMSCD, *Governors' Action*, April: 8–9.

Part 2

The core curriculum

5

English: the best combination

Sally Bentley, Judith Laurie, Peter Harrod and Kathleen Taylor

Introduction

This chapter celebrates a diversity of methods but asserts a unity of vision in the teaching of English. Writing against the background of the National Literacy Strategy (NLS) we believe that over-reliance on any one scheme impoverishes the child's literacy, and we assert the importance of flexibility in the search for excellence. In particular we look beyond the mechanics of learning to read or write, and emphasize enjoyment, motivation and the professional judgement of the teacher. In more general terms we emphasize teaching and learning rather than testing and assessment. There is a discussion of interaction with texts using a model designed to maximize speaking and listening, talk and reflection, and to lead on to writing. Although we begin with a discussion of reading, we believe this to be interwoven with speaking, listening, talking and writing. We offer our perspectives, based on classroom experience and research, without apology for the diversity but with an underlying conviction of the importance of the teacher's positive attitudes and involvement.

Teaching children to read: a vision for the future (Peter Harrod)

In the current climate of a skills-based approach to the teaching of reading and the excessive regimentation and fragmentation of the Literacy Hour in schools, I was encouraged to see in an infant school classroom a poster entitled 'Ten ways to improve your reading'. Each one of the ten headings was identical and simply contained the message 'Read'. Alongside each invitation was a picture of the cover of a quality children's book.

This deceptively simple message proclaims that we all learn to read and practise this complex set of skills by engaging in the activity itself – just as we learn any other skill, such as riding a bike or driving a car. In the case of reading, children need an experienced and sympathetic adult to help them, along with a supportive text, a climate in which they may feel free to make mistakes without fear of being punished and a non-competitive culture which emphasizes teaching and learning rather than testing and assessment.

In this section I look critically at current practices in the teaching of reading through the NLS and, in particular, at the apparent lack of emphasis on quality reading material and on motivational aspects of reading. I also seek to answer the question, 'Where have all the visionaries gone?'. I define 'visionary' as one who is able to see beyond the mechanics of learning to read, who offers a vision of reading as a holistic process which emphasizes enjoyment and motivation. It is my view that the professional judgement of the teacher in making choices needs to be restored to the equation. It is not the intention to present a summary of relevant research, since readers may refer to Adams (1990), Harrison (1996), Beard (1999) and others for such solace. My aim is to present a view of reading which places fun and motivation above skills, strategies and test scores; and while I look back nostalgically at writers who have sought to champion those values, I also claim that they have universal currency for teaching reading in particular, and for learning in general. Those who are looking for research to support this view are referred to a review of the field by Wray et al. (1999).

Although we all learn in subtly different and idiosyncratic ways, the process of reading is fundamentally the same for everyone, irrespective of intelligence or learning style. All readers need to recognize and decode the symbols on the page efficiently. This process involves a secure understanding of the relationship between sound and symbols, technically referred to as phoneme-grapheme correspondence. In addition, readers need to develop the facility to predict sequences of language (syntactic awareness) and be able to make sense of what they are reading (semantic understanding).

There is nothing new in this model. Some time ago, Durrell (1956) wrote that all three elements of reading are complementary to one another. More recent writers have refined and extended this complex process. Research by Goodman (1967) and others has shown, for example, that if sense is to be made of the print, then it is the 'predicting reader' who is more likely to achieve this basic aim of reading. Readers who struggle to read through a predominantly phonic approach tend to develop what Frank Smith (1985), in his thought-provoking book, calls 'tunnel vision', because their short-term memory is insufficient to allow them to engage with the meaning and narrative of the text. To illustrate this point, I suggest that you try punching a small hole in a piece of card, placing it over the first letter of an unseen text, and attempting to 'read' letter by letter. After reading a sentence, you will probably find that you have forgotten what you have read, because the short-term memory can only cope with small amounts of information which make no sense or have no meaning. Teachers have traditionally labelled this type of reading as 'barking at print'. Smith (1997) points out that phonics work if you have a good idea of what a word is in the first place. Elsewhere, he argues that knowledge of phonic rules provides a clue to the sound of a configuration (Smith 1994). It is this 'mediating function', as Smith calls it, which helps the process of prediction.

A study of the reading process provides parents and teachers with important insights into how we learn to read and the methods and approaches which support that task. In order to facilitate prediction strategies, I would suggest that there are three important prerequisites: the context, the adult support and the text itself. As stated earlier, the *context* must be a secure one, in which the reader has absolute trust in the adult helper, in which mistakes can confidently be made and subsequently corrected in a sympathetic and encouraging manner. I am sure that readers will agree that we all learn as much from our errors as we do from our successes. The *adult* should support the young reader both by encouraging prediction strategies and by reading with the child to help with difficult words and language constructions. Many teachers will recognize this as the 'apprenticeship' approach to teaching reading, which is rooted in the work of the celebrated Russian psychologist, Vygotsky. Such an approach is often erroneously referred to as a 'method', but in fact, like the much maligned 'real books' approach, it is a *medium* through which many methods may be employed. For example, once the story is read, problem words and expressions may be returned to, in order to use phonic and word recognition strategies to encourage what are traditionally referred to as 'word attack' skills.

It is the quality of the *text* which is often neglected in the debate about reading. The text is a key feature, not only in providing the kind of language which is highly predictable to the child, but also in motivating the child to read because of its inherent value either as a story or as a piece of information text. If the child does not engage with the text, the value of this intrinsic motive, the virtues of which are extolled in the works of great educational thinkers such as Bruner, is lost, and negative attitudes towards reading may ensue. After all, there is little point in teaching a child a skill which they are unlikely to want to use! Related to this point is the value of rereading. My experience is that many parents believe that rereading (or reading) a text which is too easy for the child is unproductive. Quite the contrary: rereading, and reading 'easy' text, allows children to practise those important skills of interpretation and fluency in reading, which is not possible when they are reading at the threshold of their ability. An analogy might be drawn with learning to play an instrument. If novice musicians were always struggling with the next most difficult piece, or simply practising scales, arpeggios and études, they would soon give up the difficult challenge of learning to play. In the same way as pianists need to play their repertoire and to develop the art of interpretation, as well as hone their skills, a reader needs to read (and reread) a combination of 'easy' texts in order to develop those very important higher order reading skills to appreciate the nuances of text, and most important of all, to enjoy reading for its own sake.

Phonological awareness (the ability to discriminate between sounds) and phonic skills are also an important and integral part of the reading process. I have emphasized other strategies because they are too often neglected in the current debate and the contemporary received wisdom surrounding the teaching of reading. Perhaps the balance needed to be restored, but not at the expense of a vision of what it means to be a reader and what reading in its fullest sense is all about. I am not alone in presenting this argument. Many supporters of a phonics-based approach have cited Marilyn Jager Adams as their champion, using selective references to her work to present a distorted picture in order to reinforce their own preference for such an approach to reading. Careful reading of Adams (1990) reveals a more balanced approach. Adams argues, and I would strongly support her assertions, that children should be given as much opportunity as possible to practise their reading, and that repeated readings of text have been found to produce marked improvements in word recognition, fluency and comprehension. She further points out that the single most important activity for building the knowledge and skills required for reading appears to be reading *aloud* to children regularly and interactively.

Many stories in fact lend themselves to the development of phonic skills through the interactive approach advocated by Adams (1990). One example is the delightful story *Each Peach Pear Plum* by Janet and Alan Ahlberg (1978). Here the different sounds which the vowels 'ea' make in the words' peach' and 'pear' may be taught within the context of a well-loved story. Equally effective are the popular and humorous Dr Seuss books, such as *The Cat in the Hat* (1958) and *Green Eggs and Ham* (1962), which can systematically teach children the sounds and spellings of key words in an interesting and enjoyable way. Writers such as Seuss have the skill and insight necessary to write highly motivating stories within the limitations of a restricted vocabulary, which emphasizes phonic sounds and blends. Moreover, the rhythms and rhymes of the stories, rather like nursery rhymes, are highly predictable, and therefore support those important prediction strategies.

Increasingly, computer software is applying the same principles. In the BBC website, bbc.co.uk/education/wordsandpictures/phonics, for example, poems are similarly employed to arouse interest in the sounds of our complicated and irregular language. I suggest that you look up the poem, 'A Meal by the Sea' for an example of how the long vowel sound 'ea' is taught in an interesting and enjoyable context. Nor should we ignore the fact that the stories and experiences of the child written down by an adult provide strong support for the reading process, and make good reading material – not only for children but also for their peers. This is known as the 'language experience approach', and is advocated as part of a balanced approach to the teaching of reading which Adams (1990) and many other experts would advocate. Margaret Meek (1991, 1994) is one highly respected and inspirational writer in the field who has consistently supported this approach. Sadly, current received wisdom appears to condemn such tried and tested practice to the recycle bin.

I argued earlier that the reading process is the same for all children, and my contention is that the approach summarized above applies to all children irrespective of their abilities. It seems sensible to me that, when a child has been diagnosed as 'dyslexic', for example, the more parents and teachers can provide interesting and motivating challenges, the more likely it is that such children will be able to overcome their debilitating handicap. Moreover, I would suggest that prediction skills are especially significant for such children, in order to help them overcome the problems which they face in handling the minutiae of print. Dickens' well-chosen words in *Great Expectations* ([1861] 1996: 59) express this sentiment with a great deal more eloquence than I can: 'I struggled through the alphabet as if it had been a bramble bush, getting considerably worried and scratched by every letter'.

Clearly Dickens was no great advocate of an approach to the teaching of reading which places phonic and other skills at the apex of a hierarchically organized taxonomy of objectives. Throughout the history of the literature on the teaching of reading a number of writers have sought to present a vision which finds such a mechanistic process dehumanizing and patronizing to children. Morris (1963) in a compelling book which many older teachers will have encountered, argues vehemently for an approach which plays down the value of phonic and word recognition approaches *per se*, and emphasizes the importance of what he calls 'context-support'. This approach stresses the fact that words have a life of their own in the mind of the individual child, and that we dress our concepts in the clothing available to us from the wardrobe of experience. Morris' support for what he calls 'responsive' reading has much in common with a social constructivist approach to learning in science, referred to elsewhere in this book. He was also one of the first writers in the field to recognize the contribution made by the psycholinguistic movement to the debate about the teaching of reading.

It was this movement, spearheaded by Goodman (1967), which offered new insights into the reading process and recognized for the first time the part that language, as well as human psychology, plays in the process. Hitherto, the debate had raged around the controversy (which still rumbles on) as to whether a phonic or 'whole word' ('look and say') method was the more effective approach. Psycholinguistics not only added to the technical knowledge of how the reading process actually works but also showed how important the text is in supporting the prediction strategies of the reader, and in drawing on the child's intuitive knowledge of how the English language system works. This point was illustrated by my daughter Katy, aged 6, reading from a well-loved story by Judith Kerr (1970) *Mog the Forgetful Cat*. Katy's initial attempt at reading 'Once Mog had a bad day', followed by two other abortive ones, came out as, 'One morning had a bad day'. She knew that this was not right because it did not conform to her expectations of the grammar of fully formed text. She was allowed time and space to self-correct and after a minute or two came up with the right match because she was able to use a combination of grapho-phonemic, syntactic and semantic cueing systems, coupled with her enjoyment of, and absorption with the text, to solve the problem. Such an analysis of a child's miscues in reading can provide what Goodman (1967) calls a window on the reading process, which allows teachers to infer how a reader's mind interacts with the text to produce a formula which not only allows the child to decode the text, but which, more significantly, encourages the child to learn the joy of being 'lost in a book'.

Unfortunately, it does not always work as smoothly as that. One child attempting to read the sentence, 'The tortoise lost its shell and was completely naked' actually read, 'The tortoise lost its shell and was completely knackered'! There is a lesson about phonics for us all to learn in this illustration.

Many of the visionary contributions referred to above have been synthesized and applied to the primary school by Margaret Meek (1994) in a challenging and influential text, to which I regularly return for inspiration. All her writing is characterized by her insistence that shared enjoyment between teacher and child is at the heart of learning to read. To Meek (1994), and to Morris (1963) before her, reading is the active encounter of one mind and one imagination with another. It is indeed truly ironic that the shared context of a one-to-one relationship is no longer favoured by the NLS, and has been replaced, at worst, by hour upon hour of teacher-led instruction, based upon isolated bits of uninspiring and demotivating text. Above all else, Meek shares with Smith the assumption that it is the reading diet of beginners which makes all the difference to their view of reading and their attitudes towards print. Perhaps this is even more crucial for older and 'reluctant' or 'remedial' readers for whom intrinsic motivation becomes paramount.

In summary, I am arguing for an approach to learning to read which teaches phonic skills in context (using high interest words, topics and language), which is supported by quality texts which match the child's interests and enthusiasms and which provide the same kind of support which would be given to the learning of any other highly complex skill. My own vision is that teaching children to read should be partly *functional* or *instrumental* – in order to empower them to gain maximum benefit from the many purposes of print – but more especially *expressive*, in the sense that they have access to a wide range of quality literature from which they can select their own preferences, or reject texts in favour of their own individual choices. Judgement of quality, or worth, is a very personal thing, of course, and should be entrusted at least partly to the child.

The NLS has much to commend it. In particular, it opens up the neglected field of non-fiction reading and its apprenticeship model is one which I enthusiastically support. Unfortunately, however, its naively eclectic approach and its obsession with pockets of time and gobbets of text, lead to the fragmentation and segmentation which I described earlier. More disturbingly, there appears to be a lack of an underlying rationale which explains and justifies its approach. Roger Beard's (1999) worthy *post hoc* attempt at such a rationale seems to do little more than confirm the NLS's lack of a consistent philosophy.

What is needed, in my opinion, is for teachers to be freed from the excessively prescriptive approach which characterizes the NLS, and to re-introduce elements of professional choice, judgement and selection. My own rationale for making such judgements would be drawn from the vision summarized above, and would take the form of an elaborated version of the poster which introduced this chapter. It does not deny the importance of what Smith calls 'mediated' phonic knowledge in the process:

1 READ for enjoyment and pleasure
2 READ responsively for understanding
3 READ purposefully for information and empowerment
4 READ to predict meaning
5 READ from quality texts
6 READ other children's work
7 READ and reread
8 READ widely
9 READ using the latest technologies
10 READ and continue to read for life

Each teacher will, rightly in my view, have their own vision, or set of guiding principles for the teaching of reading. It is this vision which puts soul into the learning process. Moreover, it affords teachers that important professional freedom and judgement to make decisions about priorities, methods and approaches in implementing objectives, which the recipe-driven NLS seems to deny them.

From 'booktalk' to guided reading (Sally Bentley and Judith Laurie)

Our work describes how guided reading can develop into a more integrated model. Guided reading has much potential to fulfil all aspects of English and other curricular areas, but this is often untapped (Ofsted 2000). We suggest a model based upon the concept of 'booktalk' (Chambers 1993) as a way to fulfil the potential of guided reading by engaging the child in a fuller conversation about the text. We offer a practical example of a guided reading session where booktalk is harnessed to specific learning outcomes in a short, intense reading/discussion activity that would fit comfortably into the NLS suggestion for an average Key Stage 2 session of 20 minutes.

Our work with trainee teachers in schools has shown that guided group reading seems to be done with varying degrees of success, in particular at Key Stage 2. Some teachers even seem unsure of its purpose, and are only half aware of its potential. We will therefore look again at the concept of guided reading and consider one way that it can effectively be implemented.

A guided reading session, when given a clear focus, can serve a range of pedagogic purposes. It can help to develop a range of both basic and more advanced reading skills (Ofsted 2000, Section 9: 24) and in addition its benefits can be felt in other areas of the curriculum:

- It develops speaking and listening skills in accordance with the aims of the NLS (DfEE 1998). In particular, it provides a secure and non-punitive environment in which less confident readers and speakers can venture ideas to peers – ideas which they might not otherwise share. It allows them to develop the skills of answering questions, arguing and debating, encouraging interaction among children and between teacher and child (Davies *et al.* 1993a, 1993b, 1994).

- It encourages children to see beyond the language, structure, information or story. Through discussion they begin to appreciate how texts are constructed. These are metalinguistic and metafictional discussions; in turn they should improve writing, because pupils with a conscious understanding of how language is used for particular effects by published authors should be able to apply this knowledge in their own writing. Group reading should, therefore, be one of the methods by which Ofsted's desired 'significant improvement in the quality of writing' is achieved (1999, Section 10: 25).
- Guided reading offers an effective context for children to explore spiritual, moral, social and cultural issues, as suggested in the NLS framework for teaching (DfEE 1998). It provides a forum in which ideas can be shared and in which pupils can learn to respect each other's points of view.
- It facilitates the development of descriptive and observational skills and pleasurably develops the sustained attention and concentration needed in so many other contexts (Davies *et al.* 1993b).

It is tempting to list many more benefits of guided reading and to heap praise upon it as a method that can both inspire and teach children. However, these benefits presuppose that guided reading involves not just some form of group or individual reading, but that the follow-up activity involves a group discussion of some kind. Unfortunately, in some situations the discussion element is held up or curtailed because of the need to complete the reading-aloud element, thus frustrating the fluent readers and limiting the possibilities of the approach.

The idea of holding group discussions about books received much attention in the early 1990s. It was argued that the process of reading 'should be an active experience, involving questioning, problem-solving, hypothesising, and imagining: pupils should make sense of a text by interacting with it. It is important not to pre-empt pupils' responses, or to suggest that there is an orthodox, accepted interpretation' (Cox 1989: 6.1, 6.2). This led to a number of initiatives such as the 'tell me' approach to booktalk (Chambers 1993). This was an attempt to get away from the traditional method of questioning designed to winkle the 'correct' answer from the child's mind. English teaching, Chambers suggested, had too often resorted to the use of the word 'Why?', leaving the child with a blank mind and a feeling of failure because they could not understand the hidden secrets of the text. Chambers wanted children to enjoy talking about the books they had read, but realized that a 'free for all' talking shop would not lead to the most fruitful discussions. Therefore, he put together a framework of questions which could be used to structure booktalk sessions, though he was quick to remind his readers that the list was not prescriptive; booktalk should not be reduced to a 'mechanical textbook programme' (Chambers 1993: 87).

The questions are many and varied, but over the years they have been reduced to a few manageable and memorable starter questions suitable for one-off sessions, such as:

- Was there anything you liked about this book?
- Was there anything you disliked?
- Who is the main character?
- What do you think the book is about?
- If you were going to recommend this book to someone else, what would you say?

We believe Chambers' questions can be adapted to help teachers make full use of guided reading and to meet the current needs of pupils. Booktalk is an open-ended activity, which puts the book at the centre of the discussion and encourages children to draw out of it what they will. This is, of course, a laudable aim. Gordon Wells (1985: 35), writing about preschool pupils, argues that 'The most enriching experience of all for many pupils is probably the open-ended exploratory talk that arises from the reading of stories'.

Enthusiasm and enjoyment can arise from children sharing and talking about books in a booktalk session. If this positive feeling can be harnessed to specific NLS learning objectives planned by the teacher (and it can!), then we have a potent model for guided reading sessions, and one which will integrate them with the other aspects of English. Mikhail Bakhtin provides a model for just such interaction, which he calls 'dialogic' (1981: 272). In such interaction the teacher, the children, the learning objectives and the book all exert their influence on the communication situation. The book is placed at the centre of a whirling discussion, which flings ideas outwards in a wide centrifugal movement. In contrast, some traditional teacher-led 'Why?' discussions applied powerful centripetal pressures to the book, which was pressed into the service of the teacher. The challenge, therefore, is to harness both forces, centrifugal and centripetal, in a rich form of interactivity.

Although harnessing specific learning outcomes to an inherently open-ended activity needs to be handled with caution, it is worth the teacher's efforts because it offers the opportunity to meet some difficult targets. For example: 'to identify social, moral or cultural issues in stories, e.g.

the dilemmas faced by characters or the moral of the story, and to discuss how the characters deal with them; to locate evidence in text' (Year 4, Term 3); 'to evaluate a book by referring to details and examples in the text' (Year 5, Term 1); 'to explore similarities and differences between oral and written story telling' (Year 5, Term 2); 'to articulate personal responses to literature, identifying why and how text affects the reader' (Year 6, Term 1) (DfEE 1998: 42, 44, 46, 50).

We can now offer an analysis of how an approach to guided group reading based on the booktalk model can contribute to raising standards in Key Stage 2. National assessment (QCA 2000) helps us to identify weak areas critical to children's further progress in reading skills. In Table 5.1 the Qualifications and Curriculum Authority (QCA) (2000: 15) targets

Table 5.1 Identified targets at Level 3, matched with booktalk questions

QCA targets	Questions
Children achieving Level 3 need to:	
• look across the text to see overall patterns, e.g. sequence, use of illustrations; • connect two different parts of the text together;	'Were there any patterns – any connections – that you noticed?'
• generalise from two or three instances;	'What does the person telling the story – the narrator – think or feel about the characters? Does she like/ dislike them? How do you know?'
• understand features and functions of page layout and organisation;	How are the text and pictures laid out? Is all the print one size and shape? Does this affect how you respond?
• make clear references to the text to support their ideas;	'How do you know?'
• identify the purpose and potential readers of texts.	'Do you know people who you think would especially like it? What would you suggest I tell other people about it that will help them decide whether they want to read it or not? Which people would be the ones who should read it? Older than you? Younger?'

Table 5.2   Identified targets at Level 5, matched with booktalk questions

QCA *targets*	*Questions*
Children achieving Level 5 need to:	
• take an overview of texts and also use evidence to support that view;	'Have you read other books like it? How is this one the same? If the writer asked you what could be improved in the book, what would you say? We've listened to each other's thoughts and heard all sorts of things that each of us has noticed. Are you surprised by anything someone else has said? Has anyone said anything that has changed your mind in any way about the book?'
• explain imagery fully by describing what the words conjure up in the imagination;	'When you were reading, did you "see" the story happening in your imagination? Which details – which passages – helped you "see" it best? Which passages stay in your mind most vividly?'
• be able to relate features of form (e.g. line length and rhyme in poetry) to theme and effect.	'Have you read other books like it? How is this one the same? How is it different? When you first saw the book, even before you read it, what kind of book did you think it was going to be? Now you've read it, is it as you expected? What made you think this? Have you read other books like it? How is this one the same?'

at Level 3 are listed on the left in an unedited form. On the right are questions, which are mostly taken verbatim from the list of suggested questions in Chambers (1993: 87–91). Those questions not given in inverted commas are our own.

The purpose of this comparison is not to provide a model for a session, but to indicate how probing some of the original booktalk questions actually were, and how ripe they are for use in this new context with very little manipulation or adjustment. On reaching Level 5, the nature of the booktalk questions becomes more open-ended, inviting deeper use of the imagination and experience – thus, a wider range of English skills will be used (see Table 5.2).

These specific booktalk questions are not the only way of addressing children's reading needs and, indeed, they would have to be supported by further questions targeted at the particular text. Chambers himself wanted teachers to devise their own questions and to use the ideas generated by the children as a springboard for further discussion. The teacher can relatively easily set up guided reading sessions focused on specific learning outcomes while still ensuring pleasurable, self-motivating discussions. Booktalk thus becomes a mode of interaction rather than an indicator of content.

To make booktalk work well, care is needed in the teacher's choice of texts. The teacher needs 'to review her reading materials in her classroom, and to borrow and buy a selection of quality fiction with at least two copies of quality books' (Davies *et al.* 1993b: 14). However, as Hunt (1999) says, there is no essential standard of 'quality'. It is much more a matter of whether the text is good for the purpose it is intended to serve. Whether the text is deemed to be 'high quality' (a phrase often associated with beautiful illustrations, a wholesome theme, realistic characterization and so on) or 'lowbrow' (fun rather than improving, a derivative media spin-off or similar) is not necessarily the primary concern. Current educational thinking requires children to be more objective readers and in this media-dominated world it is no bad thing to ensure that they are aware of how language shapes and influences us. Thus, children must understand not only themes, messages and other relatively explicit 'meanings', which standard booktalk questions elicit, but also something about how text, both as a linguistic and a graphic sign system, constructs those meanings. Stories written in a realistic mode of writing (and these include most fantasies – see Jackson 1981 for an explication of the difference between 'realistic' and 'fantastic' text) attempt to deny their own textuality and to absorb the reader into the text. The ability to be able to stand back and understand how this process of effacement takes place is, according to Iser (1978) a higher-order reading skill. The experienced reader:

> may detach himself from his own participation in the text and see himself being guided from without. The ability to perceive oneself during the process of participation is an essential quality of the aesthetic experience; the observer finds himself in a strange, halfway position: he is involved, and he watches himself being involved.
>
> (Iser 1978: 134)

In a booktalk discussion, pupils may begin by talking about the text as if it depicted a 'real' world, debating the motivation of the characters, the setting of the story, the lifestyle portrayed and so on. They may then consider how the text works as a sign system.

Booktalk activities often centre on picture books, even at Key Stage 2. While technically the approach can work with a range of texts (non-fiction, novels, poetry, plays, media texts and so on), picture books are an accessible and useful way into the concept of language. Picture books contain not only a verbal sign system, but also a graphic sign system and their value as a resource for this language work is a point we believe is worth emphasizing. The misconception, held by some parents and teachers, that picture books are only appropriate for Key Stage 1 pupils has been challenged (Marriott 1995; Graham 1997; Moss 1997). Moss (1997: 33) claims that:

- the use of quality picture books develops children's 'visual literacy', vital in today's multimedia world;
- quality illustrations encourage discrimination of the eye and mind;
- good picture books which 'can climb up and down the ladder of the years' provide a common meeting ground for higher and lower achievers.

In fact there are many picture books that are clearly intended for older readers who have the sophistication to understand the humour, wit and often serious messages. Examples of these include *Gorilla* (1992), *The Tunnel* (1989), *Willy the Wimp* (1984) and other titles by Anthony Browne. Many picture books are 'multi-layered' with storylines that can appeal to a younger audience, and qualities at a different level for older readers – for example, *Cockatoos* by Quentin Blake (1992).

Booktalk flourishes in conjunction with picture books because the relationship between print and image can encourage readers to become aware of textuality (Lewis 1990; Stephens 1991; Moss 1992; Trites 1994). These writers cite a variety of picture books which self-consciously draw attention to their status as fiction and which may be described as 'metafictive'. Metafictive books offer fertile ground for booktalk sessions, particularly when learning objectives are targeted at developing an awareness of textuality. Some proven and enjoyable metafictive texts are Anthony Browne's *Bear Goes To Town* (1982) and *A Walk in the Park* (1977), and Jon Scieszka and Lane Smith's *The Stinky Cheese Man* (1992) and *The True Story of the Three Little Pigs! By A. Wolf* (1989). As some of these titles suggest, such texts challenge the concepts of realistic story and linear narrative by subverting conventions that we normally take for granted. They do this partly to remind us that the conventions exist. However, it requires even more skill to be able to see through the conventions of realistic narratives, which try to efface their textuality. Difficult though such a task is, this is precisely what the QCA expects children to be able to do (see Table 5.1).

The first step on the road is to get children to 'see' words and pictures not as transparent conveyors of meaning but as verbal and graphic sign systems. Moebius (1990) provides useful guidelines to some of the conventions which are used regularly in picture books and which often go unnoticed by the reader:

- the right-hand page is more dominant;
- frames present a limited view of the world; rectangular frames with a strong line around them often indicate trouble, whereas round frames imply happiness and contentment;
- breaking out of a frame may be a sign of freedom or escape;
- the point of view of the artist reveals the perspective the reader is asked to take;
- a character situated low on the page has less status than one high on the page;
- smoothly shaded, soft colours imply comfort and calmness, whereas lots of fine lines and busy cross-hatching implies anxiety or uncertainty.

These guidelines are, of course, just that. Writers and artists are sometimes highly trained individuals, self-consciously crafting their work, but often they work intuitively, exploiting their culture's underlying assumptions. Either way, their work will not always conform to these guidelines. Then it becomes interesting to debate whether the artist/ writer has 'broken the rules' to good effect or whether this reveals a weakness in a text. One of Chambers' (1993) questions invites children to make suggestions for improvements (see Table 5.2).

By way of exemplification, let us look at what could be said about just one page of an ostensibly simple and accessible story. *Dear Zoo* by Rod Campbell (1984) is generally read by preschool children or those at Key Stage 1, but this is not to say that it cannot be used as a text for older pupils to discuss, as even such an apparently straightforward book uses words and pictures in a very complex way to get its message across.

The first page ostensibly has four short sentences and a lift-the-flap picture, yet is packed with clues as to how we should read it:

'I wrote to the zoo
to send me a pet.
They sent me an . . .'

The right-hand page shows a lift-up flap depicting a crate; the crate has 'VERY HEAVY!' stamped on it and bears a label 'FROM THE ZOO'.

'He was too big!
I sent him back.'

Table 5.3 shows three clusters of textual features in the left-hand column. On the right are suggestions for booktalk questions that would encourage pupils to take notice of and talk about these issues.

Table 5.3   Developing textual features of *Dear Zoo* (Campbell 1984) for booktalk

Features of the text	Booktalk-style questions which can highlight the textual features
The text indicates that the narrator is a child because: it is all in simple sentences, not compound or complex; each begins with a pronoun ('I', then 'They', 'He', then 'I') mimicking the dialogue that the inexperienced child has with the outside world as they interact, grow and learn; it is in a child-like font; is large; it uses an exclamation mark to express surprise and amazement in a place where an experienced adult might not use one; it has a naive content (writing to zoo asking for a pet).	How can you tell from the writing that the first-person narrator is a child? Rewrite this part of the story but change the narrator to an adult and make any other changes that seem necessary. Did you keep the same simple sentences? Have you changed the plot at all? What font would you use if you were printing it? Did you begin every sentence with a pronoun? Did you keep the exclamation mark?
The writing on the crate (VERY HEAVY!) imitates the style of printing on real crates. It is very thick, black and bold. The exclamation mark reinforces or emphasizes the statement. It is a minor sentence which packs extra impact because of its compressed prose.	Do you see the words VERY HEAVY! on the crate? Has anyone seen printing like this on real crates? What did it look like? Can you think of reasons why crates often have this sort of print? What does the size and shape of letters tell you about the contents of the crate?
The liftable flap is a convention which makes explicit the reader's active involvement in the reading process. That is, it reminds the reader that they have to do something to make the text meaningful. Features like this, in what Margaret Higonnet calls 'the playground of the peritext' (Moss 1992: 59) draw the reader out of a suspension of disbelief and encourage them to adopt Iser's (1978) halfway position.	What age children particularly enjoy lift-the-flap books? What do very young children sometimes *not* know about books and stories? How does a lift-the-flap book help them learn how stories work?

   All that is from one page with little text and a very 'simple' picture. Such close reading should, of course, not always be done so intensively. Other sessions might focus more on an overview of a text or a comparison of texts. Indeed, it is important that the texts and tasks are varied and clearly focused. They must also be progressive. The teacher, whatever the age or ability of the children, first needs to introduce the concept of booktalk and to teach children how to 'play the game', what the rules are and how much fun it can be, before moving on to more focused discussions with narrower learning objectives. We suggest that you develop this by taking the rest of *Dear Zoo* or some other appropriate text, identifying textual features and generating booktalk questions.

In summary:

> booktalk is a good vehicle for developing skills of literary criticism and debate. The teachers noted that as the silent, personal experience of reading fiction became a spoken response, so the spontaneous reaction became reflective. The mode changed from casual comment to considered response. The teachers observed the close attention the pupils paid to both text and illustrations in order to explain and justify their interpretations of characters' motives and actions.
>
> (Davies *et al.* 1994: 34)

The confidence and enthusiasm generated by this method can help in the development of speaking, listening, reading and, eventually, writing skills.

Attitudes to writing (Kathleen Taylor)

English teaching emphasizes reading at the expense of writing. Ofsted (1999) recognizes the need to improve children's writing at all key stages. Rising standards in reading have highlighted further the failure to achieve rising standards in writing, as national testing shows.

The first question to ask must surely be, why is writing in a weaker position than reading? One argument is that most research in English has focused on learning to read, not write (Kress 1982). The debate between 'top-down' (whole book) and 'bottom-up' (phonics) approaches has dominated the last half century. The debate was prolific and still is. While it is expected that everyone should be able to read the greatest works of literature ever written it is not expected that anyone should be capable of writing them.

The fervour and division over reading is absent from discussions of writing. There have always been lobbies, such as the call for the return of grammar teaching. There may be a popular belief that it is more important to be able to read than write. Generally people engage in much more reading than writing, and the sort of writing that most of us do is limited to such things as shopping lists, form filling or writing the occasional letter. It would not be unreasonable to say that very few people in society are engaged in writing new and original texts but it is, of course, those very few people who are most instrumental and powerful in society (Kress 1982). Being able to write offers more than the reading ticket for joining Smiths' Literacy Club – it enables one to *run* the club!

While Ofsted annual reviews over the last decade provide evidence that all is not well in the teaching of writing (Beard 1999, 2000; Ofsted 1999) the reports also provide evidence of where good practice occurs, specifically in relation to where high performance is achieved, and in this respect offer a way forward to improving standards. The reports relate high achievement in writing to discussion with the teacher before writing, to being inspired by good literature and to teachers who are confident in subject knowledge. Poor achievement is associated with decontextualized, undemanding exercises, with poor teacher intervention in the drafting process, with teachers who are weak in subject knowledge and with insufficient use of writing as a tool for thinking. The reports call for more systematic teaching of grammar, punctuation and spelling (Ofsted 1999, 2000).

Good practice in writing is notoriously hard to define, and even when defined it is hard to measure or assess: 'The best writing is vigorous, committed, honest and interesting. We have not included these qualities in our attainment targets because they cannot be mapped on to levels. Even so, all good classroom practice will be geared to encouraging and fostering these vital qualities' (DFE 1988, para. 10: 19). But if such qualities are categorically excluded, all writing and all education suffers. What emerged from the National Curriculum was a curriculum led by attainment targets. The tendency to promote skills narrowly related to specific knowledge contexts inhibited teachers from allowing children to take *ownership* of skills. Thus, for example, rather than discovering genres of writing through experiment and enquiry, the child became subject to imposed definitions of genre. The NLS does give emphasis to investigation and enquiry; but it is only through the child's desire to enquire and to communicate that investigation and enquiry can take off into significant learning about writing. The missing and essential ingredient, then, is attitude. When positive attitudes are engendered towards acquiring and expressing knowledge, the child will demand to be taught the skills in order to communicate knowledge and to develop further understanding.

So how can teachers enable children to become skilful and knowledgeable writers? A number of planning features will be discussed here, and the first is that writing must be contextualized. When decontextualized tasks are imposed, this is a rejection of the knowledge and skill children already have (Hall 1987). For a very young child the context may well be a desire for time and space to explore. Thus the child finds enjoyment and meaning in making marks, making patterns, writing their name or using formats such as lists, notices, stories and letters. In these early mark-making processes the child is formulating their ideas and attempting to be creative. The inventiveness and creativity that a child shows, as it struggles with the mysteries of written language, undoubtedly constitutes the notion of art (Smith 1982). These early marks involve real literacy (Hall 1987; Harste *et al.* 1984).

Another feature is that writing can give permanence to spoken words or thoughts. If thoughts and ideas are not recorded in some way then they may be lost in the transience of the spoken word. Smith (1982) sees the need for a permanent record as another reason for the persistence of writing. Craig (1990) remembers how it felt to see her first words in print, and the resultant positive feelings, wonder and exultation.

Children do seem to understand this notion. James, a 5-year-old, commented, 'if you don't write it in a book it just disappears, it flies away' and Daniel, also aged 5, said, 'you can't see your talk but you can see your writing'. When children have their own experiences to share or stories to tell, motivation to give them permanence is paramount. I taught three 6-year-old boys who were desperate to recount their story of 'scrumping' the previous night; they became equally desperate to transpose their spoken account into written form. They knew that the written form demanded different structures and conventions and were eager to develop their understanding. In discussion with the teacher they were able to make decisions about how to emphasize the main point in a sentence (clause structure), how to make one point appear more import-ant than another (use of appropriate connectives for subordination), how to choose words for greater impact (strong verbs) and so on.

In the earliest stages the scribe, be it parent or teacher, must provide a means of documenting the child's thoughts before they are capable of doing this for themselves. Joanne, aged 4 years and 10 months, told a story which I scribed as a big book. I now use it with adult students on teacher training courses in order to show the (often untapped) know-ledge young children possess about story structure. Joanne began her story, 'The stars came out at night, they didn't come out in the morn-ing. At night magic flowers open'. This is a startlingly sophisticated opening. Joanne adopts the voice of an experienced narrator who entices her reader into her created world. She later uses personification to introduce 'Twinkle', a 'special star', and employs a lost-and-found plot: 'One of the fairies, Mary-Diane, has lost her ring'. As the story unfolds Joanne clearly draws from the stories she knows, in particular the story of the Nativity (see also Fox 1993). Her story is not unusual, it was one of many told by the children, captured in writing by the teacher. Children have a great many stories to tell and have knowledge of a great many literary devices, but much remains locked in their heads unless teachers apportion time so that they can listen to the children and develop further their knowledge about stories and writing. The teacher's demonstration of structuring writing from speech 'scaffolds' a child's understanding of written composition, and provides the opportunity for the child to talk about learning to write (DfEE 2000).

Teacher demonstration, teacher scribing and supporting composition are methods advocated in guidance for the NLS (DfEE 2000). The guidance clarifies and makes explicit those methods while stressing that the teacher should not 'over scribe' for the child. The child must want to take over, must be desperate to take up the pen for themselves. Writing cannot be forced upon a child – the child must *want* to write. This desperate desire comes about when a child sees writing being done and realizes what writing can do (Smith 1982).

Just as experience and speech can produce the desire to write, so also writing changes experience and speech. As children see how written language is composed and how it works, they begin to get in on the craft of writing (McKenzie 1986). They are able to see that writing is to do with shaping, organizing and revising ideas, an 'iterative' process (DfEE 2000). Scribing releases the child from difficulties and competences associated with writing, enabling them to focus on what they are trying to write (Perera 1984). The scribe is therefore enabling the child to organize and develop possibilities in their own mind (Smith 1982). This interaction between the writer and the writing happens in whatever context the writing is taking place.

Children do not always want to use writing to communicate. Sometimes they have no other reason for writing than the desire to invent and create and to see tangible evidence of their thoughts and words on paper. Their writing is therefore similar to thinking (Whitehead 1990). This process can include older children using cartoons and bubbles to strengthen the impact of what they write. It is purely for their own personal use that they write – this is why so many like to keep secret scribblings in private books or diaries (as did the Brontës) and why so many teachers organize their classrooms to accommodate this type of private writing.

Writing, therefore, is not always done for the express purpose of communication, and perhaps if this personal writing were to be given greater value in schools there would be less pressure for the child always to perform correctly. This is only a pleasure when the child succeeds, and lack of success is a possible reason for the lack of writing that takes place when children leave school.

We have seen that, at its best, learning to write is an expression of talking and thinking which in itself shapes talking and thinking. Scribing involves dialogue: talking and listening between teacher and child. Communication via the written word is very much an active process. It requires not only to be instigated by the person desiring to communicate but also for the intended recipient to partake in the process. In verbal communication it is possible to see if the communication is failing, and often to understand how it is failing. Then adjustment can be made in response to the reactions. In written communication no such instant feedback is possible. Nevertheless, children communicate successfully with each other in writing from an early age. A high degree of commitment to writing was seen in a change from a non-literate home corner in a nursery class into a literate home corner, with dramatic effect (Hall 1987).

While communication is being effected at this stage, accuracy is not foremost in the children's approach to writing. It is quite obvious that rudimentary writing will suffice for communication purposes. In my own classroom, children would often place notices on partly-built models for others not to touch: 'do nt tch'. Similar strategies are cited in Bissex (1980). Where there is an urgent, contextualized desire to communicate, children succeed in making themselves understood in written form. Note that it is the communication of the message that is important and the unconventional means of writing is of no significance to the meaning.

The question then arises that if children's communication is successful in its existing form, what is the incentive to develop their writing skills to a more conventional or more sophisticated form? To address this question we need to examine what is happening in the situations cited above. First, the children had very strong feelings and second they chose writing as the appropriate medium for expressing those feelings; they wanted to make an impact! This brings us back to motivation. We have seen how an interesting, urgent context motivates the child to communicate. A teacher whose classroom ethos is about communication is more likely to motivate children to want to be accurate in their communications. The danger lies in those classrooms where correctness comes first, especially when the children do not know the process by which the teacher evaluates. Often, the expressive aspect is ignored because the teacher is more interested in the mechanical skills and evaluates the writing according to what is expected from a particular child at a particular time. Children frequently acquire a fear of being wrong and become afraid to write. These are the children who constantly look for teacher approval and ask for help over every word they want to write. Needless to say, this leads children to reject writing, or produce writing merely in order to get by in the classroom.

The remedy has to be in the hands of a sensitive teacher who organizes time in order to be fully involved in the drafting and redrafting process. It is *only* the teacher who can offer ways for children to evaluate their writing, and indeed to extend ideas. The drafts should be seen as being as important as the finished product in order for the child to know that their writing has developed and improved. Disregarding the drafts is like disregarding an artist's early sketches. Just as an artist develops sketches a writer must develop drafts and see them as valuable in their own right.

Built into a strategy for writing must be the enabling of children to evaluate and self-correct. Children need to know that there is more to this process than spelling and punctuation checks; they need to be able to evaluate the literary content of their writing. The teacher has to provide a model of demonstration whereby the children see the skills necessary to evaluate a piece of writing – otherwise, the children will only understand the mechanical right or wrong and will only perceive their writing in those terms, which demotivates them from literary expression.

Progress towards more conventional and sophisticated writing may also be affected by issues around the pupils' personal choices. Graves (1991) found that children wrote more when they could address topics they themselves had negotiated and when the teacher was able to be flexible in the amount of time provided for writing. It is unfortunate, to say the least, that at present such activities are given prescribed times within the classroom timetable (i.e. usually 20 minutes at the same time each day, every day of the school week, every week in the school term). This in itself creates in children the feeling that writing is merely a mechanical exercise and very directed. The opportunity for spontaneity and self-selection is highly limited. I believe that teachers must ask themselves how they can respond to the communicative urgency children feel. If we deny children this human need we may, in future, have accurate technicians rather than creative and effective writers.

Another motivating factor towards progress is an identifiable audience. This is noticeable when young children write to one another, especially when an older child writes to a younger child. Dialogue and communication are important in scribing and are vital also in assessment and progress. Perhaps the worst response to written communication is that of a tick or grade. The writer, in this situation, has no indication of the teacher's criteria and is thus unable to make adjustments that will improve the quality of communication. Neither party can be reassured that either are contributing to some kind of human relationship, which is necessary if the child is to feel any sense of motivation. Instead of teachers seeing themselves as the sole providers of content, the sole controllers of script, they need to see themselves as advisers, collaborators, facilitators and models. In this role teachers can advise on content, form, grammar, spelling and punctuation. They therefore intervene at the point of writing, and in the writing act.

Finally, example is crucial to progress. It is a rather odd phenomenon if the teacher, a presumed expert, is never actually seen engaged in writing! Craig's (1990) childhood memories were of her father typing. The writing was not of an incidental nature (i.e. paying bills or answering letters) but was in an environment where people were writing for a living. I see the teaching profession as offering an opportunity to teachers to become writers. Surely, developing one's own reading and writing is an ongoing prerequisite for being able to teach others. The notion of learning for life, promoted through education, seems ironic if the very promoters are not engaged in the process themselves. I work with students in initial teacher training. They tell children a story, then help the children change it into written form. It becomes a bound storybook for children, to be used as a starting point for writing. The response from children is always to admire the work of the student author and want to take up the role of author themselves. There is a difference here between modelling writing and a model writer. The first involves a demonstration of the process of writing, the second demonstrates what can be achieved by writing. It is the latter that fosters the ambition to write. This can only be effected by those closest to the child. If vigour, commitment, honesty and interest are immeasurable, perhaps only the teachers can supply them, and match them to the national directives of the day.

It is often said that being a good reader does not necessarily result in being a good writer. Reading will not simply rub off on the reader and equip them with the skills to become a good writer! Explanations are required. Booktalk, the process described and developed earlier in this chapter by Sally Bentley and Judith Laurie, can be a step from reading, through talking and listening, to writing. For example, discussion of plot structures may help to draw children's attention to similarities and differences in authors' styles. A structure such as a collection of three characters, one big, one middle, one small, is seen in many children's stories, but used in different ways. Although the authors may use a similar format, the stories are unique in characterization, themes, use of individual imagination and style of writing. Finding out about these devices seizes the attention. The children will then have an urgent need to identify where they occur, to see them working, to communicate about them and to use them.

For example, in my classroom many children responded well to using very basic writing frames in early readers from which to construct their own stories. One particular example was Amy's book which she made as a present for me. Her basic reader (*Ginn 360*, 1980) is limited to a few words ('Look', 'No, not in here') until the very end when 'Yes' is used. The story is told in pictures, showing a child trying to find his treasure chest of sweets. The child searches to no avail until, at the very end of the story, he finds what he is looking for. Amy constructed her book in similar style, but with adaptations reflecting her experience. On each page she wrote 'Look in here' on a flap cut out in the shape of various household fittings (a cushion, curtains, wardrobe, and a treasure chest). When I lifted the flap I saw written, 'No, not in here!'. On the last page Amy added my name: 'Look in here Mrs Taylor'. I remember her copying my name from the label on the classroom door. The insertion of my name added just the right amount of tension – underneath this special flap, which was a Christmas tree, the search might end. Hence she proudly offered me the book and I read it while she watched. To my surprise and delight when I lifted the Christmas tree there was a little Bourneville chocolate around which was written: 'Yes, in here!'. This has clear associations with the process described by Bruner and Watson (1983) as 'scaffolding' where one uses somebody else's structure to discover one's own voice.

Enabling children to have at their fingertips devices and conventions, patterns and formats used by famous and respected authors allows them to develop their own sense of authorship. The engaging of children in creating of storybooks, either individually or collaboratively in pairs or groups, allows them to take on the role of author. Children's own storybooks and class storybooks provide the personal kind of reading that is highly motivating.

Learning to write depends upon attitude. It cannot be separated from reading and conversation; it springs from them and enriches them. It depends on the enthusiasm, commitment, skill and interaction of the teacher. Finally, it is the supportive nature of the pupil–teacher relationship and the environment that will enable children to take on writing and all its risks and pleasures.

References

Adams, M.J. (1990) *Beginning To Read: Thinking and Learning About Print*. Cambridge, MA: MIT.

Ahlberg, J. and Ahlberg, A. (1978) *Each Peach Pear Plum*. Harmondsworth: Kestrel.

Bakhtin, M. (1981) Discourse in the novel, in M. Bakhtin, *The Dialogic Imagination: Four Essays*, trans. C. Emerson and M. Holquist. Austin, TX: University of Texas Press.

Beard, R. (1999) *National Literacy Strategy: Review of Research and Other Related Evidence.* Sudbury: DfEE.

Beard, R. (2000) *Developing Writing 3–13.* London: Hodder & Stoughton.

Bissex, G. (1980) *GNYS AT WRK: A Child Learns to Write and Read.* Cambridge, MA: Harvard University Press.

Blake, Q. (1992) *Cockatoos.* London: Jonathan Cape.

Browne, A. (1977) *A Walk in the Park.* London: Hamilton-Penguin.

Browne, A. (1982) *Bear Goes To Town.* London: Hamilton-Penguin.

Browne, A. (1984) *Willy the Wimp.* London: Hamilton-Penguin.

Browne, A. (1989) *The Tunnel.* London: Hamilton-Penguin.

Browne, A. (1992) *Gorilla.* London: Hamilton-Penguin.

Bruner, J. and Watson, R. (1983) *Child's Talk: Learning to Use Language.* Oxford: Oxford University Press.

Campbell, R. (1984) *Dear Zoo.* London: Penguin.

Chambers, A. (1993) *Tell Me: Children, Reading and Talk.* Woodchester: Thimble.

Cox, B. (1989) *English for Ages 5 to 16.* London: DES.

Craig, F. (1990) *The Natural Way to Learn: The Apprenticeship Approach to Literacy.* Upton Upon Severn: Self Publishing Association Ltd (One to One Publications).

Davies, P., Karavis, S. and Monk, J. (1993a) Becoming a reader: 1, *Language and Learning*, September: 5–7.

Davies, P., Karavis, S. and Monk, J. (1993b) Becoming a reader: 2, *Language and Learning*, November: 12–15.

Davies, P., Karavis, S. and Monk, J. (1994) Becoming a reader: 3, *Language and Learning*, January–February: 32–5.

DfE (Department for Education) (1988) *English for Ages 5–11: Proposals of the Secretary of State for Education and Science and the Secretary of State for Wales.* London: DES.

DfEE (Department for Education and Employment) (1998) *The National Literacy Strategy.* London: DfEE.

DfEE (Department for Education and Employment) (2000) *Grammar for Writing.* London: DfEE.

Dickens, C. ([1861] 1996) *Great Expectations.* Boston, MA: St Martins Press.

Dr Seuss (1958) *The Cat in the Hat.* London: Collins.

Dr Seuss (1962) *Green Eggs and Ham.* London: Collins.

Durrell, D.D. (1956) *Improving Reading Instruction.* London: Harcourt, Brace & World.

Fox, C. (1993) *At the Very Edge of the Forest: The Influence of Literature on Storytelling by Children.* London: Cassell.

Ginn 360 (1980) *Here* (the Ginn Reading Programme). Aylesbury: Ginn and Company Ltd.

Goodman, K.S. (1967) Reading: a psycholinguistic guessing game, *Journal of the Reading Specialist*, 4: 126–35.

Graham, J. (1997) Imagined lands, *Language Matters*, 2: 17–21.

Graves, D. (1991) *Build a Literate Classroom.* Portsmouth, NH: Heinemann.

Hall, N. (1987) *The Emergence of Literacy.* London: Hodder & Stoughton

Harrison, C. (1996) *The Teaching of Reading: What Teachers Need to Know.* Royston: UKRA (United Kingdom Reading Association).

Harste, J., Burke, C. and Woodward, V. (1984) *Language Stories and Literacy Lessons.* Portsmouth, NH: Heinemann.

Hunt, P. (ed.) (1999) *Understanding Children's Literature: Key Essays from the International Companion Encyclopedia of Children's Literature*. London: Routledge.

Iser, W. (1978) *The Act of Reading: A Theory of Aesthetic Response*. London: Routledge.

Jackson, R. (1981) *Fantasy: The Literature of Subversion*. London: Methuen.

Kerr, J. (1970) *Mog the Forgetful Cat*. London: Collins.

Kress, G.R. (1982) *Learning to Write*. London: Routledge & Kegan Paul.

Lewis, D. (1990) The constructedness of texts: picture books and the metafictive, *Signal*, 62: 131–46.

McKenzie, M. (1986) *Journeys into Literacy*. Huddersfield: Schofield & Simms.

Marriott, S. (1995) *Read On*. London: Paul Chapman.

Meek, M. (1991*) On Being Literate*. London: Heinemann Educational.

Meek, M. (1994) *Learning to Read*. London: Bodley Head.

Moebius, W. (1990) Introduction to picturebook codes, in P. Hunt (ed.) *Development of Children's Literature: The Development of Criticism*. London: Routledge.

Morris, R. (1963) *Success and Failure in Learning to Read*. London: Oldbourne.

Moss, E. (1997) Picture books throughout the primary school, *Language Matters*, 2: 13–16.

Moss, G. (1992) Metafiction, illustration, and the poetics of children's literature, in P. Hunt (ed.) *Literature for Children: Contemporary Criticism*. London: Routledge.

Ofsted (Office for Standards in Education) (1999) *An Evaluation of the NLS*. London: The Stationery Office.

Ofsted (Office for Standards in Education) (2000) *The Annual Report of Her Majesty's Chief Inspector of Schools*. London: DfEE.

Perera, K. (1984) *Children's Writing and Reading*. Oxford: Basil Blackwell.

QCA (Qualifications and Curriculum Authority) (2000) *Standards at Key Stage 2: English, Mathematics and Science: Report on the 1999 National Curriculum Assessments for 11-year-olds*. London: QCA.

Scieszka, J. and Smith, L. (1989) *The True Story of the Three Little Pigs! By A. Wolf*. London: Penguin.

Scieszka, J. and Smith, L. (1992) *The Stinky Cheese Man*. London: Puffin.

Smith, F. (1982) *Understanding Reading*, 3rd edn. New York: Holt, Rinehart & Winston.

Smith, F. (1985) *Reading*, 2nd edn. London: Cambridge University Press.

Smith, F. (1994) *Understanding Reading*, 5th edn. Hove: Lawrence Erlbaum Associates.

Smith, F. (1997) *Reading Without Nonsense*, 3rd edn. New York: Teachers College Press.

Stephens, J. (1991) Did I tell you about the time I pushed the Brothers Grimm off Humpty Dumpty's wall? Metafictional strategies for constituting the audience as agent in the narratives of Janet and Allan Ahlberg, in M. Stone (ed.), *Children's Literature and Contemporary Theory*. Wollongong: New Literatures Research Centre, University of Wollongong.

Trites, R. (1994) Manifold narratives: metafiction and ideology in picture books, *Children's Literature in Education*, 25: 225–42.

Wells, G. (1985) *Language and Learning: An Interactional Perspective*. London: Falmer Press.

Whitehead, M. (1990) *Language and Literacy in the Early Years*. London: Paul Chapman.

Wray, D., Medwell, J., Fox, R. and Poulson, L. (1999) Teaching reading: lessons from the experts, *Reading*, April: 17–22.

6

But where is the mathematics?

Harriet Marland

Introduction

This chapter explores the elusive quality of mathematical success in the primary classroom. Examples of children's work are used to distinguish emergent insight from more humdrum acquiescence to taught procedures. Skills deemed to be characteristic of mathematically able pupils are compared with the reasoning skills embedded in successive versions of the National Curriculum for mathematics. A case is made for raising expectations for pupils' mathematical reasoning from the earliest years and throughout Key Stages 1 and 2. It is suggested that all primary pupils should be expected to explain their mathematical insights and justify their reasoning through considered (yet informal) definitions, generalizations and argument. Routine exposition of pupils' mathematical reasoning within the plenary session of daily mathematics lessons could be a way forward. This demands a shift in the teacher's perspective from valuing individual answers and particular strategies to probing pupils' understanding of the structure of mathematics and challenging their emerging concepts of proof.

A first look

Imagine yourself walking into a primary classroom that you do not know well. Even when the children are not in the room you can find out quite a lot about the teacher's expectations and the pupils' individual achievements. Look at the walls. There will certainly be artwork on display. Perhaps pupils have been exploring a new medium or learning a specific technique. Initial attempts at gaining control over the materials and tools may be visible alongside more complex final pieces using what has been learned to create a picture or design. If you are lucky, the whole process will be annotated by questions and explanations, which evolved in the class as the work took place. Stand back and you can see how the children have learned from their own explorations and from each other. You can also see that, while all (we may assume) have striven to succeed, some show flair, talent and artistry in their results while others remain diligent but dull.

Look too at the writing. Whether it is poetry or prose, extended writing or simply a list of words, you will gain insight into the learning objectives of the teacher and the varied proficiency of the children. You could, for example, rapidly sequence the pieces to show a gradient in handwriting skills. Alternatively, you might sort them to reflect the complexity of words used, though any spelling weaknesses may well have been edited out before they were put on the board. You could almost certainly suggest a cogent reason why each piece was deemed a 'good effort' and worthy of display. Perhaps one child had shown more persistence than usual; another more meticulous presentation; another deliberately extended the vocabulary employed; a fourth succeeded in sequencing events logically and so on. Whatever the task set and the specific objectives shared, you will also be able to tell very rapidly both who has an insight into the subject matter and who has an ear for language. It will be scarcely harder to tell the pedants from the poets than it was to distinguish the scribblers from the scribes or the artisans from the artists.

Peep out of the classroom window to where the children are engaged in physical education (PE). You will observe children challenging their own comfort levels and aiming to extend what they can do. Again you should see that each child is striving to improve particular skills, but there will undoubtedly be some who achieve this with a grace and gamesmanship that quite eludes the others.

Now what of the mathematics? You would be lucky to find much direct evidence of mathematical activity at all, and even then you would need to be a determined detective to piece together the clues to give you an overview of the range of achievement. In many classrooms the mathematics may be completely invisible. In others there may be a display of activities to do, indicating the type of work in progress, but it is less likely that there will be any children's work on the walls. Let us suppose, however, that this class was actually engaged in mathematics just before leaving the room, and that their activities and written work has been left out on the tables. What insights can you gain from these? You might note, perhaps, that some were using larger numbers or more (or more complex) operations in a game – but are these children actually better at mathematics or simply more adept at calculations? Many such games leave no product to guide your investigations further than an examination of the materials used to generate the situations requiring a numerical response. If there is a written record, what might you see then? Perhaps jottings indicate that some children still struggle to form neat numerals or to incorporate mathematical symbols, belying the hand-writing competence visible on the walls. Two children sitting side by side may have recorded the same results, structured into similar number sentences. Yet it would be rash to infer from such evidence that their mathematical understanding was similar at all. The written script on its own seldom provides unambiguous clues about the thinking that produced it. As teachers we need to develop skills of reading between and beyond the lines of arithmetical calculations, just as pupils need to learn to extract inferences and implications, as well as information, from a written text.

Mathematical insight is so peculiarly elusive in the primary classroom that even negative evidence is often a bonus. In some ways we might think ourselves lucky to find partial or incorrect answers. Even though they are clearly not what we actually want to see, they often indicate something about how a child is thinking. If we are not both careful and canny as teachers we are left with the paradox that increasing competence may actually disguise, rather than illuminate, a child's mathematical insights and errors of reasoning.

In this chapter I want to explore how teachers can develop a discerning eye, ear and mind for mathematical achievement which will allow them to discriminate as surely for mathematical insight as they do for art, language or movement. I will start with some examples of children at work.

Getting it right

The trouble with getting the answer right is that the result is so tediously predictable. The answer itself tells us little about the thinking behind it, yet it is in the reasoning that mathematical confidence or confusion may be found. To find out how an answer is reached, it is not enough to look into a classroom: we need to watch and to listen to the children at work.

Let's look at Leanne. She has been taught a procedure and performs this with serious intensity. Meticulous deliberate actions accompany her steady repetitive monologue. 'Four less than seven is . . . ?' she intones, reading out an incomplete number sentence. 'Seven' is said assertively, as she covers the numeral 7 on a number track with her index finger. 'One . . . two . . . three . . . four', she counts, moving her finger in deliberate steps from right to left. 'Three' is announced emphatically, as she uncovers the numeral under her finger on the fourth square. She then carefully writes a '3' to complete the original number sentence. 'Two less than seven is . . . ?' Leanne begins the procedure again without another glance at the sentence she has just finished.

In a similar fashion she plods and points her way down her page. But the observer should not be distracted by other events in the classroom assuming that Leanne will continue in just this manner. Something else may occur, and indeed it does. On the very last number sentence Leanne completes the answer quite differently, and so fast that an unwary watcher might miss this significant moment of mathematical incisiveness. Without so much as a peep at the number track for this one, Leanne simply writes out the concluding sentence: 'Five less than seven is two'.

How has Leanne achieved this final answer? Perhaps she just knows, although it is surely a strange fact to recall. Perhaps she has seen a link with the statement immediately above: 'Two less than seven is five' and has realized the significance of reversing the two numbers that make seven. Perhaps she has internalized the finger-pointing procedure in some way and has seen the answer independently formed in her mind's eye. As the watcher in question I could not tell how she had done it, but I was able to ask her. Her reply was a little clumsy in its construction, but mathematically astute. She indicated the first statement she had written: 'Four less than seven is three', and then explained the last one thus: 'Five is one more than four, so the answer is one more less than three. That's two!'

In another class Neil was more forthcoming than Leanne and volunteered his own insight without being asked directly. He was happily adding pairs of numbers that he generated from dice, but then suddenly stopped and grinned. 'I don't have to do this one!' he declared. I looked at his book, looked at the clock and then looked at his face. I could see no instantly obvious answer to the question he had set himself and it was certainly not yet time to pack away. Neil responded to my puzzled expression. Pointing to another calculation already completed somewhere else on his page he explained patiently: 'You see, the first number is two more but the second one is two less. The answer is just the same'. I had assumed he meant that he did not have to complete the number sentence at all, whereas he had realized that he could do so through reasoning but without the effort and the risk of calculation.

MacNamara and Roper (1992) have written tellingly of pupils' attainment that is 'unrecorded, unobserved and suppressed' within the classroom. Certainly, from the written answers alone, I would never have known that there was one point on each pupil's page where meticulous mechanical rigour was ousted by a moment of mathematical insight. In each of these two cases the children produced one answer in a completely different manner from any of the others. The answer itself could not have shown the distinction since it was simply correct. Only watching, questioning and listening made the change in method apparent. When asked, the children not only explained how they had reached the answer, but each articulated a powerful generalization about the underlying structure of arithmetic. Algebraic notation was not within their mathematical vocabulary at this stage, but the syntax of generalized arithmetic was clearly present.

Leanne's explanation extended:

	$7 - 4 = 3$
so	$7 - 5 = 2$
if	$a - b = c$
then	$a - (b + 1) = c - 1$
and	$a - (b + n) = c - n$

Neil's assertion extended:

	$23 + 46 = 69$
so	$25 + 44 = 69$
if	$a + b = d$
then	$(a + 2) + (b - 2) = d$
and	$(a + n) + (b - n) = d$

Looked at in this more formalized way, both children seem to be quite confidently using equivalence or balancing strategies. Leanne's is particularly impressive because it involves adding to a negative; something which many of us still find counterintuitive as adults. Such strategies have been seen by some writers as elusive and essentially difficult (e.g. Thompson 1999) and by others as key strategies which should be taught (e.g. Threlfall and Frobisher 1998). My concern here, however, is not which particular strategies should be explicitly taught and when, but how more pupils might be encouraged to articulate the relationships they themselves perceive and to phrase them into powerful general statements. Leanne and Neil did not just describe a particular procedure, but provided a clear rationalization of their strategies. It is this ability to synthesize a way to generate such speedy and accurate results, avoiding the hazards of counting and calculating, that is particularly significant. Such insights provide the learner with power over the field of arithmetic through presenting strategies they can use, adapt and extend in the future. The sadness is not only how easy it is for teachers to miss such moments, but that the pupils themselves do not necessarily see them as especially significant and may suppress the nature of their achievement, content in simply arriving at a correct answer.

Her Majesty's Inspectorate of Schools (HMI) made the point forcefully some 15 years ago (HMI 1985: 3) in the influential series 'Curriculum Matters' which was a precursor to the National Curriculum:

> In very simple terms *mathematics is about relationships* . . . And yet there is a danger in school mathematics that this fundamental feature of mathematics might not be appreciated by pupils as they become preoccupied with trying to master the details. At whatever level pupils are working the aim should be to enable them to appreciate that there are relationships between the different aspects of mathematics structure. There is no doubt that this would facilitate pupils' progress.

HMI is calling here for a determination to help pupils perceive the broader picture of mathematics within which they are operating. It must then have been disappointing when the early versions of the National Curriculum for mathematics seemed to provide a sequence of topics applied to steadily more complex situations rather than stressing the structure of arithmetic and the conceptual links between different areas of mathematics. A study contrasting the impact of different teaching styles (Askew *et al.* 1997) further corroborated HMI's assertion by distinguishing teachers who made the relationships within mathematics explicit as some of the most effective at raising standards in numeracy.

However, despite the robust and overtly optimistic statement from HMI, there are times when a limited appreciation of mathematical structure can actually make matters worse. A partially correct insight into particular relationships between numbers, accompanied by an inadequate understanding of the system as a whole, can lead to a network of errors that needs to be disentangled just as urgently as more successful strategies need to be probed and appreciated.

Getting it wrong

Incorrect answers are always fascinating. Some may seem to suggest momentary lapses of memory or concentration, but many others indicate deeper errors in the procedures followed or the generalizations used. Unfortunately, although the errors may follow a coherent pattern, it is not always easy to discern the reasoning or to distinguish between faults. In fact the most perfidious of errors can result in answers that are often correct, but founded on ill-conceived generalizations and unsustainable strategies. The difficulty for the teacher is finding the cause of the problem, especially if several of the answers are nonetheless accurate. The following examples highlight some of these difficulties.

Three boys, Adam, Brian and Charlie, were adding single-digit numbers using a number line. At first glance the work of the first two looks similar, and the third appears to be correct except for a single error that you might imagine was just a careless slip. However, appearances here are deceptive. In this case the similar answers have been generated by very different lines of thinking and the apparently random error of the third child is part of a consistently applied strategy which means that even the 'correct' answers rely on seriously flawed logic. I have written below the answers each child gave to the same set of questions in order to bring out the similarities and differences between their scripts. See if you can unravel the thinking behind each set of answers before reading the explanation below.

Adam

$3 + 4 = 6$ $7 + 2 = 8$ $2 + 4 = 5$ $3 + 0 = 2$

Brian

$3 + 4 = 6$ $7 + 2 = 8$ $2 + 4 = 5$ $3 + 0 = 3$

Charlie

$3 + 4 = 7$ $7 + 2 = 9$ $2 + 4 = 6$ $3 + 0 = 4$

Adam uses a methodical, if unwieldy, strategy. He counts along the line to the first number then counts on for the second number. Finally, when he stops counting, he finds the answer under his finger. Unfortunately his first count of 'one' coincides with him pointing to the beginning of the line, or zero. Every single answer is therefore consistently one less than it should be.

Most of Brian's answers are the same as Adam's, but for a different reason. Brian uses a somewhat more sophisticated strategy in that he starts by finding the first number on the line, rather than counting to it. However, when he counts the second number he always begins by pointing to the first number as he says 'one', and only then moves his finger on. His answers will therefore also be one less than they should be, except when he has to add zero, in which case his incorrect strategy should erroneously produce a correct answer.

Adam's and Brian's strategies are at work in many classrooms. The large number of errors they produce and the very visibility of the ponderous methods, accompanied as they are by physical movements along a number line, should ensure that they are soon seen, discussed and dismissed. But are they? Charlie's flawed reasoning is almost invisible, and yet it is a devastating indictment of the dangers of superficial correction, which can inadvertently delay effective understanding. Charlie was using Brian's strategy just the day before this exercise, methodically miscounting the second number and consequently getting each answer one less than it should be. Although his teacher spotted and 'corrected' this error, what Charlie actually learned from this experience was that all his answers fell exactly one short of what was required. He therefore evolved what must have seemed a failsafe system: to continue exactly as before, but then to 'add one for teacher' before recording an answer. So he now has a laborious system with two specific faults: that he begins to count on in the wrong place and that he adds an arbitrary extra one at the end. Yet he gets almost every answer right. His errors, seen and shared the day before, have been driven further underground. He has learned a system to generate correct answers, which, unless deliberately explored and challenged, will effectively curtail any development of understanding of the structure of the number system itself.

Charlie was intent on getting the answers right – he is a tick-dependent child who has learned to control the reward system of the classroom, but not to understand how numbers work. Other children seem to have a misplaced ambition simply to please their teacher, even though this may mean carrying out a misconceived or misinterpreted rule without scrutinizing its logic. Such pupils are the very obverse of Neil and Leanne who, at least momentarily, asserted their logical analysis over and above a learned procedure.

Two further examples of tensions created between adult and child logic illustrate the point. Both come from a classroom where a well-meaning teacher had instructed the class to 'carry the little one' when completing vertical addition with column exchange. Try to make sense of each child's precise mathematical interpretation of this phrase when you analyse the examples below.

Julie

27	43	36	12	24
+ 12	+ 18	+ 49	+ 38	39
= 39	= 61	= 85	= 41	+ 18
				= 72

Bob

26	17	39	38	246
+ 31	+ 34	+ 41	+ 25	+ 319
= 57	= 51	= 71	= 81	= 511

Julie gets most of her answers right when adding two numbers. Errors only begin to surface when digits add up to 10 or 21. In these cases she moves the units digit into the next column, something that Bob apparently does all the time. But why? Is it carelessness or is there a logic to each set of answers?

In fact the reasoning of each child is a valiant attempt to apply their own secure but limited understanding of arithmetic in order to obey the teacher's misleading mnemonic. Both children interpret 'the little one' to mean the smaller of the two numbers in a two-digit number, rather than a small suffix of the numeral '1'. Julie, however, ignores place value and always carries the numeral representing the smaller number because this is 'the little one' when you compare the two. Meanwhile Bob, with considerable mathematical sensibility, carries the units digit consistently because he knows it must always represent a number smaller than 10. For Bob, the digit in the units column is 'the little one' since it is smaller than the number represented by any digit in the tens column.

Both of these children have developed a partially accurate, but limited, sense of mathematical relationships between numbers. Nonetheless they have put themselves in a precarious position whereby they apply their own growing logic of numbers to a new situation without testing the coherence of the whole system thus created. They fail to scrutinize the final answer as a solution to the initial question, focusing rather on the steps in between. Both children could justify their methods because they believe they are doing what their teacher told them to do. Their mistake is that they have not questioned or comprehended the instruction, nor checked the consistent accuracy of the results.

The National Numeracy Strategy

The National Numeracy Strategy (NNS) should help to avoid the conflicts of logic and language experienced by Bob and Julie. Indeed the rationale for delaying the introduction of column addition and other standard algorithms explicitly acknowledges the need to ensure that pupils develop confidence in their mental strategies first, and that they then use these to sieve out impossible answers generated by half-remembered procedures (DfEE 1999a: 7). We might therefore expect both Bob and Julie to realize that some of their answers were too large and to scrutinize these again. However, such scrutiny would not necessarily lead them to challenge and alter their erroneous procedures, only to accept that on occasions they do not actually lead to the correct answer!

Stressing the evolution of more efficient methods beyond prelim-inary counting should also help Adam and Brian to improve their plodding procedures. Routine retelling of how pupils reached their answers may even help to uncover the tangle of errors embedded in the strategies adopted by each child. However, this may not be as automatic as one might suppose. Several researchers have reported pupils' ability to maintain two conflicting systems: one of 'school maths', which generates answers according to a prescribed rule, but is at odds with their personal 'real maths' (Papert 1981; Nunes and Bryant 1996). In such cases pupils assert with conviction that the incorrect answer gen-erated is the one that the school requires even though, of course, they get a different answer pursuing their own logic. Charlie, Julie and Bob may still be caught between extending their own sense of the system of mathematics and reflecting that which they believe their teachers espouse.

However, perhaps of more concern is that stressing the preeminence of mental calculation will not necessarily make the powerful mathem-atical insights of Leanne and Neil any more public or prolific. The numeracy framework lays down a selection of strategies which pupils should learn to use, set out year by year in a steady sequence of com-plexity. The structure of the daily mathematics lesson encourages pupils to choose the method they use and to be able to explain clearly what they have done. However, neither the learning programme nor the teaching procedures would necessarily ensure that children move from selecting a strategy to formulating strategies, or from describing what has been done to articulating why it must work. It is this subtle shift of emphasis from the particular to the general, from the actual past to the possible future, which is a peculiarly significant ingredient of effective mathematical thinking. It is not enough for teachers to use careful language, imagery and strategies; we need to acknowledge and welcome the fact that pupils will readily make their own generalizations and then be adamant and explicit in encouraging them to share, test and refine these.

The plenary section of a daily mathematics lesson provides a wonder-ful opportunity to do just that. A time when the class are reconvened after their own intensive working is a time when individuals might well have an insight to share, a general statement to propose, a definition to refine, or a conjecture to test. It is disheartening to learn that both teachers and classroom observers often say that the plenary is the hard-est and least satisfactory part of many lessons.

Just as an art lesson puts new techniques to use in creating pictures, and a PE lesson puts practised skills under pressure in games and com-petitions, so too mathematics lessons would do well to tackle difficult cases, as a deliberate extension to the more routine ones. As a wise child said to me recently in a student's class: 'I shouldn't be doing these – 'cause I know I'll just get them all right!'

It was no mere chance that the final number sentence '3 + 0 = ?' was the one that yielded the most interesting and varied results for Adam, Brian and Charlie. It was thus also the one that allowed a reader of their scripts to distinguish the strategies used by the first two boys and to discern that something is awry with Charlie's reasoning. Working with zero is often a testing case for the strategies used. It is a lost opportunity that it is so often omitted from dice, number lines, 100 squares, texts and talk in the classroom. The application of a technique to a new and demanding number domain: larger, fractional, negative or simply zero is one way of focusing on internalized strategies and generalizations – sometimes extending them further, sometimes testing them to destruction.

A facility for formulating and using generalizations has long been perceived as one of the characteristics to be expected of mathematically able children of any age. Lists of criteria for mathematical ability cited, for example, in Straker (1983) and Lumb (1987), are derived from Krutetskii's work with the mathematically gifted (1976) and the School Council's more general compilation on recognizing children's exceptional abilities (Ogilvie 1973). The criteria include a somewhat repetitive list of 'classroom pointers' such as:

- use very sophisticated criteria for sorting and classifying;
- show great powers of reasoning, of dealing with abstractions, of generalizing from specific facts, of understanding meanings and seeing relationships;
- have an ease of grasping the essence of a problem;
- display an ability to process information with clear thinking and economy of solution;
- be able to see pattern in number and to use that pattern on future occasions.

However, while these are suggested as 'pointers' indicating ability or potential, there is seldom any detailed advice on how to perceive them beyond offering opportunities for pupils to display independent and sustained reasoning strategies through investigations and problem solving activities. The National Curriculum of England and Wales is rare in requiring that such skills should be specifically observed, taught and assessed. One justification is that 'mathematically able pupils are in every school and among all ethnic and socio-economic groups' (DfEE 2000) – but should we also infer that specific attention to reasoning skills in mathematics could have a far-reaching potential for raising the attainment of all?

Reasoning in the National Curriculum

The mathematics working party was the first subject group to report and present a draft National Curriculum (DES & WO 1988). As a prototype it was unwieldy and incorporated no less than 15 attainment targets clustered into three profile components. However, it was also groundbreaking. In tracing the evolution of the National Curriculum for mathematics through three major revisions it is interesting to note how several of the apparent anachronisms of early versions have been re-established at a later date as part of the orthodoxy of the National Curriculum as a whole.

From the very first version, the National Curriculum for mathematics has provided not only the expected lists of specific knowledge and skills to be taught and practised, but has also made a valiant attempt to clarify what it actually means for pupils to engage in mathematical activity. The content areas of mathematics presented in the first two profile components were thus juxtaposed in 1988 to a third profile component for the practical application of mathematics. This third profile component proposed three separate attainment targets: using mathematics, communication skills and personal qualities. However, the mathematics group balked at producing the required ten-point scale of statements of attainment for these particular targets. They admitted the difficulty of distinguishing clear progressive levels and recommended instead a 'best fit' model based on teachers' professional judgements of the range of problem solving skills demonstrated by pupils over a period of time. In 1995 this notion of 'best fit' became a part of the assessment of the whole National Curriculum, but in these early stages the presentation, intentions and proposed importance of mathematics profile component three were perceived as being out of step with the overall development of a common framework.

In this early curriculum proposal, reasoning skills were presented as a gradual formalization of essential common sense. While common sense was presented as natural, inherent and necessary, reasoning skills were deemed desirable and in need of strategic development. The document provided a useful list of attributes of reasoning (DES & WO 1988: 50) which once more reflected Krutetskii's work on giftedness. The working party was thus implicitly proposing that a deliberate effort to encourage clarity of mathematical reasoning in pupils of all ages would help to extend mathematical attainment generally:

> The development of reasoning ability should be fostered: pupils need to be encouraged and challenged to think and reason at levels appropriate to them. We would expect pupils to develop their ability to,

- sort and classify objects;
- describe objects or processes unambiguously and give definitions;
- make conscious assumptions and conjectures;
- test definitions and conjectures systematically, using counter examples or other means;
- use increasing rigour in argument;
- recognise the meaning of 'true', 'false' and 'not proven'.

(DES & WO 1988: 50)

These traits were proposed as being applicable to all ages and stages of mathematical development, yet it remains a challenge to provide positive examples of the later statements in primary classrooms. Pupils, such as Leanne and Neil, may subliminally recognize the generality of the statements they make, but they are seldom routinely encouraged to make these consciously, systematically and rigorously.

By the end of 1988 this innovative aspect of the mathematics curriculum had already been radically reworked (NCC 1988). The desirability of having distinctive attainment targets for the application of mathematics was broadly supported by the majority of respondents to the consultation process and perceived as a means to emphasize the importance, and ensure the relevance, of mathematics as a subject of study. However, the separate profile component was dismantled, and reappeared in essence as a single attainment target for using and applying mathematics, located within each of the two remaining profile components. The original separate attainment targets of profile component three now became three strands embedded within the new attainment targets 1 and 9: application, communication and reasoning. Thus the original, more general, 'personal qualities' had given way to the more distinctively mathematical qualities of 'reasoning'.

One critical result of the sleight of hand in dismantling profile component three was that the weighting for the application of mathematics within the overall assessment of the subject tumbled from a proposed 40 per cent to just 14 per cent, a proportion considered more acceptable by the Secretary of State for Education. However, it should be noted that the inclusion of any specific, assessed, targets for application and problem solving is rare within the national curricula of Europe (Howson 1991).

In an attempt to ensure that using and applying mathematics would 'inform all the work undertaken by pupils in mathematics and . . . [be] given appropriate emphasis at each level' (NCC 1988: 19), the curriculum document provided explicit statements of attainment at ten distinct levels. The National Curriculum Council (NCC) recognized that more work on this would still need to be done and, in particular, suggested that the 'communication' strand might usefully become a cross-curricular attainment target at some future date. Indeed, the year 2000 saw the inclusion of 'key skills', including communication and problem solving, and 'thinking skills', including reasoning, within the National Curriculum as a whole. Back in 1988, however, the NCC was certainly right in perceiving the sequencing of statements of attainment in these particular skills as only a preliminary draft. Although there were 'unique statements of achievement corresponding to each point of the 10-point scale' (NCC 1988: 19) the sequencing of these statements sometimes appeared random rather than progressive, and the interpretation of pupils' work remained fairly arbitrary. Many primary teachers were duly baffled that 'estimating, checking and considering results' did not appear until Level 3, yet were intrigued to find that they might exult in any pupils' argumentative examples of 'disproof by counter example' as incidents of putative achievement at Level 9. One statement – 'to respond to questions of the form "what would happen if . . . ?"' had been relocated from Level 8 in the proposals to Level 2 in the final version. The precise position of other statements seemed every bit as haphazard.

A simple sorting and classifying activity that I presented to teachers and students (to reconstruct the whole attainment target from its separate statements of attainment) proved impossible to achieve. It produced a great deal of discussion, a fair amount of frustration, but certainly no agreement about progression. Indeed, many teachers reflected the sentiments of the original working party, suggesting that reasoning skills should be developed as a whole within each key stage, rather than searching for instances of specific sub-skills as evidence of a particular level of attainment. However, while teachers and students might agree this as a principle, evidence was mounting that it was seldom achieved in practice. A mathematics evaluation project commissioned by the NCC (Askew *et al.* 1993) found that the attainment targets for using and applying mathematics were not well understood by primary teachers. While many believed that the application strand was adequately addressed through routine practical activities including the use of apparatus, the communication and reasoning strands received little focused attention and teachers often expressed only a hazy idea of how progression in these areas might be planned for or assessed.

In secondary mathematics the assessment of communication and reasoning skills was more securely embedded in the whole notion of sustained mathematical investigations. However, the suggested progression within the National Curriculum from predictions (Level 1), through statements (Levels 3, 4), and generalizations (Level 6), to chains of reasoning (Level 7) and ultimately to proofs (from Level 8) may in fact have been counter-productive. Certainly there was an increasing backlash from teachers of mathematics at A level and beyond, who claimed that investigational work for GCSE was a poor foundation for further study (Gardiner 1995; Wells 1995; Roper 1999). Although attainment target one endorsed the use of investigational work, it also inadvertently limited teachers' expectations through specifying assessment against these levels. Thus, predicting, spotting patterns and recording them in algebraic symbols were perceived as specific goals for the majority of pupils, rather than reaching an understanding of the underlying structure of the system and working towards justification and proof. The retelling of what was seen took precedence over any emerging sense of why it must be so.

One particular difficulty for teachers was that the early versions of the National Curriculum for mathematics did not include distinctive programmes of study. Instead of providing a sense of the flavour of the proposed teaching style, the printed programmes of study merely produced a topic list, or syllabus, for each level in turn. It was not until the 1995 version, following the Dearing review of the whole curriculum, that programmes of study covering a complete key stage were introduced to give clear indications of pupils' entitlements to a varied experience of mathematics (SCAA 1994; DfE 1995). The number of statements was also radically reduced to a mere 20 per cent of the previous version, and the whole mathematics curriculum was reshaped into just three attainment targets at Key Stage 1, with four at Key Stage 2 and five thereafter. This in itself must have been a tremendous sorting and classifying task for the working party, and it certainly resulted in a curriculum document that was more coherent and succinct than earlier versions had been.

The reasoning strand became ever more distinctive in successive versions. By 1995 there were more definite indications of the appropriate degree of formality to elicit within pupils' work. For example, the programme of study stated that all pupils in Key Stage 1 should have the opportunity to 'explain their thinking to support the development of their reasoning', even though the ability to 'explain their reasoning' was still first specified as a descriptor of achievement at Level 3. Progression within each strand also became more explicit. Thus, explaining thinking (Level 3) leads to explaining reasoning (Level 5) and on to giving mathematical justifications (Level 6), before pupils are finally expected to comment constructively on the reasoning and logic employed (Level 8).

The latest version of the National Curriculum (DfEE 1999b) marks another structural shift. Using and applying mathematics has been dismantled and no longer appears as a separate item in the programmes of study. Instead it is embedded within each of the other areas of mathematics. The curriculum thus specifies how every aspect of mathematics should be used and applied as it is taught. However, there is still a separate attainment target for using and applying mathematics at the end of the document which specifies achievement at eight levels. This shift in presentation emphasizes that, while using and applying can only take place within an actual mathematical context, the specific skills drawn out should be scrutinized and assessed for each pupil.

The main changes to attainment target one in this version provide a more distinctively mathematical description of the type of reasoning required. The whole language of expression has altered from a quasi-scientific search for pattern in evidence to a more determinedly mathematical quest for logical rigour through abstract reasoning. Thus, a whole new vocabulary of 'solutions', 'conclusions' and 'arguments' is introduced to strengthen the more familiar one of 'pattern', 'results' and 'evidence'. These changes are most marked at the lower levels. For example, Level 2 now includes a forceful new demand for pupils to 'explain why an answer is correct'. While, towards the end of Key Stage 2 'search for a pattern' becomes 'search for a solution' (Level 4), and 'make general statements' (Level 5) has been strengthened to 'draw simple conclusions'.

These changes may seem slight and subtle, yet they do have enormous significance. In effect the National Curriculum 2000 is underwriting two strong claims: first that an ability to reason, justify and prove is central to all mathematics; and second that this is as true for work in the primary years as it is for continued mathematical study. It demands a shift of perspective so that teachers see and present mathematics as an interrelated set of ideas, rather than a string of arbitrary strategies. Work in primary school cannot be seen as a preliminary, pragmatic set of basic skills leading to the study of 'real' mathematics at a later date. Instead the challenge is to ensure that even the earliest work is essentially mathematical.

Proof in the primary school

To claim that reasoning and proof are central to mathematics is scarcely controversial. Gardiner and Moreira (1999: 17) open their article on proof in schools with the statement that 'mathematics without proof is an impossibility: proof is the key aspect that sets mathematics apart from other kinds of knowledge'. However, there have been repeated assertions that reasoning and proof have a very tenuous place even in the mathematical diet of the most successful secondary pupils (Tall 1989; Porteous 1994; Waring 2000). Ongoing research into able pupils' perceptions of proof at Year 10 suggests that they have considerable difficulty in even recognizing rigour and distinguishing it from erroneous reasoning (Hoyles and Healy 1999a). Successive versions of the National Curriculum have nonetheless both refined and extended expectations of mathematical reasoning so that proof is seen as an essential part of mathematics teaching at all ages. How is this requirement to be made a reality?

Intriguingly, although little is explicitly written about primary pupils' abilities to justify and prove, reflections on proof activities at secondary school increasingly suggest that primary pupils might be rather good at them, provided that clarity of reasoning is allowed to take precedence over formality of presentation. Thus Perks and Prestage (1995: 45) ask: 'Is it possible that we leave working on proofs too late? If a young child can use pictures to justify results, perhaps we should encourage pictorial explanations, so that algebraic proofs become an extension of our skills of proof rather than the only "accepted" ones'.

Hoyles and Healy (1999b: 11) conclude a brief report of empirical research in progress with a similar cautious conjecture:

> These results could be interpreted to suggest that, in classes which follow a more challenging mathematical curriculum where proof is given a more explicit focus, students, regardless of their general mathematical attainment, engage better in the game of deduction and logical argument. Our interviews with teachers and students even suggest this should be started at an earlier age than at present.

The key change that is proposed is that pupils should be expected and encouraged to use reasoning logically: to define terms carefully, to see their results as part of a larger system of mathematics, and to justify the truth of one statement following on from that of another.

Conclusion

Nick Tate, the government's chief adviser on the school curriculum for several years, wrote a newspaper article shortly before leaving this post (Tate 2000). Although the focus of the article is on his own subject, history, one general comment has a bearing on the argument here about mathematics. Tate (2000: 4) writes:

> The rhetoric of education professionals in recent years has often implied that content is unimportant or at least secondary, and that all that matters is transferable skills. This is a mindset that sits comfortably with postmodernist intellectual currents that wash around us. It sits uneasily with high quality education and with the aim of maintaining continuity across the generations.

For mathematics at least, the skill of deductive reasoning is fundamental to high quality education. It is also, incidentally, our line of cultural continuity stretching back to at least Euclid and the ancient Greeks. The National Curriculum as a whole has provided a sense of unity and structure across all its subjects, but perhaps it is now appropriate to reassert and to celebrate the distinctive and demanding disciplines of each one. The introduction to the mathematics curriculum 2000 achieves this through a strong statement of the importance of mathematics as both a wondrous tool and a dynamic discipline (DfEE 1999b: 60):

> Mathematics equips pupils with a uniquely powerful set of tools to understand and change the world. These tools include logical reasoning, problem-solving skills, and the ability to think in abstract ways . . . Mathematics is a creative discipline. It can stimulate moments of pleasure and wonder when a pupil solves a problem for the first time, discovers a more elegant solution to that problem, or suddenly sees hidden connections.

The immediate challenge is to ensure that the mathematical insights, which lead to elegant solutions, are made visible, and that the logical reasoning which reveals hidden connections is made audible in every daily mathematics lesson.

References

Askew, M., Brown, M.L., Johnson, D.C. *et al.* (1993) *Evaluation of the Implementation of National Curriculum Mathematics.* London: SCAA.

Askew, M., Bibby, T. and Brown, M.L. (1997) *Raising Attainment in Numeracy: Final Report.* London: King's College.

DES & WO (Department of Education and Science and the Welsh Office) (1988) *Mathematics for Ages 5 to 16: Proposals.* London: DES.

DfE (Department for Education) (1995) *Mathematics in the National Curriculum.* London: HMSO.

DfEE (Department for Education and Employment) (1999a) *The National Numeracy Strategy.* London: DfEE.

DfEE (Department for Education and Employment) (1999b) *The National Curriculum: Handbook for Primary Teachers in England.* London: QCA.

DfEE (Department for Education and Employment) (2000) www.standards. dfee.gov.uk/numeracy/NNSresources/ablepupils/intro/(accessed 12 September 2000).

Gardiner, T. (1995) The proof of the pudding is in the . . . ?, *Mathematics in School*, 24(3): 10–11.

Gardiner, T. and Moreira, C. (1999) Proof matters, *Mathematics Teaching*, 169: 17–21.

Her Majesty's Inspectorate (HMI) (1985) *Mathematics from 5 to 16*. London: HMSO.

Howson, G. (1991) *National Curricula in Mathematics*. Leicester: Mathematical Association.

Hoyles, C. and Healy, L. (1999a) Students' views of proof, *Mathematics in School*, 28(3): 19–21.

Hoyles, C. and Healy, L. (1999b) Can they prove it?, *Mathematics in School*, 28(4): 10–11.

Krutetskii, V.A. (1976) *The Psychology of Mathematical Abilities in School Children*. Chicago: University of Chicago Press.

Lumb, D. (1987) *Teaching Mathematics 5 to 11*. London: Croom Helm.

MacNamara, A. and Roper, T. (1992) Unrecorded, unobserved and suppressed attainment: can our pupils do more than we know?, *Mathematics in School*, 21(5): 12–13.

NCC (National Curriculum Council) (1988) *Consultation Report: Mathematics*. York: NCC.

Nunes, T. and Bryant, P. (1996) *Children Doing Mathematics*. Oxford: Blackwell.

Ogilvie, E. (1973) *Gifted Children in Primary Schools*. London: Macmillan.

Papert, S. (1981) *Mindstorms: Children, Computers and Powerful Ideas*. Brighton: Harvester Press.

Perks, P. and Prestage, S. (1995) Why don't they prove?, *Mathematics in School*, 24(3): 43–5.

Porteous, K. (1994) When proof is seen to be necessary, *Mathematics in School*, 23(5): 2–5.

Roper, T. (1999) Pattern and the assessment of mathematical investigation, in A. Orton (ed.) *Pattern in the Teaching and Learning of Mathematics*. London: Cassell.

SCAA (School Curriculum and Assessment Authority) (1994) *Mathematics in the National Curriculum: Draft Proposals*. London: SCAA.

Straker, A. (1983) *Mathematics for Gifted Pupils*. York: Longman.

Tall, D. (1989) The nature of mathematical proof, *Mathematics Teaching*, 127: 28–32.

Tate, N. (2000) They come not to praise England but to bury it, *Sunday Times*, 27 August: 4.

Thompson, I. (1999) Mental calculation strategies for addition and subtraction part 1, *Mathematics in School*, 28(5): 2–4.

Threlfall, J. and Frobisher, L. (1998) *Starting Mental Maths Strategies*. Oxford: Heinemann.

Waring, S. (2000) *Can You Prove It? Developing Concepts of Proof in Primary and Secondary Schools*. Leicester: Mathematical Association.

Wells, D. (1995) Investigations and the learning of mathematics, *Mathematics Teaching*, 150: 36–40.

7

Is there still a place for primary science?

Keith Bennett, Peter Crowther and Jane Johnston

Introduction

Not only has the nature of primary science within the curriculum changed over the past ten years, but the importance placed upon it has altered too. As one of the first curriculum areas to be introduced within the National Curriculum, it became an area of rapid growth and has been hailed in inspections as an area of successful development. There has been a change in emphasis from process to a combination of process and conceptual understanding. This has led to science in the primary school being a unique combination whereby understanding develops through motivating, practical experiences.

This chapter will look at the success story of primary science and consider whether continued successful development can be retained within a changing curriculum. Particular questions which will be explored within the chapter are:

- Can we successfully develop scientific skills and attitudes alongside knowledge and conceptual understanding?
- Is there a danger that the awe and wonder of science will be lost in the new curriculum?
- What are the effects of whole class teaching and learning strategies on practical, exploratory or investigative science?
- Are there different types of interactive science teaching and learning?
- Can cross-curricular science be effective?
- How can we teach difficult and abstract scientific concepts?

Exemplars from the primary classroom will illustrate the features of effective science teaching and learning, focusing on:

- Good learning which is motivating, experiential, interactive and focused.
- Good teaching in which the teacher is a good role model for learning and facilitates learning through focused interaction.

Scientific development

Science has been a major success of the National Curriculum. From 1989, when science became a core subject, its place in a broad and balanced curriculum has been recognized (ASE 1997). Since that time inspection and national assessment have shown progress in science to be steady (Ofsted 2000). However, this progress has been adversely affected by new curriculum initiatives and changes in teaching and learning (ASE 1999). Changes in the science curriculum have occurred at regular intervals and led to different teaching and learning requirements and different curriculum emphases. Changes in teaching and learning methodologies, with the introduction of the National Literacy Strategy (NLS) and National Numeracy Strategy (NNS) have resulted in science teaching often neglecting the more practical aspects of development. Teachers lacking in scientific knowledge or confidence often resort to science lessons which merely impart information (Ofsted 2000). In many cases the awe and wonder of science is not being conveyed to children. The result of the changes is a great deal of confusion among teachers, which leads many to doubt the status of science. Is it a core subject in name only? Has the raising of standards in English and mathematics led to science being relegated from the premier to the first division?

Science, at all levels, is concerned with exploring and recognizing 'features of living things, objects and events in the natural and man made world and looking closely at similarities and differences, patterns and change' (SCAA 1996: 4). Understanding of the world begins to develop before birth, as we listen, feel and remember. Children develop scientific skills, attitudes, knowledge and understanding through both formal and informal experiences throughout their lives. Piaget and Bruner shared the belief that children are 'born with a biological organisation that helps them to understand their world, and their underlying cognitive structure matures over time, so that they can think about and organise their world in an increasingly complex way' (Gross 1992: 762).

Science teaching in the primary school is a rich and rewarding process which involves a wide range of cognitive skills from children who are at their most receptive and curious. Young children are actively involved in constructing their understanding of the world, based upon their unique experiences of life, formed at home and in the community. They bring to the classroom a broad range of experiences, which, in turn, become their starting points for the acquisition and development of scientific concepts, skills and attitudes. This learning will modify their maturing and developing cognitive structures.

Preschool children explore the world in which they live through play experiences. They may have encountered living and non-living things through playing in the garden and observing 'mini-beasts', or leaves falling from trees. They may have experienced sliding on ice; burning their fingers on hot objects; or discovered gravity at first hand when dropping or throwing objects, or falling down themselves. These discoveries, through play, may be seen as random, unstructured experiences, but they all influence the initial concepts that are being formed.

Most children, prior to entering school, will have a basic understanding or an awareness of many scientific concepts. They may have experienced the arrival of younger siblings or witnessed the birth of a kitten, and as a consequence acquired a rudimentary appreciation of the life cycle. Some children will have been actively encouraged to grow plants from seeds and then care for them by watering and feeding them. All these examples result in children coming to school with the beginnings of scientific understanding.

There are a number of factors which affect the quality of learning in these early, play-type explorations (Johnston 1996; Johnston and Gray 1999). Most important are exploration, time, novelty and interaction. Exploration (or 'structured play') (Johnston 1996) is the way that young children learn about the world around them and is a prerequisite for subsequent scientific enquiry. Through exploration children develop specific scientific skills such as observation, raising questions, classification, handling resources, interpretation and communication. Children of all ages need quality time to explore the world around them. In the youngest children, time to explore and time to interpret from explorations is essential, but even older children need time and exploration to enable them to plan productive investigations. For young children many experiences in the world around them are novel. Motivating, fun experiences, which encourage children to look at their world in different ways can help develop positive attitudes to learning generally and to science specifically. As de Bóo (2000) has said, it is these experiences which lay the foundations for the future. Interaction is an essential element of good early education (QCA/DfEE 2000). Young children need to interact with their environment, scientific phenomena, each other and especially adults who can support learning. It is 'through such interaction that early learning becomes the partnership envisaged by policy makers' (Johnston and Gray 1999: 5).

Children in the early years are not aware that they are developing knowledge and skills in particular curriculum areas. They are exploring the world around them or playing. For example, in a Nottingham nursery, children were making play dough and exploring the properties of the different ingredients and how they changed when mixed or heated. They looked and felt all the ingredients, using their own words to describe them. Josh said the flour was 'fluffy' and Lucy said it was 'like powder'. The word 'powdery' was then used to describe it. The children then mixed the ingredients together in a big bowl and the teacher encouraged them to describe how it had changed. 'It's all gooey now!' said Lucy, while Shari said, 'Ugh! It's all sticky'. The children then helped to put the mixture in a saucepan and the teacher heated and stirred it, showing it to the children at intervals as it solidified into a malleable mass. 'What's happening to it now?' asked the teacher. 'It's all sticking together', replied Josh. A little later, when it was cool enough to handle, the children played with it and used it to make shapes. They noted that it was cooling down and 'all stuck together' and that 'the colour was mixed up' (see Figures 7.1 and 7.2).

Science in the primary school

On entering school, children encounter a much more structured world of timetables, core and foundation subjects, Literacy and Numeracy Strategies and break and lunch periods, and some of these have been found to have an adverse effect on scientific development (Cassidy 1999). Within this complex structure, children will rediscover many of their past experiences in primary science. Part of the structure is the National Curriculum, which identifies the knowledge and skills to be transmitted to children (DfEE 1999; QCA/DfEE 2000). Teaching and learning science in school can take many different forms and styles which may include observations, explorations, investigations and development of factual knowledge, practical work, visits, data handling and research from secondary sources. The teacher should aim to build on children's natural curiosity, experience and inclination towards enquiry, encouraging them to increasingly draw upon accepted scientific knowledge while still retaining the value of their own experience and understanding.

The key to effective teaching and learning in science is the interrelationship between the practical and the theoretical, that is, the development of knowledge and understanding through practical experiences. There are a number of different types of practical science work, all

Figure 7.1   Children in the early years making play dough

Mix together in a large saucepan:

- 2 cups of flour
- 1 cup of salt
- 2 cups of water
- 2 tablespoons of oil
- 2 teaspoons of cream of tartar
- 1 tablespoon of powder paint or a few drops of food colouring

Cook over a medium heat, stirring all the time to prevent sticking.
Remove from the heat when the mixture comes away from the sides
of the pan. Knead and use. It keeps well in an airtight container.

Figure 7.2   A recipe for play dough

involving the child in interacting with ideas, resources and scientific phenomena. *Demonstrations* can have a place in the primary classroom, especially where the activity has safety or organizational implications. For example, when looking at balanced and unbalanced forces, it is probably wise to show children by demonstration that air exerts sufficient pressure to break a ruler or keep water in an upturned cup (see Figure 7.3). The alternative is a large class of 30-plus children all spilling cups of water, with the resultant slippery floors and chaos! Good demonstrations should be used sparingly and involve all the children in an interactive way, through questioning, participation and especially interpreting what they have observed.

Explorations involve children in observing the world around them, asking questions, formulating hypotheses and developing some basic scientific skills. Explorations can be included in the structured play activities that occur in any Key Stage 1 classroom and can form the first part of investigations, where children plan their work. Young children can explore mixing salt and sugar with water and watching it dissolve. They can compare salt dissolving in warm water with margarine melting in warm water. Older children may undertake the same explorations before planning an investigation to see what factors affect the rate at which these substances dissolve.

Investigations can stem from children's observations and hypotheses. In investigations the children take responsibility for the work, making decisions about the focus for investigation, the resources they will need, how they will implement their plans and how they will record the data collected. Some examples of investigation topics might be:

- What affects the bounce of a ball?
- What affects the speed of a vehicle rolling down a ramp?
- Which paper towel is best?
- What affects the rate at which salt and sugar dissolve?
- How does exercise affect you?
- Which fabric is best?

Investigative work helps children to clarify their ideas, make sense of the world around them and develop basic and more advanced skills in science. However, it should be noted that not all scientific work will lead to good investigations. An investigation involves the *systematic control* of variables. The *key variables* are those which define the investigation; the *independent variables* are the things that can be changed during the investigation; and the *dependent variables* are the results of the investigation. Finally, the *control variables* are those which need to remain constant throughout the investigation in order to collect accurate results.

If the stick (ruler), placed on the table under a sheet of newspaper, is hit, it will break because of the air pressure exerted on the newspaper

The water stays in the cup because the forces are balanced. The air pressure exerted on the card is equal to the downward force exerted by gravity

Figure 7.3 Demonstration of scientific phenomena

Problem solving is a highly motivating form of practical scientific work and can therefore help to develop useful scientific attitudes as well as apply and develop skills and knowledge in a context. Children can make a powered vehicle to travel across the floor, or an alarm system to tell them when someone enters the classroom, or, using chromatography, find which black pen wrote a note.

Science is a process which consists of a number of skills. The process is cyclic in which many parts are revisited to ensure complete understanding. The process usually begins with observation, exploring and raising questions. This leads to planning in order to answer the questions, and investigating. Investigating involves following plans, measuring, handling variables and recording data. The final part of the process is interpreting data and communicating results. Practical science helps to develop the skills involved in the process. Some of these are generic skills, which are necessary in other areas and in later life. Observational and group work, and analytical skills are all examples of generic skills which are needed throughout education and life. Some skills are more science specific, for example, classification, handling variables and measuring.

In schools in the UK we have become very good at practical science, but our recent practice has highlighted some difficulties. These are discussed in the following sections.

Misunderstanding the process and attempting to develop the whole process at once

The scientific process is not a recipe to follow from beginning to end. Rather, it contains a series of mini-processes within a larger process and, as mentioned above, is cyclic rather than linear in nature. Young children may observe, raise questions and then attempt to answer them through exploration. They will then need to analyse and interpret their observations and explorations in order to make sense of them. Communication will help to consolidate their understanding. After initial observation and exploration, older children raise questions which they can plan to answer through investigations. At various stages in the process they may return to an earlier stage. They may decide to reconsider their plan, or take additional or new measurements, or rethink predictions (see Figure 7.4).

It would be impossible to develop all the skills in the scientific process in any one practical activity or indeed over a short period of time. It is better to focus on one skill at a time and develop this skill in a coherent way. This does not mean that you cannot work within the

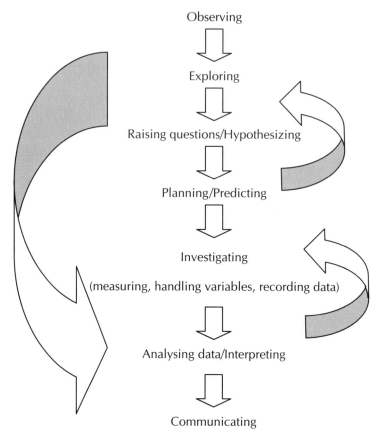

Figure 7.4   The scientific process

whole process, but rather that you should focus on the development of one skill during science activities and identify this skill as your learning objective.

Not understanding the skill and how it develops

In order to focus on the development of one particular skill you need to know what the skill involves, how it might develop and how you can aid that development. You also need to know how to provide structure to an exploration or investigation to enable one particular skill to be developed. As examples, we will focus on two of the most important skills in science: observation and interpretation. Observation is an important part of the scientific process and is necessary for other process skills to develop – for example, raising questions, classification and handling variables. Observation involves more than just looking. It involves:

- using all the senses;
- identifying similarities and differences between objects;
- seeing patterns in objects and phenomena;
- identifying sequences and events in the world and in observed phenomena;
- interpreting observations.

We can develop children's observational skills if we:

- give them opportunities to observe collections of objects and to explore scientific phenomena;
- encourage them to use all their senses (where safe) in their observations;
- help them to enhance observations by giving them magnifiers, binocular microscopes, projection screens, stethoscopes, colour charts, etc.;
- ask them to describe their observations, giving them new vocabulary as appropriate;
- encourage them to look for patterns, sequences of events, similarities and differences in their observations; this is important for other scientific skills such as hypothesizing, classification, recognition of variables and interpretation;
- allow them to describe the patterns, sequences and their own interpretations of events;
- ask them questions about their observations;
- allow them time to draw details of their observations.

It is essential that children are given time to think about their explorations and investigations and are given opportunities to express ideas emerging from their practical work. Reflection and interpretation enables them to sort out any muddled thinking, to clarify their ideas and reach a better understanding. Children need to clarify their ideas in order to communicate them to others and communication often encourages them to evaluate their ideas. We often undertake scientific activities with children but forget to think carefully about the ideas being developed. Without the opportunity to reflect on observations, explorations and investigations and interpret from them, it is likely that learning will be impaired.

We can develop the skills of reflecting, interpreting and communicating in children if we:

- allow time at the end of science explorations or investigations to reflect, interpret and communicate;
- encourage children to share their findings;
- discuss interpretations with the children;

- make use of carpet time, circle time or whole class discussions;
- encourage children to pose new questions, perhaps for others to answer in a new investigation;
- question children about their investigation;
- encourage children to identify what they have learned.

Misunderstanding the nature of scientific practical work

There is a misunderstanding in primary education that any scientific activity has to be investigative. It is important that children are active and practical in their learning so that conceptual understanding develops with scientific skills and attitudes in a coherently interrelated manner. This does not mean that every scientific activity needs to include an investigation. Indeed, it is difficult, if not impossible, to be really investigative in all aspects of science. As described above, practical science can take a variety of different forms. Some activities may be observational, some exploratory and some experimental or demonstrative. All are appropriate, especially if the children are actively engaged in the learning.

Not recognizing the importance of exploration and interpretation in the process

Practical science without an opportunity to explore before formally investigating or experimenting is educationally poorer. This is because we all need time to acquaint ourselves with new experiences, to play, mess about and bring to the forefront of our minds our previous knowledge and experiences which may be helpful. We also need opportunities to reflect on experiences after any practical work, otherwise learning is much less likely. The scientific process can therefore be said to be like a sandwich, where we eat the filling and disregard the bread. For a healthy educational diet we need to remember that exploration and interpretation are also important.

Practical science activities also help in the development of attitudes – both positive attitudes towards science as an activity or subject, and scientific attitudes. Positive attitudes support children's learning. Curiosity helps children to become motivated and to want to find out about the world around them. Perseverance helps children to repeat measurements and persist in investigations that appear to be going wrong. Tolerance helps children to respect differing ideas and to work with others. Respect for evidence helps children to understand that their ideas and predictions may not be correct and tentativeness helps children to see that there may be other interpretations. Most importantly, good practical science helps children to retain an interest in the world around them and develop a continuing love of learning. Children have a natural curiosity. They will experience awe and wonder with scientific phenomena. This can be lost if school science becomes too formal, too rigid, too structured. As the curriculum has become more structured and teachers teach rigidly to national schemes of work, there is a real danger that the quality of science teaching will be reduced and that science learning will regress towards mediocrity.

Cross-curricular science

The amount of time devoted to primary science has to be considered alongside the needs of other curriculum areas and the teacher has to consider how much time is devoted to whole class lessons, group activities and investigations and individual research. With the onset of the NLS and NNS, consideration may have to be given to cross-curricular links so that scientific activities are given appropriate amounts of time for pupils to receive 'quality experiences' rather than complete a worksheet with limited opportunity provided for planning, obtaining, presenting and evaluating evidence. In the 1990s, cross-curricular work received considerable criticism for being unfocused and a move towards subject teaching followed. This too is not without its educational problems, for science as a separate subject can appear to be irrelevant to many children. A combination of cross-curricular and subject science, well planned and prepared and with clear learning objectives can solve some of the problems of coverage, relevance and focus.

At Key Stages 1 and 2, Sc1 (Scientific Enquiry) and Sc2 (Life Processes and Living Things) (DfEE 1999: 78) can provide the teacher with the opportunity to plan a range of cross-curricular activities which support and enhance the science programme to be taught. The study of the relationship between animals and plants and their surroundings provides primary children with opportunity to observe and investigate how animals and plants live together in communities and habitats.

Young children may be able to experience environment trails and sound walks which build upon previous experiences. They should be encouraged to become more conscious of their observation skills and this can be supported by the use of sketch books, photographs and video recordings. Children can be introduced to simple sampling techniques which contribute to the construction of a transect line (a sample line of vegetation, which is then studied). This may illustrate a range of environmental issues including erosion, pollution, weathering and human

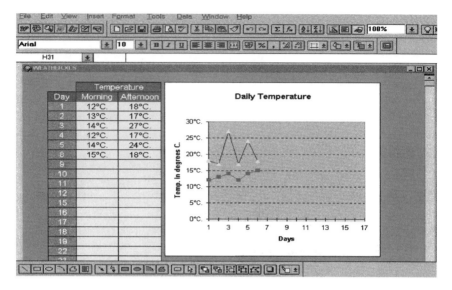

Figure 7.5 A weather chart created by children on the computer

influences (for example, walking on flower-beds, parking on the grass, and litter). Pollution and the ways in which humans impact upon the environment are essential topics which support the development of notions of citizenship. The observation of birds, animals, insects, fish and pond life; the collection of leaves, cones, seeds, flowers, plants, feathers, stones, pebbles and soil samples; and the investigation of woodlands, orchards, hedgerows, walls and environmental areas all utilize a range of cross-curricular skills and ideas. Observational drawings, colour matching, making casts, recording sounds, taking photographs, drawing maps, making wormeries, writing about discoveries, sorting, classifying and counting are skills and processes which are found in art, English, music, mathematics, geography and history. Investigations which incorporate plotting and charting trees, hedges, and the types of grass, plants, mosses and lichens to be found within a quadrat, lead children to become aware of the value of information and communication technology (ICT) through the construction and use of simple databases and spreadsheets which can, in turn, be interrogated and interpreted. ICT can also be used to support a census of trees, plants, animals and insects, to record the rate of growth of seeds and plants and to provide daily information on weather conditions. All such activities rely on the observation and measurement skills of children.

A spreadsheet (see Figure 7.5) provides children with the opportunity to record information based on their own observations and measurements, which can then be explored and interpreted. Science teaching involves the teacher and children becoming aware of the cross-curricular nature of the skills, attitudes and knowledge that are being transmitted.

In a Doncaster primary school, a Year 2 class were investigating 'growth'. The topic began with the story *The Very Hungry Caterpillar* (Carle 1970), so enabling children to consider the life cycle of the butterfly (egg – larva – chrysalis – butterfly). This was followed by setting up an environment for the children to observe caterpillars and the changes in their life cycles. Observations were made daily and were entered in small logbooks, sometimes in the form of annotated pictures. The children were encouraged to form questions and seek answers from textual sources, which were used to support their work. The class used a clipart package to design their own butterflies. At the same time the children were investigating changes in their own lives as part of a history topic, looking at Key Stage 1 historical enquiry (DfEE 1999). A display of photographs was constructed using pictures of the children as babies, toddlers and infants. Comparisons were drawn between the insect and human life cycles. The work in science linked with and reinforced the work undertaken in history related to chronological understanding. The cross-curricular nature of this work on growth highlights the value of devoting a period of time, in this case half a term, to observation and sustained record-keeping. The importance of drawing upon the child's past experiences and understanding of growth and life cycles is made apparent through the choice of the science and history foci.

Primary school science should have relevance to the children and their lives. Concepts set in familiar and concrete contexts are easier for a child to comprehend than concepts set in unfamiliar contexts, taught in an abstract way. There are many science projects which involve primary children in scientific work relevant to their everyday lives. Some of these can also develop learning objectives in other curriculum areas. One example would be children developing understanding of health and food. Children can:

- Keep a daily diary of food/drink intake (links with English).
- Identify the characteristics of a balanced diet through:

  (a) the construction of healthy sandwiches (links with design technology, art, mathematics);
  (b) the design and making of sandwiches/salads (links with design technology, art);
  (c) an investigation into the contents of lunchboxes and the class design of a healthy/nutritious lunchbox menu (links with art, mathematics, ICT, design technology).

- Conduct a food and drink survey within the class/school (links with mathematics, ICT, speaking and listening).
- Taste different types of bread and record observable properties and likes/dislikes.
- Design and conduct an investigation into the fluid intake of an individual/ the class.
- Observe the changes that occur when chocolate, bread, water, sugar and eggs are heated or cooled.
- Consider the changes taking place when cooking a packet of soup.
- Conduct an investigation into the most nutritious breakfast cereal (consider fat/sugar/energy content and cost per gram).
- Chart their teeth with the aid of a mirror/partner; investigate the most efficient method of cleaning away deposits of plaque.
- Describe their 'partner'; draw, colour match, paint or model parts of the body (links with art, language).
- Sort the members of the group according to their own criteria; record the data collected in their investigation and complete a table, 'Facts about me' (links with mathematics, language).

Not all science topics lend themselves to cross-curricular work and content specific topics may be achieved within a relatively short period of time – for example, three/four hours over two weeks. Where time is a constraint it is vitally important that quality time is allowed for children to plan their investigations and consider the sources of information required to answer the questions raised. Time should also be allowed for children to consider how to make a fair test, how to record and then how to present their evidence. In this way, the children are developing valuable scientific skills, understanding of the scientific process (Sc1) as well as scientific understanding (Sc2–4). If children are presented with a ready-made record or worksheet to be completed, this learning will not occur.

Constructivist teaching in the primary school

Understanding of how children learn in science has been important in helping the development of science teaching and learning. A constructivist teaching methodology (Scott 1987) supports children in constructing meanings from their scientific experiences. Teachers introduce the concept to the children by setting the scene (orientation phase). They use a variety of techniques to find out the children's existing ideas (elicitation phase), recognizing that children will have already begun to develop scientific concepts. They then use this knowledge of the children to plan to develop, modify or change ideas (restructuring phase).

Real learning is said to occur when children can apply their ideas, implying a need for understanding rather than knowledge.

A class of Year 4 children in a Mansfield school were working on developing understanding of circulation. The children were asked to think about the functions and purposes of the heart. They were encouraged to discuss what they already knew about the heart and pulse rate. In the constructivist teaching process this is the elicitation phase (Ollerenshaw and Ritchie 1993: 10). Time was given to enable the children to raise questions and consider how they might plan and carry out a fair test. The class was asked how various activities (ranging from 'non-active' tasks to increasingly 'active' tasks) affect their pulse and breathing rates. The class was split into groups and invited to construct and plan an investigation and to consider how best to record their findings. A blank record sheet was provided for each group to identify suitable passive and active tasks and space was left for each group to consider how best to measure and record their findings. After much group discussion and planning, a whole class plan was agreed so that a consistent and fair approach to the testing of activities was arrived at. Each pupil completed their own chart using a common format. The

Name		Age			Height		Weight	
Reading out loud		**Climbing stairs**			**Washing up**			
Pulse @ rest		Pulse @ rest			Pulse @ rest			
Pulse after activity		Pulse after activity			Pulse after activity			
Recovery time		Recovery time			Recovery time			
Writing		**Run to end of playground**			**Change for PE**			
Pulse @ rest		Pulse @ rest			Pulse @ rest			
Pulse after activity		Pulse after activity			Pulse after activity			
Recovery time		Recovery time			Recovery time			
Walking for 3 minutes		**Reading out aloud**			**Warm up for PE**			
Pulse @ rest		Pulse @ rest			Pulse @ rest			
Pulse after activity		Pulse after activity			Pulse after activity			
Recovery time		Recovery time			Recovery time			

Figure 7.6 Spreadsheet compiled by a Year 4 child

data was then put onto a spreadsheet, so that conclusions could be drawn from the class results (see Figure 7.6).

This investigation began with a clear starting point from which a series of questions and statements were to be tested. Children were encouraged to predict outcomes and then plan and carry out their tests, using measurements and collecting data. Finally the data was displayed, the results were interpreted and the groups' findings were communicated. In this particular investigation the children discovered that 'reading out aloud' to the whole class resulted in an increased pulse rate!

Teachers organizing science activities face a dilemma: does effective science teaching and learning involve whole class or individual and group practical activities? Whole class practical work can be very disorganized and behaviour and learning may be difficult to manage. As a result many teachers may resort to imparting knowledge to the whole class or demonstrating an experiment, which the class write up. This does little to develop scientific skills or understandings and can produce negative attitudes towards science. Individual and group work is equally ineffective unless it has clear objectives and is well planned and prepared for. Effective learning in science can include some structured tasks, which involve children in limited research tasks and the completion of worksheets, and do not necessarily have cross-curricular links. For example, if developing understanding about the human body children may be asked to:

1 Locate and name the various joints in the body on the blank outline.
2 Locate and name the organs of the body (e.g. lungs, heart, liver) on the blank outline.
3 On the blank outline of the skeleton mark the major bones (e.g. ribs, tibia, skull).
4 Construct from card the arm/elbow joint and the leg/knee/ankle joint.
5 Identify the joints used in the following everyday activities. Observe, describe and measure the movements and angles of turn involved in some of the processes:

- standing from sitting;
- getting out of bed;
- cleaning teeth;
- walking upstairs/downstairs;
- swimming breast stroke (arms and legs).

6 Construct a simple diagram of the heart. Label the chambers, the position of the valves and arteries and the veins which lead to and from the heart.

7 Make a simple stethoscope and listen to your heart. How would you describe what you are hearing?

Not all activities are so structured and focused. Many teachers make use of a variety of curricular areas to support and inform their teaching. With the rapid development of ICT and the provision of the Internet and the National Grid for Learning (NGfL), teachers and pupils have access to a wide range and variety of pictorial, textual and aural sources which may be used to support investigation and research.

A variety of CD-ROMs and websites are available and provide stimulating and informative materials for young children to access. Written materials may be transferred from a website and placed into a child's personal document so that they may be subsequently edited. Pictures and graphics may similarly be inserted into documents from the Internet, digital cameras and scanners. A range of ICT facilities are available for teachers to construct professional working documents, spreadsheets and databases for children to access. The availability of spreadsheets and Microsoft PowerPoint enable teachers to provide custom-made teaching aids to support scientific investigations and teaching packages for children to access in their own time. These materials provide the teacher with the opportunity to encourage children to access records that have been designed specifically for a particular scientific investigation. PowerPoint may be used to display information taken from textual sources, diagrams, photographs and even interactive worksheets, which can also be used for assessment purposes.

Difficult and abstract scientific concepts have always been hard to teach in the primary school, as young children are not able to engage with abstract ideas. It is for this reason that science in the primary school should be highly practical. One way of facilitating interaction with abstract concepts is through the use of models, for as the DfEE (1999) have said, scientific method involves children in interpreting from evidence and in modelling.

Using scientific models to develop understanding

In many ways, scientific knowledge can be thought of as a language for explaining 'reality' and how it works. Ever since the foundations for modern science were set by Galileo, science has evolved largely through experimentation and the development of models. In this context, a model is a mental picture of how some aspect of science works. It is a way of envisaging a particular scientific concept or theory. According to Gribbin (1999), the way to tell a good model is to test it and see if it works for every situation. Any model will have limitations and when these are reached it will have to be replaced by another. For example, in looking at the concept of particles (or atoms), the simplest model would be of spherical objects which are constantly moving (vibrating in solids and freely moving in gases). We can use this model to explain the pressure caused by gas particles in a container. However, if we want to explain how particles join together (how molecules are made from atoms) then we need a more complex model in which we visualize a central nucleus surrounded by electrons. To explain radioactivity, we need to take it a stage further by envisaging a model in which the nucleus is made up of different components (protons and neutrons). As children learn about the structure of atoms they need, therefore, to build up more and more complex models. When attempting to develop understanding in difficult and abstract concepts, it is an important role of the teacher to help pupils develop such models in a way which is understandable to them.

Consider teaching the concepts of floating and sinking. Although the National Curriculum (DfEE 1999) makes no direct reference to these concepts, few teachers would disagree that consideration of them is a valuable aid to the understanding of many of the underlying concepts relating to forces and their effects. Consequently, floating and sinking is a favourite topic within both Key Stages 1 and 2. It is of course impossible to see forces – we can only observe their effects. Consequently we can directly observe whether an object will float or sink in water but we cannot see what is causing this to happen. However, activities can be carried out to enable children to build up appropriate models to explain what is happening. It is essential that these activities should be carried out in a logical sequence to enable children to build up models which they can easily understand.

When teaching the concepts of floating and sinking, there are a number of key ideas the children need to grasp. These are that:

- 'heavy' objects sink, 'light' objects float;
- objects placed in water experience a downward force (gravity);
- objects placed in water experience an upward force due to the water (upthrust);
- an object will sink when the downward force is greater than the upward force;
- it is the nature of the object (what it is made of) rather than its size or shape which determines whether it will float or sink (ignoring for now the effects of surface tension or the presence of air in the object);
- the property of an object to float or sink can be determined by comparing the mass of the object with the mass of an equal volume of water – if the mass of the object is greater, it will sink;
- an object floats when it displaces its own mass of water.

There are three different ways of 'explaining' floating and sinking:

- *Explanation 1*: an object will sink when the downward force of gravity is greater than the upthrust exerted by the water.
- *Explanation 2*: an object will float if its density is less than the density of water.
- *Explanation 3*: an object will float when it displaces its own weight of water.

Of course, these are not really 'different', but 'alternative' ways of looking at floating and sinking and, consequently, each will require a different model.

Most teachers of Key Stages 1 and 2 would probably choose to work towards a model relating to Explanation 1, but they might choose to lay the foundations for appropriate models for Explanations 2 and 3 by introducing the ideas of 'heavier than water' (density) and displacement, without developing the full model. This would support learning within this abstract concept at a later stage of development. It is important that teachers understand the learning development within a concept. Primary teachers need not only to understand the ideas underpinning learning at their key stage, but also how children have developed in previous stages and how teaching and learning will take them deeper into conceptual understanding. This knowledge prevents teachers from teaching misconceptions, which are difficult to dispel in later life.

There are also a number of what we might classify as 'subsidiary ideas' relating to floating and sinking. These are:

- the presence of air in an object may cause it to float;
- surface tension may allow objects which are denser than water to float;
- different liquids have different densities to water and therefore objects placed in them may behave differently.

These ideas will of course involve modifications of the basic models.

Unless these subsidiary issues are taken into consideration when teaching floating and sinking, they will inevitably arise during lessons and cause confusion in the children's conceptual understanding. One way of dealing with these subsidiary issues is to adopt strategies to prevent them occurring until the children have had the opportunity to build up a basic model.

In a Year 5 class in Lincoln the pupils were investigating floating and sinking. The following scheme was used in an attempt to allow the children to build a suitable model for Explanation 1 and to introduce the concepts of density and displacement. The teaching involved a series of activities designed to enable the children to develop the 'key ideas' (see list on p. 116).

Key idea 1: 'heavy' objects sink, 'light' objects float

The children were provided with a tank of water and some carefully chosen solid objects (avoiding those which contain air or which may float due to surface tension). The children were asked to predict whether each object would float or sink, to explain their prediction and then test it out. This led to the general conclusion that 'heavy' objects (or, even better, that objects which are heavier than water) sink, while 'light' objects float.

Key idea 2: objects placed in water experience a downward force (gravity)

The children were asked to drop a coin, first in air and then into water. This helped them to realize that gravity 'exists in water'. They had some previous experience of gravity and its effects – i.e. that things fall towards the earth when released – but most of them had never considered whether gravitational force exists in water. This simple activity helped to convince them that gravity was evident even in water.

Key idea 3: objects placed in water experience an upward force due to the water (upthrust)

The children were asked to hold a block of wood under water and release it. They immediately observed the effect of the upthrust of the water pushing the wood to the surface. By this stage the children were aware of the two forces which act upon objects in water and the directions in which these forces act. To complete the model they needed to consider the relative sizes of these forces.

Key idea 4: an object will sink when the downward force is greater than the upward force

The children were given two objects, one which floated and one which would sink. They were asked to place them in the water and think about the two forces acting upon them. They were given two diagrams showing the two objects in water and were asked to show the forces on the diagrams and to compare their relative sizes. Some time was taken here to ensure that the children were able to represent forces and the direction in which they were acting by using arrows.

Key idea 5: it is the nature of the object (what it is made of)
rather than its size or shape which determines whether it will
float or sink (ignoring the effects of surface tension or the presence
of air in the object)

The children were given a number of balls of Plasticine ranging in size from about 3mm in diameter to 30mm in diameter. They were asked to predict which would float and were then invited to test their predictions. The majority of them were amazed to find that they all sank. This, of course, led to some confusion because both 'heavy' and 'light' pieces of plasticine sank.

At this stage, the majority of Key Stage 2 teachers will probably feel that they have achieved their aim and will not progress further in building a model. However, we recommend that they tackle the subsidiary ideas at this stage if they have not already arisen during lessons. This will consolidate the children's ideas and help them in further developing the concept at a later date. In the Year 5 class in our example, these ideas were developed through the following activities.

Subsidiary idea 1: the presence of air in an object may cause
it to float

The children were given a variety of objects which clearly contained air (polystyrene, balsa-wood, cork) and were asked to predict and then find out whether they floated in water. The majority of the children predicted correctly and said that they floated because they contained air. This was probably because they had already undertaken the main activities and were beginning to develop their model for floating and sinking. They were then given a piece of Plasticine and challenged to make it float. Many of them produced a 'boat shape', which if made carefully was able to float. The majority of them were not able to explain why their 'boats' floated and help was given by suggesting that they draw a sideways picture of the boat in the water and consider exactly what was floating *on* the water. One or two suggested that the Plasticine boat contained air.

Subsidiary idea 2: some objects float due to surface tension

The children were asked to make a pin float. This was found to be impossible. They were then introduced to the trick of floating the pin on a piece of paper in the water and then carefully removing the paper. This allowed the pin to float. The children were then introduced to the idea that water behaved as if it had a 'skin' and that very light things were not able to pass through the 'skin'.

Finally, it was decided to attempt to introduce the children to the concepts of density and displacement and their importance in determining why some objects float in water while others sink.

Key idea 6: the property of an object to float or sink can be determined by comparing the mass of the object with the mass of an equal volume of water – if the mass of the object is greater, it will sink

The children were provided with a number of blocks of different materials each having the same volume. Using an arm balance, the children compared each block in turn with an equal volume of water and recorded whether each object was heavier or lighter than the water. The children were then asked to determine which of the blocks floated in water. These results were then put into a table. From the table, the children were able to see that those objects which were heavier than the water sank, while those which were lighter floated.

Key idea 7: an object floats when it displaces its own weight of liquid

The children were asked to place a cube of metal (which would sink) into the water in a displacement can and collect and measure the water displaced. They were then asked to compare the volume of water displaced with the volume of the block of metal. The purpose of this activity was to introduce the children to the concept of displacement and show how it can be used to measure the volume of a solid. The children were then instructed to place a piece of wood onto the surface of the water in a filled displacement tank and to collect and measure the water displaced. They were then asked to compare the weight of water displaced with the weight of the wood. From their measurements the children were able to see that the two weights were equal.

These activities introduced the children to the alternative explanations about floating and sinking. They were able to develop models to help them understand the concepts. These ideas can now be further explored at Key Stages 3 and 4.

Conclusion

In this chapter we have argued that science for primary aged children should be very practical and motivating, reflecting science in the world around us. As teachers, we have a duty to teach a wide range of skills and knowledge. Teaching in other curriculum areas should not be at the expense of science. Coverage of the science curriculum should not be at the expense of understanding and the development of skills and attitudes.

References

ASE (Association for Science Education) (1997) *ASE Policy Statement. The Place of Science in a Balanced Curriculum.* Hatfield: ASE.

ASE (Association for Science Education) (1999) *ASE Survey on the Effect of the National Literacy Strategy on the Teaching of Science.* Hatfield: ASE.

Carle, E. (1970) *The Very Hungry Caterpillar.* Harmondsworth: Penguin.

Cassidy, S. (1999) Science sacrificed on the altar of literacy, *Times Educational Supplement,* 25 June.

de Bóo, M. (ed.) (2000) *Laying the Foundations in the Early Years.* Hatfield: ASE.

DfEE (Department for Education and Employment) (1999) *The National Curriculum: Handbook for Primary Teachers in England.* London: QCA.

Gribbin, J. (1999) *Almost Everyone's Guide to Science, the Universe, Life and Everything.* London: Phoenix.

Gross, R. (1992) *Psychology: The Science of Mind and Behaviour.* London: Hodder & Stoughton.

Johnston, J. (1996) *Early Explorations in Science.* Buckingham: Open University Press.

Johnston, J. and Gray, A. (1999) *Enriching Early Scientific Learning.* Buckingham: Open University Press.

Ollerenshaw, C. and Ritchie, R. (1993) *Primary Science: Making it Work.* London: David Fulton.

Ofsted (Office for Standards in Education) (2000) *Annual Report of Her Majesty's Chief Inspector of Schools. Standards and Quality in Education 1998/9.* London: The Stationery Office.

QCA/DfEE (Qualifications and Curriculum Authority/Department for Education and Employment) (2000) *Curriculum Guidance for the Foundation Stage.* London: DfEE/QCA.

SCAA (School Curriculum and Assessment Authority) (1996) *Nursery Education: Desirable Outcomes for Children's Learning on Entering Compulsory Education.* London: DfEE.

Scott, P. (1987) *A Constructivist View of Teaching & Learning Science.* Leeds: University of Leeds.

8

Information and communication technology: the fourth core subject?

David Fox

Introduction

Information and communication technology (ICT) has been available in British schools since the 1980s. At that time teachers were told that they were on the edge of a revolution in teaching and learning, but the nature of development has been uneven and inconsistent, evolutionary rather than revolutionary. There have been dramatic developments in ICT, but schools have shown a great capacity for maintenance of the status quo. Computers have introduced new dimensions to the curriculum, but it is questionable whether they have radically changed the nature of teaching and learning. Yet they have the capacity to do so.

In this chapter it is argued that the development of ICT has been restricted by a lack of confidence on the part of teachers, lack of equipment and increasing restrictions on the use of time. However, the National Grid for Learning (NGfL) and Internet access for all schools provide the opportunity for significant advances in teaching and learning. Teachers play a critical role in extracting the learning potential from technology, but require support and encouragement from school managers. Given appropriate strategic management and confident teaching, the potential of ICT is very considerable and still largely untapped.

The importance of ICT has been stressed in every version of the National Curriculum. As the communication dimension has grown, ICT has developed from an esoteric adjunct of design technology into what many see as the fourth core subject. The emphasis of the programmes of study has progressively shifted from the technology itself towards the ways in which it can be used.

The National Curriculum 2000 (DfEE 1999) requires primary children to use ICT to:

- find things out;
- develop ideas and make things happen;
- exchange and share information;
- review, modify and evaluate their work.

It is expected that children will develop skills in the subject itself and use these skills in all other areas of the curriculum. ICT is therefore a means of investigation and expression as well as a subject in its own right. It is seen as parallel with literacy or numeracy, a key skill to be developed and used across the primary curriculum. Its fundamental role in the curriculum (and life) has led to it being described as the fourth core subject. In fact, this nomenclature was never used in the published versions of the National Curriculum, a decision that may have been driven by resource constraints as much as educational philosophy.

In recent years the scope of ICT has moved away from desktop computers towards laptops, notebooks and hand-held devices, as well as programmable toys, voice recorders and video machines. Through this chapter I refer to 'computers', but this should be taken to include the variety of devices listed above.

The impact of ICT on schools

Though the world in which we live has been transformed by the ICT revolution, the effect in schools has been uneven. The greatest impact has been on the way schools are managed, rather than in the classroom. Most schools now have fax machines. The video is standard. The photocopier has replaced carbon paper. The mobile phone accompanies school trips. Standards of presentation of school documentation have improved hugely, and word processing has facilitated regular revision. Financial and administrative systems depend on ICT. Government publications are routinely delivered electronically rather than on paper. Access to performance information is rapid, and analysis is infinitely more sophisticated than it was. However, we still have many classes where children rarely use a computer, and then only for low level and unchallenging activities, while in others 9-year-olds are engaged in complex creative thinking facilitated by ICT. We have a National Curriculum that requires every subject other than physical education (PE) to contribute to the development of primary children's ICT capability, but the practice is still uneven. ICT can make radical contributions to subject teaching, but still many teachers never use it.

In my view, ICT is underused because of poverty of resources, lack of confidence and awareness on the part of teachers, and the demands of other curriculum developments. It is ironic that the growing emphasis on a child's entitlement to ICT experience in the various versions of the National Curriculum has been accompanied by increasing restrictions on the use of time. The tight structure of the Literacy Hour, for example, has reduced the extent of ICT in English lessons.

Lack of resources is frequently blamed for the underuse of ICT. However, government initiatives such as the NGfL and lottery funding, coupled with the growth of the world wide web, mean that quite suddenly schools have much higher levels of resources and relatively fast and inexpensive communication networks. At the same time, the development of digital cameras, hole-in-the-wall cash machines, e-commerce and the Internet has resulted in much increased teacher awareness and confidence in the use of ICT in everyday life. This combination of conditions may finally mean that, if we manage it correctly, a genuine unleashing of children's potential is about to occur. In the sections that follow, I shall try to reconcile the competing demands of a structured curriculum with the exploratory use of ICT, and show how this technology can genuinely support and invigorate children's learning.

It has been argued that the introduction of computers into schools was a case of a technology seeking an application. Indeed, the first computers were introduced into English primary schools by the Department of Industry (DoI), not the Department for Education (DfE) (Smart 1996), and probably had more to do with the need to revitalize the British microelectronics industry than education. Many primary teachers could see very little point in the initiative. I can vividly recall my scepticism when we decided to spend £700 on a computer. The computer duly arrived – one, for the whole school. In her enthusiasm to get the machine working the science coordinator (for ICT was seen as a branch of science or technology) connected the earth wire of the monitor mains lead to the live pin on the plug, with predictable and spectacular results. The only programs were two demonstration tapes and lists of BASIC code which had to be meticulously typed and recorded on cassette tape. Few teachers had the time to do this, or saw it as useful; those who did became absorbed and obsessive. A colleague regularly stayed up until 3 a.m. plotting his biorhythms and writing routines that would generate addition sums for his class the following day. Loading the program took several minutes and required dexterity in juggling the volume and tone controls on the cassette player. The display consisted of big square blocks of solid colour. One program, in which the user had to defend a village against thieves and the flooding of a river, raised interesting possibilities, although few teachers regarded the new computer as a realistic teaching tool. However, we were excited by the new information age and the cassette recorder was very handy indeed!

Warning notes were sounded. The danger was that teachers would use new technologies with little consideration of their educational possibilities. This dilemma illustrates some fundamental issues that we are still reconciling today, namely:

- What is the place of ICT in primary education?
- Can it (and should it) be harnessed in support of children's learning?
- Does the technology work and do what teachers want it to do?
- Do teachers know how best to use it?
- How can schools develop a strategic approach to the management of ICT?
- How can small numbers of machines impact on the learning of large numbers of children?

Of course, the situation developed rapidly. It was soon realized that programming was a waste of teachers' time and a specialist educational software industry grew up. As the power of the equipment increased, the price remained stable in spite of inflation, and the numbers of machines in schools steadily rose through the 1990s, leaping with the NGfL funding at the end of the decade. Successive versions of the National Curriculum have imposed requirements on teachers to make use of ICT in their teaching, though it was only with the 2000 curriculum that the requirement finally became statutory.

The rationale for including ICT in the primary curriculum was initially somewhat hazy. At the beginning, familiarity with computers was seen as an end in itself, an essential preparation of children for a digital society (hence the involvement of the DoI). In-service courses for teachers focused on how to turn the machines on, and paid little attention to why you would want to do so (Tagg 1995).

The development of ICT has been characterized by increasing emphasis on its role as a tool for learning and an enabler for other subjects. Through the early 1990s, attention turned increasingly to making 'better and fuller use of the education potential' of ICT (Smart 1996: 2). This implies a shift in focus from the technology to the curriculum and the learner. The technology does not merit a place in the classroom because it exists, but because it serves the needs of the child.

As I write this chapter, the tension between the needs of the child as learner and the child as future citizen continues to be debated and there is increasing emphasis on the communications dimension of ICT.

Familiarity with ICT is being promoted enthusiastically by the government, which is sponsoring computer access in supermarkets, pubs and the homes of the unemployed in order to promote citizenship in the age of 'edutainment', e-commerce and e-learning. But the driving reason for ICT in the primary curriculum has to be the contribution it can make to children's learning.

ICT and teachers

Whatever the official pressure, the extent to which children will benefit from the use or non-use of ICT will always depend on a teacher's professional judgement. ICT can contribute to children's learning in many ways, but it is rare to find its potential being fully exploited. Structured learning packages give untiring practice and reinforcement. Investigations and adventure games provide opportunities for problem solving. Databases, spreadsheets, word processing, graphics and presentation software give children ways of expressing, refining and presenting their ideas. Communications and database technologies give children access to information and ideas. Group work around the computer facilitates speaking and listening, as well as interpersonal skills. All this amounts to a rich and versatile resource that the skilled teacher can use to support and stimulate children's learning (Cook and Finlayson 1999; Ager 2000). This resource should not be used blindly. Teachers are accountable for children's progress and the quality of learning. It is essential that they apply the same quality standards to their choice (or rejection) of ICT resources as they do to other aspects of the classroom experience.

Most teachers base their decision on whether or not to use ICT on the availability and reliability of the technology, and the extent to which they believe that the potential benefits outweigh the hassle and the risk of it going wrong. It is essential that the machinery works. While the latest Internet-ready multimedia computers certainly offer possibilities for independent learning, there is still enormous potential in the older equipment that is often to be found gathering dust on a trolley in the corner of a classroom. There are thousands of computers standing idle because minor problems have occurred: someone has fiddled with the printer driver, the paper feed is jammed, the start-up disk has been mislaid or corrupted. Ongoing management of the resource is essential if ICT is to be cost-effective.

In the early years of primary school computing, it was expected that the technology would be unreliable. Many teachers will recognize the scenario of printers not working, frustrated children and precious educational time taken up tackling technical problems. There is still a tendency for some teachers to abandon ICT because of such difficulties, or to limit themselves to things that work for them.

A further problem is lack of equipment. Until recently the average primary-school teacher has had access to only small numbers of machines, so implementation of ICT has involved systems of pupil and task rotation. This leads to a host of access issues.

Limited resources also militate against the teaching of the skills that children need if they are to develop the ICT capability demanded by the National Curriculum. Children need to be taught the basic operations of word processors, spreadsheets, databases or presentation packages if they are to be able to select appropriate ICT solutions to learning problems for themselves. The teaching of skills is a great deal easier where they can be demonstrated on a large display, and enough machines are available for the children to be able to practise while the demonstration is fresh in their minds. This usually involves a dedicated lesson in a computer suite. This is not to say that we should abandon the good practice that has developed when ICT is seen as a component of other subjects, but all too often the ICT is seen as a self-sustaining activity that receives little teacher input once it has started. However, dedicated computer lessons have the disadvantage of restricting the casual access of the ICT-capable child to machinery that could help them learn.

Teachers' decisions about when and when not to use ICT are affected by their attitude to the technology. There is a significant need for support, training and leadership as teachers tackle an area in which they may well feel vulnerable (Tagg 1995). Teachers' decision making is discussed by Cook and Finlayson (1999: 76) – as their confidence grows, teachers increasingly take control of the technology and adapt it to suit the learning needs of children, moving 'from a position where ICT is slotted into traditional teaching sequences towards one reflecting a complete change of curriculum emphasis through new possibilities'. Initially teachers tend to employ packages that make minimal demands on themselves or their pupils. Often, early finishers are allowed to use the computer with little guidance. There is little connection between the ICT and the general classroom activity. As confidence increases, teachers use packages that support planned work and fit in with the existing curriculum, but they do not go out of their way to seek out relevant resources. Later the computer begins to be used as a classroom tool, with computer-based activities being planned as an integral part of the teaching sequence rather than as an optional extra. Finally, the teacher has the confidence, and the children the capability, for ICT to be used to enhance and deliver elements of the curriculum (Cook and Finlayson 1999). This has a radical effect on the teacher's role, and leads to a reconceptualization of their view of children's learning.

ICT and theories of learning

Confident teachers need to make professional decisions about when and when not to use ICT in their teaching. They need a clear understanding of the potential of the application to promote the learning objective. Programs should not be chosen simply because they are available and are known to work! This is not as straightforward as it might at first appear. 'What is important for us to understand as educators is that the computer is not neutral, but that it will exercise an active influence on the learner' (Underwood and Underwood 1990: 15). The influence stems not only from the nature of the activity, but also from the values and theories of learning that are implicit in its design (Bonnett 1997).

Skills and drills programs and many programmed learning packages are rooted in behaviourist psychology. SuccessMaker,[1] for example, gives pupils repeated practice in mathematics and English, analysing errors and providing appropriate reinforcement, remediation or extension questions. Intervention by the teacher is minimal once the system is set up, though diagnostic and summative reports are provided. Generally, the pupil works alone wearing headphones. Teachers report significant gains for many pupils, but no opportunity for creativity. This contrasts with the exploratory approach advocated by Papert (1980), the inventor of LOGO. LOGO is most commonly applied in primary schools to enable children to control the movement of a screen or floor 'turtle' by issuing commands such as FORWARD 100 or RIGHT 90. Complex problems can be resolved as a series of procedures to be explored and mastered individually. Papert uses the concrete example of juggling. Keeping three or more balls in the air is a near impossibility for most of us until it is divided into the distinct processes of 'throw left', 'throw right' and 'catch'. Each process can be mastered individually and then assembled into a complex spectacle, giving ordinary individuals the ability to demonstrate impressive circus skills.

Papert anticipated that if children were immersed in computer-rich environments, LOGO would give them a tool through which they could analyse, understand and control their 'microworlds'. The results of several evaluations of the impact of LOGO (e.g. O'Shea and Self, 1983; Grabe and Grabe 1996; Lawler 1997) may be simply summarized as 'LOGO programming can accelerate a child's normal course of cognitive development' (Underwood and Underwood 1990: 37). In this case, children are controlling the computer rather than being controlled by it. The full potential of LOGO has rarely been realized in primary classrooms. Though it is recognized as valuable and appears in the National Curriculum, most children meet it only briefly in mathematics lessons, and prefer to move a pointer on the screen by dragging it with a mouse.

While we are now closer to the resource levels that Papert envisaged, a tightening of the curriculum has reduced the time available for exploratory investigation, and the ubiquitous mouse removes the need to program the computer to make a pointer move, making this fundamental dimension of LOGO seem a bit pointless to children. The potential of LOGO remains, but it requires a determined teacher to really harness it.

Most primary ICT applications lie somewhere between the reinforcement provided by SuccessMaker (Research Machines) and the exploratory immersion envisaged by Papert (1980). Lawler (1997), Cook and Finlayson (1999) and Ager (2000) explore the connection between ICT applications and theories of learning in greater depth, reviewing previous work and placing it securely in a primary-school context. They present a picture of learning with ICT that places the learner in an active role at the centre of the learning process, actively constructing meanings, and learning. McFarlane (1997: 9) summarizes this 'constructivist' approach as follows: 'we currently believe that children must construct a view of their world, and that this is largely a social process. By working with ideas, materials and objects learners come to a point where they develop certain beliefs'.

Learning is not about digesting predetermined chunks of information. The teacher seeks to support the learner as they construct meaning and move towards independence. Talk and social interactions play a critical part in the process: 'It is social interactions mediated by talk which cause changes in learning' (Cook and Finlayson 1999: 92). Certain types of ICT activity facilitate this type of learning. Talk around an adventure game, for example, involves children in problem solving, negotiation and decision making. Programming a Roamer (a programmable vehicle that moves around the floor using a simplified set of LOGO commands) to move around the classroom promotes collaboration and reflection. Young children can dress it up as an animal or vehicle, which helps them to identify with it, and have shown remarkable problem-solving abilities (e.g. Cook and Finlayson 1999: 53), surprising their teachers by their ability to handle numbers. While much of this learning is mathematical, it should be noted that 'The real value of using computers with these young children is that it encourages them to communicate with each other' (Tagg 1995: 15).

If children are to construct meanings using ICT, it is important that the strong links are made between the ICT activity and everything else that is going on in the classroom. ICT, with all its benefits, needs to be set in a 'whole life' context. ICT is an extremely valuable part of life, but is not life itself. Cunningham (1997) advises that its use must be sparing, selective and reflective. The computer represents only a part of the learning environment (Bonnett 1997), over which the teacher must exercise control and responsibility. Children need to experience things first hand, although computers can help take learning further. For example, the nineteenth-century census data for Saltaire (a 'model village' near Bradford) is available in a spreadsheet which children can interrogate. This gives them access to historical information that would rarely be possible by conventional means, but this must not be children's only contact with historical sources. They need to handle objects and deal with the evidence at first hand. Digitized census data allows children to track individual families or test hypotheses. It can be done on a rainy day and you do not need a coach. A CD-Rom gives a bank of pictures, newspaper reports and diary accounts of Saltaire life, which is a wonderful resource for a skilled teacher, but it cannot replace the first-hand experience of a genuine local study.

Allen (1993: 43) highlights the potential for ICT to diminish the richness of human experience: 'Think how different history may have been if Samuel Pepys had possessed a Psion Organiser. History consigned to a chip! Think how readable Chaucer would have been if he had been given a Spell Checker by the Wife of Bath'. Allen goes on to set children's interactions with computers alongside their experience with class pets. The use of ICT gives a tool for classification, analysis and communication of information to remote audiences, but does not replace the kind of experience children have when they 'prod and poke the gerbils, weigh them, sort their food, draw graphs of tail length against time' (Allen 1993: 45).

Compare the richness of this experience (for the children if not the gerbils) with another scenario. Children are undertaking early database work. Mrs Clayton has set up a database program with a file on the class's pets. Fields include species, colour, skin type, food and size. As she wants children to be able to classify and produce charts and is aware of the problems caused by misspelling, Mrs Clayton has restricted entries in the colour and food fields to choices from a list of words such as 'grey' and 'brown'. This is good practice in database terms and will guarantee that meaningful use can be made of the data once it has been collected. However, the experience of children, as they handle the gerbil and describe how it looks and feels, is potentially diminished by imposing the simple label 'brown' on it. As Bonnett (1997: 154) comments, ' "database mentality" must be strongly countered by a sense of the poetic, the power of the metaphor to break the mould of imposed categories . . . Here a space is preserved for awe, wonder, mystery and the inspiration of things themselves'. This is why the role of the teacher is so vital. The skilful teacher will balance the conflicting demands of precision and poetry, will inspire and motivate the children as they explore, classify and explain their environments, and communicate their findings to a worldwide audience.

Awe, wonder and the world wide web

A similar dilemma is raised by developments in communication technologies such as email and the world wide web. In skilful hands, these offer an immense resource for learning, and I am an eager advocate of the contribution these technologies can make to primary education. However, there is a danger of a repetition of the naive assumptions of the early 1980s, when it was assumed by some that the single microcomputer in each school would transform education.

Email and the Internet offer children a worldwide audience and access to huge volumes of information, but their use in school must be moderated by discerning and professional teachers, with a genuine sense of purpose: 'Imagine proposing a library for children that contains pornography, is unedited, organized like a second hand book shop after an earthquake, costly to use and may or may not be open' (Davies 2000: 16). It is clear that teachers need to be more than one step ahead of the children if they are to harness the potential of the web. Government initiatives are promoting web connections for all schools, and this is only the start. Despite the reservations expressed earlier about hyperbole, the potential is genuinely awesome. Those with access skills will be able to requisition learning programmes from sources that are remote in time and location. And this *will* change the relationship between the learner and the teacher. It is already happening in adult education and for older school students. In Lincolnshire it is difficult for rural schools to maintain viable sixth-form classes for many subjects and transport can be difficult. Schools are already using video conferencing to link remote schools, so a teacher in one school can simultaneously interact with students elsewhere. With the web, 'elsewhere' could be anywhere. In higher education and industry, training modules are available on demand and the trainee is able to select according to their needs from any provider irrespective of geographical constraint. This has implications for primary education. Even primary children can obtain electronic information from anywhere, but will they want to, and will they be able to do anything with it?

Few primary children have the dedication to seek structured teaching on the computer without the encouragement of a teacher or parent. Furthermore, a base level of access skills and screen literacy (the ability to read a screen and operate a browser, the visual and intellectual discernment to identify appropriate leads, the ability to skim and scan, technical proficiency) is required before a person can learn from a web-based course. Though primary education provides these skills, along with fundamental literacy and numeracy, this is not its only role. A key facet of primary education is the social and affective development of children, the inculcation of the love of learning, friendship and self-respect. These are learned from people. Teachers will, however, increasingly have to take note of the fact that they are not the unique providers of information to children. Children already get much of their information from television, and through ICT children can, if they have the patience and the wherewithal, get information from anywhere. This should not be a problem for teachers who take a constructivist view of learning, but can be unsettling for those who do not.

We need to enable children to access and process appropriate information and to generate their own lines of enquiry. The quality of information can be dubious. The Internet has been described as a goldmine, but . . . 'as in real mines, the nuggets could be mixed with a good deal of dross' (Cook and Finlayson 1999: 9). We need to educate children and teachers in scepticism. There is a tendency for children to print out the appropriate section of a CD encyclopaedia for their homework, with the approbation of gullible adults. Smith (1999: 226) poses the key question: 'Is there a risk that children may come to regard the possession of information, on paper or on disk, as a substitute for actual knowledge? There is no value in children downloading quantities of information without engagement in the content'. But despite all these reservations, there are already many examples of good practice to be found.

Children in one remote Lincolnshire primary school have an email link with a school on Kangaroo Island, Australia. The children have their own correspondence partners. They have their photo, taken on a digital camera and sent across the web. This gives them a real sense of audience for their writing. Studies of their locality take on an important meaning for the children when they know that strangers (or, better still, correspondence partners) will be reading them. The 'Travel Buddies' project offers similar potential. The website describes the project as follows:

> Travel buddies are soft toys or puppets that travel the world as representatives of your class. They may go on a cultural exchange with a single school or travel widely on a path chosen by those who forward [him/her] to friends and relatives in other places. They go instead of sending the children, an expensive and unrealistic proposition for most schools.
>
> (Travel Buddies 2000)

The receiving class photograph the toy in their home settings and communicate about its activities. The children who posted it send questions and receive rapid answers. This immediacy contrasts with the frustrations of the conventional correspondence partnerships that were the bane of my life when I was a French teacher.

These projects do not stand alone. They encourage children to go to atlases as well as computerized sources of information. There is the potential to view satellite images of the foreign location, collect real-time weather information, find details of the air-travel arrangements and in some cases to see live video of the location through webcams.

Conclusion

In my view, it is unlikely that the average child would benefit from unfiltered access to all this information. The role of the teacher is enhanced, not diminished, by global communication technologies. Already teachers filter information, give it meaning, challenge children to explore and think, inspire and assess. The web merely makes this role more acute. The availability of information means that a teacher must more than ever apply professional judgements to direct children to appropriate resources in pursuit of investigative enquiries. Knowledge of children and knowledge of learning are the predominant professional skills in an information age, though they must be complemented by the ability to manage the technology.

ICT is the enabling technology that will allow this learning to take place. Children who do not develop confidence in its use will be deprived. Knowledge of ICT is a new literacy, and as a discipline in school I believe it deserves to be seen as the fourth core subject. If the potential is to be achieved, school managers will need to ensure that teachers are equipped and competent to take advantage of the possibilities. Clear aims and values will have to be verbalized if they are not to be swamped in a flood of information. With these in place, ICT may genuinely 'create a community of learners and co-learners able to share the outcomes of their learning' (Smith 1999: 217).

Note

1 SuccessMaker is an integrated learning package produced by Research Machines Plc. Details are available from their registered office at New Mill House, 183 Milton Park Road, Abingdon, Oxfordshire OX14 4SE, telephone +44 (0) 1235 826000, fax +44 (0) 1235 826999.

Bibliography

Ager, R. (2000) *The Art of Information and Communications Technology for Teachers.* London: David Fulton.

Allen, D. (1993) Information technology and childhood, in J. Fields (ed.) *The Challenge Ahead: Information Technology in the Primary School Curriculum*, pp. 43–50. Chur, Switzerland: Harwood Academic.

Bonnett, M. (1997) Computers in the classroom: some values issues, in A. McFarlane (ed.) *Information Technology and Authentic Learning: Realising the Potential of Computers in the Primary Classroom*, pp. 145–59. London: Routledge.

Cook, D. and Finlayson, H. (1999) *Interactive Children, Communicative Teaching: ICT and Classroom Teaching.* Buckingham: Open University Press.

Cunningham, P. (1997) IT and thinking skills in humanities, in A. McFarlane (ed.) *Information Technology and Authentic Learning: Realising the Potential of Computers in the Primary Classroom*, pp. 63–77. London: Routledge.

Davies, D. (2000) Do primary pupils need computers?, *Times Educational Supplement*, 29 September: 16.

DfEE (Department for Education and Employment) (1999) *The National Curriculum: Handbook for Primary Teachers in England.* London: QCA.

Fields, J. (ed.) (1993) *The Challenge Ahead: Information Technology in the Primary School Curriculum.* Chur, Switzerland: Harwood Academic.

Grabe, M. and Grabe, C. (1996) *Integrating Technology for Meaningful Learning.* Boston, MA: Houghton Mifflin.

Graham, D., McNeil, J. and Pettiford, L. (2000) *Untangled Web: Developing Teaching On The Internet.* Harlow: Pearson Education.

Heinrich, P. (1995a) The school development plan for IT, in B. Tagg (ed.) *Developing a Whole School IT Policy*, pp. 51–71. London: Pitman.

Heinrich, P. (1995b) Sharing responsibility, in B. Tagg (ed.) *Developing a Whole School IT Policy*, pp. 72–94. London: Pitman.

Lawler, R. (1997) *Learning with Computers.* Exeter: Intellect Books.

Leigh Star, S. (1995) *The Cultures of Computing.* Oxford: Blackwell.

Loveless, A. (1997) Working with images, developing ideas', in A. McFarlane (ed.) *Information Technology and Authentic Learning: Realising the Potential of Computers in the Primary Classroom*, pp. 121–44. London: Routledge.

McFarlane, A. (ed.) (1997) *Information Technology and Authentic Learning: Realising the Potential of Computers in the Primary Classroom.* London: Routledge.

O'Shea, T. and Self, J. (1983) *Learning and Teaching with Computers: Artificial Intelligence in Education.* Brighton: Harvester.

Papert, S. (1980) *Mindstorms.* Brighton: Harvester.

Smart, L. (1996) *Using IT In Primary School History.* London: Cassell.

Smith, H. (1999) *Opportunities for Information and Communications Technology in the Primary School.* Stoke-on-Trent: Trentham Books.

Stephenson, P. (1997) Using control information technology, in A. McFarlane (ed.) *Information Technology and Authentic Learning: Realising the Potential of Computers in the Primary Classroom*, pp. 38–51. London: Routledge.

Straker, A. (1989) *Children Using Computers.* Oxford: Blackwell.

Tagg, B. (ed.) (1995) *Developing a Whole School IT Policy.* London: Pitman.

Thwaites, A. and Jared, L. (1997) Understanding and using variables in a variety of mathematical contexts, in A. McFarlane (ed.) *Information Technology and Authentic Learning: Realising the Potential of Computers in the Primary Classroom.* London: Routledge.

Travel Buddies (2000) website: http://rite.ed.qut.edu.au/oz-teachernet/projects/travel-buddies

Trend, R., Davis, N. and Loveless, A. (1999) *QTS Information and Communication Technology.* London: Letts.

Underwood, J. and Underwood, G. (1990) *Computers and Learning: Helping Children Acquire Thinking Skills.* Oxford: Blackwell.

Ward Schofield, J. (1995) *Computers and Classroom Culture.* Cambridge: Cambridge University Press.

Webb, L. (1997) Investigating science, in A. McFarlane (ed.) *Information Technology and Authentic Learning: Realising the Potential of Computers in the Primary Classroom,* pp. 78–94. London: Routledge.

Part 3

The curriculum as
a foundation for learning

9

From somewhere to eternity: the journey towards good quality in religious education

Mark Chater

The teacher's role is not to give answers, because
there are no answers which are universally agreed.
It is rather to help the children to move along in
the process of finding their own meaning.

(Bastide 1987: 33)

Introduction

There may be some teachers who find the above statement liberating, and others for whom it creates uncertainty. We do not have to know all the answers, that is a relief, but what *are* we supposed to teach, and how on earth do we 'help the children to find meaning'? This chapter is written in the widely-held belief that, while primary religious education (RE) is steadily improving, most teachers know there is still room for further improvements. It is my personal belief that once teachers see good practice in RE, and understand the *point* of the subject in the curriculum, they find it much easier to take ownership of it, to operate on their own professionalism and produce other examples of their own which are as good or better.

We will begin, then, with one example of good practice, in the section entitled 'Tuesday afternoon at Somewhere School'. I shall invite you to comment on the example, identifying its strong points and being critical too. In the next section, 'The road to Somewhere', we will find out about the educational aims of RE. Two further sections offer advice on planning. The section on 'Frequently asked questions' can be used as the basis of a staff discussion in school, or for continuing professional development.

Tuesday afternoon at Somewhere School

The bell has just rung for the end of lunch. Miss Howe is lining her Year 4/5 class up to go into the classroom. There is a special sense of anticipation in their noise today. 'Have you all got your gifts ready?' she asks them, but really there's no need, as they've been asking each other the same question for the last two or three minutes. 'I'll just check I've still got the marbles and those cards,' murmurs George; and 'Are you really giving that picture?' enquires Stephanie of her friend. Then silence falls, and they're ready to go in.

The classroom takes them by surprise. There's some very peaceful music playing, it's dark, but a line of candles stands on a row of desks in the centre. Illuminated by the candles, and gazing down on the children, are images of Ganesh and Krishna. The children already know, from previous weeks, that Ganesh the elephant god is the bringer of good fortune and the remover of obstacles, and that Krishna, playing his flute, is a playful figure with a serious message about the beauty and love of God.

Once everybody is on the carpet, Miss Howe does a brief spoken explanation about the ceremony of Arti, the act of worship using light and other offerings. Through questioning she reminds them of the significance of the gifts they will bring; these are offerings to the deities, signs of respect and love. She chooses three children to bring their gifts forward and one more to hold the special candle holder, moving it slowly round in a circle. Everybody wants to have a go at that, and there is a slight breeze of restlessness every time she looks for a new person to do it. But everybody is also looking forward to offering their gift and putting their special written wish or prayer at the feet of the deities, half hoping it will come true, even though Miss has said this is a pretend Arti.

Later, with the lights back on and the desks back in place, the pupils write about 'Our *Arti* ceremony'. George writes:

> The deities looked very special and a sort of mixture of strict and kind. I liked the way the candles made the room mysterious. We all acted the *Arti* ceremony which is part of Hinduism. We did what Hindus do, we gave offerings. I gave two marbles and my best cards. I chose them because they are very special and it took ages to collect the cards and I wanted to offer something really important to show how much I love Krishna. I asked Krishna to help me with my younger sister who annoys me. I don't know if he will.

At this point Miss Howe passes by and congratulates George on his piece. She invites him to say something about how the ceremony made him feel. George continues:

I felt excited when we were going in. The chanting music went round and round in circles in my head, just like the candle. I felt proud giving my things away even though I knew I'd get them back. I was hoping to have a go with the candle but I didn't. I'm glad I put something sensible in my prayer.

A day later, George's work is up on display, together with that of several other pupils.

What was good about the lesson? It may include aspects that you have tried, and others that you would like to try. We can identify the elements which strike us as good practice by making a list. Get a pen and paper and make your own list. Then compare your list with mine, which appears below.

- The lesson was prepared, part of a planned unit with information on Hindu deities and *Arti*, leading up to the ceremony itself. Classroom preparation included artefacts and music which are commercially available.
- The pupils, though excited, had been clearly briefed about appropriate behaviour and feelings, and they had enough interest in the topic to be able to match their teacher's expectations.
- Explanation and reminder helped the children to focus their thoughts at the outset. This was done through question-and-answer, allowing the children to be involved and to demonstrate their understanding. Experience and atmosphere made the activity powerful and memorable. The darkness, music, images of deities, and the activity of offering gifts and prayers, amounted to a rich experience of something quite solemn, but also fun.
- Exploration of the pupils' own lives was included. The activity was not only about what Hindus do, it was also about George and his sister. Pupils had an opportunity to allow the sense of meaning and mystery in the activity to touch their own lives, without being forced into any particular response.
- Lastly, there was a sense of boundaries around the activity. The children's behaviour was kept appropriate. They were aware of the specialness, but also knew they were not taking part in a real *Arti*. They accepted that the activity was designed to be enjoyable and to help them understand something about Hinduism and something about prayer. This sense of boundaries is especially helped when the teacher has a good relationship with the class and when they have known each other for some time.

The road to Somewhere

RE has not always been like this. In keeping pace with social and educational changes, RE today may look very different to its forebear in the primary classrooms of our own childhood, and this may sometimes disorient us, but it has been necessary. The opening up of a multi-faith society in Britain has made older, exclusively Christian forms of RE inappropriate in county and borough schools. Globalization brings the huge varieties of belief and lifestyle on the planet closer to us through faster transport and information technology. *Arti* belongs in the classroom because India is at the end of the street.

Another factor has been the evolving scholarly and professional understanding of RE. The methods of the 1950s and early 1960s made frequent and often heavy-handed use of Bible stories and teacher explanation (Sutcliffe 1984: 48; Copley 1997). According to the Office for Standards in Education (Ofsted), traces of this approach are still to be found, for instance in the over-use of Bible stories in Key Stage 1 (Ofsted 1997). RE began to move away from this approach because educational research found it ineffective (Goldman 1964). Mainstream Christian churches supported a change, knowing the old model of RE to be neither tenable nor useful (Ramsey 1970). Out went the emphasis on top-down instruction and the exclusively Christian assumptions; religious instruction was dead.

Amid some uncertainty as to what might replace the old model, RE entered an eclectic period including a popular world religions approach. There developed the view that RE must do something more radical than simply teach about world religions. It must 'go beneath the systems, Christianity, Islam, Judaism, to the age-long insecurity of man' (Mumford 1979: 27). The books and photopacks of the Westhill Project invited pupils to study the festivals, practices and beliefs of a religion, while also challenging them to reflect on their own and others' life issues (Read *et al.* 1988). Ofsted praised those schools which combined stimulating information with opportunities for discussion and personal response (Ofsted 1997).

Church schools, meanwhile, were encouraged to allow their own distinctive practice of RE to evolve. World religions began being taken seriously by both Anglican programme writers (Brown 1992) and Roman Catholic writers (Byrne and Malone 1992). The faith nurturing and celebratory element in church school RE was not lost, and became part of these schools' thinking on spiritual and moral development (Brown and Furlong 1996).

The 1988 Education Act reaffirmed RE in its unique curricular position: a compulsory subject, neither core nor foundation, but locally determined through a standing advisory council on religious education (SACRE). The SACRE in each local education authority (LEA), composed of representatives from the teaching profession and the local faith groups, is responsible for writing and monitoring the locally agreed syllabus of RE. Their work has been supported by central government

through the publication of model syllabuses (SCAA 1994), exemplification of standards (QCA 1998a) and non-statutory guidance including
level descriptions and exemplar lesson plans (QCA 2000a). Agreed syllabuses have typically settled into a balanced definition of good quality,
emphasizing both the study of a variety of religions and the personal,
spiritual or experiential element. This is summed up in the model syllabuses (SCAA 1994: 7) which use the phrases 'learning about religions'
(meaning factual study of their beliefs, rituals, stories and so on) and
'learning from religion' (meaning personal response to the feelings and
experiences of being religious). This balanced definition is seen in most
recent syllabuses.

Influenced by cultural and social changes, and guided by scholarly
and professional thinking, the subject has been through several phases,
each of which leaves its mark on the present model. To judge the earlier
models as inadequate is easy, but hardly the point. Earlier models seemed
more or less adequate to practitioners at the time; they still influence
those of us who are practitioners now, in varying ways, depending on
who we are and when, how and where we were trained.

The balanced definition ('learning about', 'learning from') is in many
ways a resolution of those earlier evolutions. It challenges the teacher to
handle a range of religious traditions with professional detachment. It
also requires the teacher to create space for spiritual and moral growth
through personal reflection and response to the religious traditions. The
logic is that RE remains incomplete if either 'learning about' or 'learning from' are emphasized at the expense of the other. Any RE which
balances the two elements has a greater chance of bridging the cognitive
and affective faculties, reaching both head and heart.

Attractive though this balanced definition may be, it is not the last
word. RE continues to evolve in its understanding of its task. Influenced by postmodernism and secularism, Jackson (1997) offers a new
model. His interpretive approach is based on principles of ethnographic
investigation and researcher–subject interaction. It moves RE away from
the study of religious systems and more towards an encounter with
religious experience. It envisages that pupils who used to study Sikhism
will now meet and interact with Sikhs. This approach is reflected in the
pupil texts of the Warwick RE project (Robson 1995) and to some
extent in other reliable resources (Clarke 1984).

To arrive at the kind of good practice seen in Somewhere School, RE
has had to evolve, and continues to do so. When RE is good, it reflects
some of the richness of its journey; when individual teachers produce
good RE, it is because they themselves have grappled with some of the
twists and turns of the journey, and have reached a balanced place. In that
place they are neither confused nor complacent. They continue to learn.

Planning a scheme

If teachers are aware of the journey RE has made, they are much more likely to plan it creatively in their school. I believe that the profession as a whole has absorbed the lesson about the importance of objectivity and inclusiveness in relation to the religions, and strives hard to achieve this. Some teachers have gone further, seeing the limitations of objectivity and asking themselves how they can make RE personally important to the pupils. Fewer have arrived at a point of balance in which world religions' content is stimulating and stretching and is accompanied by opportunities for reflection and growth. This is a personal view, although the underemphasis on 'learning from' is attested to elsewhere (QCA 1998b). Standards in RE seem to be rising, but there is still room for growth in the depth of work offered at Key Stage 2, as well as in assessment and the use of information and communication technology (ICT) in RE (QCA 2000b).

Planning RE begins with a determination to have it as a visible and meaningful element of the child's day and week. It will not do, for instance, to 'pin' RE to the history topic on Tudors and Stuarts – what kind of impression of religion would be gained if we did? Ofsted has helped RE considerably by drawing attention to the dangers of allying RE with too many other themes or subjects, and the benefits of focusing on a limited range of religions and concepts in a key stage (Ofsted 1997), with the result that pupils' learning is deeper and more secure.

For instance, a scheme on rites of passage which covers Christian baptism, Jewish and Muslim circumcision, confirmation, Sikh baptism, bar and bat mitzvah and certain Hindu samskaras (a total of say eight ceremonies in five religions) cannot deliver much depth of content and is likely to remain at the 'this is what they do' level of thought. This is an exaggerated example, but not by much. This sort of scheme will move at such speed that it leaves a blurred picture. The pupil is not enabled to distinguish between religious traditions, has little time to enter the thought- or feeling-world of the believer, and cannot pause to ask why or to ponder on important moments in their own life.

By contrast, when teachers focus on one issue ('What is really important in life?') in a limited range of religions (for instance, Islam and Christianity); when pupils are asked to explain the meanings of beliefs and practices (such as those summarized in the five pillars of Islam); when they are challenged to articulate difficult concepts (such as declaration of faith); when they are pushed to the edge of their own meaning-making through engaging in inclusive, supportive discussions ('if these beliefs are true, why doesn't everybody believe them and follow them?'); when they are met with precisely worded tasks and the right kind of

---

Match up as many as you can

Aims	Content
Appreciate the beliefs behind . . .	Singing an Easter hymn
Ask questions about . . .	Bar and bat mitzvah
Develop an attitude of . . .	Hindus
Consider the importance of . . .	*Tefillin*
Describe what happens in . . .	Racism, other prejudices
Describe the duties of . . .	A parable
Develop an awareness of . . .	Sikh baptism
Discover the meaning of . . .	Daily prayer for Muslims
Explain their feelings about . . .	Awe towards the universe
Explain the connections between . . .	A Muslim on pilgrimage
Identify reasons for . . .	Respect for the planet
Join in a celebration of . . .	Non-violence
Know about the beliefs about . . .	A Buddhist prayer-wheel
Know how to use . . .	A Passover *seder*
Recognize the message of . . .	The River Ganges
Understand the significance of . . .	Death and the afterlife

Figure 9.1   Generating some precise learning outcomes

support, and challenged to extend their self-expression in writing ('use this word bank to write the diary of a boy going on Hajj') – when these things happen, pupils' interest in the subject and in the questions it raises will deepen, and the standard of work produced will sometimes surprise.

Like any other subject, RE needs a clear sense of what the pupils should achieve. While aims such as knowledge, understanding or experience (e.g. of a visit, a discussion or an artefact) are useful general areas, it is wise to attempt a more specific identification of aims. Try using Figure 9.1 as a way of identifying several quite precise statements of the kind that could be used as learning outcomes in an hour's lesson. It is designed so that several variant connections can be made.

How many connections did you make? If you connect every aim with every piece of content, you'll get 256 statements, but not all of them fit. For instance, I would consider invalid connections like, 'Consider the importance of Hindus' as too vague, and, 'Know about the beliefs about awe towards the universe' as not matching. Even so, I counted over 100 possible statements. For instance, 'Identify reasons for . . .' could go with 11 out of the 16 content areas, including, 'Singing an Easter hymn', '*Tefillin*', 'Racism, other prejudices', 'Daily prayer for Muslims', 'A Muslim on pilgrimage' and 'Respect for the planet'.

Racism and other prejudices	A Passover *seder*
Hindus	The River Ganges
Non-violence	A Buddhist prayer-wheel
Singing an Easter Hymn	Death and the afterlife

There are two other possible connections between the areas of content listed in Figure 9.1. See if you can identify them.

Figure 9.2   Making legitimate connections: some examples

'Understand the significance of . . .' can be attached to almost any content, whether it is an issue such as death or a religious ritual such as bar and bat mitzvah. Just over halfway down comes the aim, 'Explain the connections between . . .'and here we should be careful. By and large it is a good idea to teach the religions in their own terms rather than referring them to each other or comparing them. This means avoiding, where possible, statements such as, 'A synagogue is a Jewish church' or, 'Jesus started Christianity and Mohammed started Islam'. When teachers make statements of this sort, they almost always intend well; they want to explain the unfamiliar by connecting it to the familiar. In religious terms, however, the comparisons are not always apt. More importantly, the comparisons (or contrasts) are not the main point: the most important focus for the pupils should be on the religious practice, belief or issue in itself, not on the degree of its possible resemblance to something else. Where explanation of connections can properly be used is in drawing together content areas which have some connection already (see Figure 9.2).

Let us now imagine that you are going to cover one religion with a class for half a term. We'll choose Sikhism, as it is often under-represented in primary schools. It helps to identify the kind of content you might hope to cover in six to eight weeks: in this case of a study of Sikhs, it will probably be as shown in Figure 9.3.

If Sikhism is thoroughly unfamiliar to you, try identifying eight content areas for another religion, then attempt the two tasks at the foot of Figure 9.3. Make a note of the results: these can be a useful template for further planning. When you have finished, ask yourself: have I included a sufficient balance of 'learning about' and 'learning from'?

Long-term planning

So far our focus has been on the short-term planning of a few lesson approaches. There is also medium- and long-term planning, through a

- Belief in one God and the symbol which demonstrates it
- The significance of Guru Nanak
- Stories which elucidate Nanak's attitude to wealth and power
- The ritual of Sikh baptism
- The story behind Sikh baptism
- The Gurdwara and the worship which takes place in it
- The holy book (the Guru Granth Sahib)
- A Sikh child's daily life, feelings and attitudes

In what order would you take these content areas, and why? Match the content areas to aims from the list in Figure 9.1.

Figure 9.3   Content areas in a study of Sikhs and Sikhism

year or a key stage, and through an entire primary school. There are several strategic issues to face when doing this. How many religions should be covered at each key stage? Should the approach be based on a religious concept, such as sacrifice or love? Or should it start from a human experience, whether personal or universal? Is it best to adopt sometimes one approach, sometimes another, and use each programme to try reaching from one to the other? What is the best way to ensure a coherent, growing experience for the children?

My personal belief is that coverage of all six major religions is not necessary. An agreed syllabus must certainly cater for all six, but a school need not deliver all six. To attempt it in the limited time available will normally result in superficial coverage and confusion. Better to tackle some in depth, and to trust that the skills of understanding and empathy inculcated thereby will be transferable in subsequent study. It is usually expected that Christianity will be covered at each key stage, with one or perhaps two other religions.

Where a unit leads with a religion it should go on to raise important human or moral issues. For instance, a unit on Sikhism might raise issues of religious toleration, and a unit on Judaism might lead through Passover to a discussion of freedom. Units based on a human or moral theme, say on belonging, celebration, fairness or conflict, can also be introduced. Where a unit leads with such a theme, it should draw the pupils into looking at a religion, for instance, a unit on belonging will often lead to baptism and/or other ceremonies of initiation, and a unit on conflict might look at Hindu and/or Christian practice of non-violence. Recent Qualifications and Curriculum Authority (QCA) advice offers three planning approaches and emphasizes that they are not mutually exclusive (QCA 2000a). There is space for almost endless permutation and adaptation. Within a year and a key stage the range of approaches should be varied, the range of issues and religions should be kept limited, and time should be allowed for discovery, discussion and reflection to suitable depths.

We need not be afraid of revisiting a religion or topic. In 1998, the QCA reported that Key Stage 2 pupils found RE more positive when taught a topic or religion for a second time. A cyclical system of returning to a religion or topic and dealing with it at greater depth will add coherence and a sense of progression.

Schools have the freedom and responsibility to choose religions and themes for a long-term plan. They can do so taking into account the social and religious context, the moral and spiritual themes pupils need to have raised, the availability of places of worship and artefacts, and the knowledge and understanding of the teachers.

Effective planning and implementation depend on the school's priorities. The commitment and expertise of the coordinator is essential in providing a clear programme, modelling good practice and offering advice. But this is not enough on its own; management support is also necessary (Ofsted 1999), especially in the form of resources and decisions about staff development.

Frequently asked questions

For reasons of space the questions must be few and the answers brief – and because brief, necessarily partial. It is well worth consulting one or more of Bastide (1987), Read *et al.* (1988) and Arthur (1990) for more thorough discussions.

How can I teach RE when I'm not religious?

This is the wrong question. Who said you had to be an athlete to teach PE or a French citizen to teach modern foreign languages? All that is required of you is that you teach the curriculum so that it reflects the full scope of human existence, which includes the religious dimension of life. Ask yourself, 'How can I be a teacher and not help pupils with their sense of meaning, value and purpose?'

How do I use an agreed syllabus?

Understand its structure, familiarize yourself with how it sets out the religions. This is frequently done via sub-themes such as festivals, beliefs, writings, founders, etc.. Look for, and stick to, repetitions of the 'learning about, learning from' formula. If the syllabus offers non-statutory schemes of work, spend time understanding their content, adapting them in consultation with your colleagues, and finding appropriate resources to deliver them.

May I connect RE with collective worship?

No, if you're trying to do curricular RE through whole-school collective worship, the two are distinct in law. Yes, if you're making thematic connections between them, for instance using collective worship as a way of starting a unit, sharing key concepts and celebrating pupils' understandings and responses. So long as they remain distinct in your mind, you can benefit from having cross-fertilization.

What about opting out of RE?

Parents and guardians have the right to withdraw their child from RE. If they do so, they are responsible for providing alternative religious education.

Can I use artefacts to simulate worship or rituals without causing offence?

The general rule is: yes, this is good practice provided you and the pupils are clear that this is not real worship. For instance, it is popular and enjoyable for pupils to participate in a role-played *seder* (the Jewish Passover meal), a baptism or a wedding. Artefact suppliers such as Articles of Faith or Artefacts to Order provide both the artefacts and explanatory material for teachers, with practical ideas for approaches. Artefacts are good as an initial stimulus, for questions, as a focus for reflective stillness, and as an assessment exercise. Avoid using a Koran in Arabic, a Guru Granth Sahib or the consecrated bread (the Host) from the Christian Eucharist.

What do I do if a pupil asks a 'deep' question?

Ultimate questions can offer some of the most important and educative moments in school life. They raise ancient and perplexing human issues on death, meaning, forgiveness, anger, science and evolution, eternity, wonder, belonging, the nature of God, the nature and destiny of humanity . . . to name just a few. They are creative questions. It is vital to realize that, although the child treats you as a source of reliable knowledge, neither you nor anyone else knows the answer to an ultimate question. Therefore the best service you can render the child is to avoid giving a definite answer and instead help the class to see the size of the question. Get them to glimpse some of the possible answers and to realize there is room for faith, doubt, honest disagreement and humble searching. These are qualities you can model. (There is further advice of a practical nature in QCA 2000a: 19–20.)

Is it legitimate to share my own beliefs?

Yes, so long as you are planning and delivering a balanced RE syllabus, and so long as you make it clear that they are *your* beliefs. See especially the issue of ultimate questions (above).

What should I do about the negative aspects of religions such as persecution and sexism?

Essentially there are three choices. You can teach about negative aspects such as the divisions in Christianity, but this runs the risk of creating negative impressions. Alternatively you can teach only the tolerant, open, non-sexist and progressive faces of religion (e.g. bat mitzvah and churches which ordain women), but this is misleading if it allows pupils to assume there is little or no persecution or sexism in religions as a whole. Finally, you can teach both the negative and positive faces of religions, and raise the issue with the children from time to time, in order to stimulate a thoughtful discussion. This would be a good example of 'learning from'.

Should I assess RE?

Yes, if this covers knowledge and understanding. It is a consensus view that beliefs and practices ought not to be tested. Whether there is room for the assessment or monitoring of reflective, responsive work (of the sort written by George at the start of this chapter) is an ethical question. Assessment is not only a judgement on pupil progress but also an indispensable indicator of the effectiveness of teaching. In general there is probably too little of it in RE. But it requires considerable care.

Conclusion: starting somewhere else

Are we any nearer to a practical vision of good RE and a sense of how to achieve it? Figure 9.4 provides a brief summary of some of the qualities of good RE planning which have been discussed in this chapter. How many of these qualities are visible in your school? It might be

- Limited range of appropriate content, supported by resources, confident teacher knowledge and positive attitude
- Opportunities for reflection on meaning and sharing of pupils' own response, not just teaching the facts – not just 'learning about' but also 'learning from'
- Allowing religions to raise issues and issues to lead to religions
- Teaching religions through the lives of individuals rather than through belief systems – e.g. Muslims rather than Islam
- Planning of vivid learning experiences – e.g. use of artefacts, visits – avoiding only teacher talk
- Questioning which stretches and challenges the pupils
- Taking each religion on its own merits, not comparing or referring

**How many of these qualities are visible in your school's RE?
Can you amend or add to this list?**

Figure 9.4   Checklist of good RE planning

an interesting exercise to share this list with your colleagues. Ask them to amend it too, it is by no means complete. Other developments such as assessment of understanding in RE, catering for children with special needs in RE and delivery of progression and differentiation are still in their infancy.

To the task of developing and teaching good RE, each teacher brings their experiences of religion and the spiritual and moral dimension of life, as well as specific beliefs, values and practices. These may constitute unhelpful 'baggage' if they are not acknowledged by the teacher. On the other hand, if there is self-awareness, particularly of fears and reservations, then that is the beginning of positive progress towards good RE. In the end, personal beliefs and experiences can be a part, but only a part, of what the teacher shares with the children, accompanied and qualified by the structure of the agreed syllabus and the school's programme.

There is still much to do. However, let us not forget how far RE has come, how seriously it takes its educational role in a changing world, how richly it contributes to the overall development of the whole child and how rewarding it can be for the teacher.

Bibliography

Arthur, C. (1990) *Biting the Bullet.* Edinburgh: St Andrew Press.
Bastide, D. (1987) *Religious Education 5–12.* London: Falmer Press.

Brown, A. (ed.) (1987) *Shap Handbook on World Religions in Education*. London: Commission for Racial Equality.

Brown, A. (1992) *Religious Education*. London: National Society/Church of England Board of Education.

Brown, A. and Furlong, J. (1996) *Spiritual Development in Schools: Invisible to the Eye*. London: National Society/Church of England Board of Education.

Byrne, A. and Malone, C. (1992) *Here I Am*, vols 1–5. London: HarperCollins.

Clarke, B. (ed.) (1984) *I am a Muslim*. London: Watts.

Copley, T. (1997) *Teaching Religion*. Exeter: Exeter University Press.

Goldman, R. (1964) *Religious Thinking from Childhood to Adolescence*. London: RKP.

Grimmitt, M. (1973) *What Can I Do in RE?* Great Wakering: Mayhew.

Grimmitt, M. (1987) *Religious Education and Human Development*. Great Wakering: McCrimmons.

Hammond, J., Hay, D., Leech, A. *et al.* (1990) *New Methods in RE Teaching: An Experiential Approach*. Edinburgh: Oliver & Boyd.

Hyde, K. (1990) *Religion in Childhood and Adolescence*. Birmingham, AL: Religious Education Press.

Jackson, R. (1997) *Religious Education: An Interpretive Approach*. London: Hodder & Stoughton.

Mumford, C. (1979) *Young Children and Religion*. London: Arnold.

Ofsted (Office of Standards in Education) (1997) *The Impact of New Agreed Syllabuses on the Teaching and Learning of Religious Education*. London: The Stationery Office.

Ofsted (Office of Standards in Education) (1999) *Standards in Primary Religious Education*. London: The Stationery Office.

QCA (Qualifications and Curriculum Authority) (1998a) *Exemplification of Standards in Religious Education*. London: QCA.

QCA (Qualifications and Curriculum Authority) (1998b) *Analysis of SACRE Reports*. London: QCA.

QCA (Qualifications and Curriculum Authority) (2000a) *Religious Education: Non-statutory Guidance on RE*. London: QCA.

QCA (Qualifications and Curriculum Authority) (2000b) *Religious Education and Collective Worship: An Analysis of 1999 SACRE Reports*. London: QCA.

Ramsey, I. (1970) *The Fourth R: Report of the Commission on Religious Education in Schools* (the Durham Report). London: SPCK.

Read, G., Rudge, J., Teece, G. *et al.* (1988) *How Do I Teach R.E.?* Cheltenham: Thornes.

Robson, G. (1995) *Christians* (Interpreting Religions series). London: Heinemann.

Schools Council (1971) *Religious Education in Secondary Schools* (Working Paper 36). London: Methuen.

SCAA (School Curriculum and Assessment Authority) (1994) *Model Syllabuses in Religious Education* London: SCAA.

Smart, N. (1973) *The Phenomenon of Religion*. London: Macmillan.

Sutcliffe, J. (ed.) (1984) *A Dictionary of Religious Education*. London : SCM Press.

10

Historical perspectives on the history curriculum

Jean MacIntyre

Introduction

History has an interest in enquiry into people, places, times and objects. It helps to deliver and sharpen a battery of skills, particularly critical enquiry, investigation, the evaluation of evidence, and a range of attitudes, among them a commitment to truth. This chapter aims to begin a reflective process so that the reader can critically evaluate how the teaching of history happens in the classroom, and can begin to form opinions on how it might develop. There are implications here for the development of the subject in the twenty-first century. There are challenging questions about the role of the teacher and about the nature of knowledge and understanding. It is, as always, to be hoped that teachers and trainees can combine commitment to present models of best practice with an equally dedicated search for improvement in response to the issues raised.

In the late twentieth century the government came to some momentous decisions about the future form of primary history education. They surveyed a broad sweep of predominantly British history and decreed which significant parts should be imparted to the primary child. The decisions that they made were, of course, influenced by their age and their culture. They knew then that the passing of time would alter the perceived significance of their choices. They accepted that in subsequent years new governments would review and revise their decisions. They also understood that the choices they had made would shape a whole generation's perception of history.

The choices made were not only of particular events, personalities and even centuries. The emphasis placed on evidence and in particular the material world was most significant. The focus on museums and gallery collections is still a major feature, as is the commitment to historical objects. The new National Curriculum (DfEE 1999) refers to them as 'artefacts' but I prefer the word 'objects'. Here, at the very start of the twenty-first century, we have the opportunity to examine some of the effects of this emphasis and identify the best practice that may be achieved.

Learning from objects

The new National Curriculum is not the only document to suggest that objects are a rich source of historical knowledge, skills and understanding for children. Many recent publications promote objects as accessible and exciting for the primary child to handle and as an immediate proof of past lives. Gail Durbin and her colleagues have written one of the best primary source books on the subject (Durbin *et al.* 1990) which is widely and well used in the primary classroom. Handling and touching objects, questioning them and hypothesizing about them is now commonplace in the primary child's pursuit of history. It is frequently praised in Office for Standards in Education (Ofsted) reports (Lomas 1999). Learning from objects takes place in a range of contexts. For example, museums nationwide are striving to make their collections more immediately accessible through exhibitions and outreach work, and historic houses often have objects for visitors to examine during visits. Schools can also borrow artefacts from their LEA for use in the classroom.

Despite this, the use of objects is problematic. In recent years, museum curators and educators have acknowledged the problems posed in the interpretation of an object within museums and galleries. But few teachers or academics seem to have seriously considered the problems of 'making history through things' in schools. At their best, objects provide positive proof of the way that people interacted with the physical world. At their worst, objects fail to reveal the vast majority of their history and children touching, smelling, drawing and describing them can only decipher a fraction of their historical meaning. Objects are seductive. Set up as a display in the classroom, they signal that history is being tackled, but the truth is often rather different.

The problem is as follows. There are hundreds of thousands of everyday objects that we do not and cannot know the provenance of. We may understand the way a meat-mincer works. We may be able to establish the date of its patent registration from the patent number on the base. We may also recognize the material used, which will help to date it and to place it in the chronology of developments in metal manufacture. But there are many things that we do not know, and most of these are about its function and particular history. We do not know who used it, where it was used, for how long it was used or where it has been over time. Some writers have suggested systems and lists that will help to structure an investigation. Keith Andrettiti, for example, has provided a great deal of useful information on how to structure an investigation into the form of an object but his comments on function, on how the object was used, are more limited (Andrettiti 1993).

Some primary practitioners would suggest that we charge the children with the task of finding out the things that they do not know – with our assistance, of course. But very few of these pieces of information can ever be retrieved. The provenance of the mincer, who used it and how they came by it, may simply be untraceable. Some primary practitioners encourage pupils to engage in the development of hypotheses, seeing the process of problem solving as almost an end in itself (Nulty 1998). This certainly has the added benefit of supporting the English curriculum through history. But if the hypothesizing runs unchecked, the 1920s meat-mincer that came from the kitchen of a small terrace house in Lincoln may be misconstrued as a Victorian gadget from the kitchen of a stately home, or, worse, a child who misconceives it as an early example of a mousetrap is never corrected. Objects can confuse and confound the child rather than adding to their understanding of history. There is another problem. Surviving objects are not necessarily a representative collection of our past lives. They may simply be the most durable or storable. Many things from the past are rarely available to schools. They are also under-represented in museum displays or inaccessible in museum stores.

It may be argued that the list of things we do know is sufficient – that children have learned a satisfactory amount about an object's general history, form and function. Yet even these facts are sometimes not uncovered. The presence of an object in a classroom display may signal an interest in the history of material culture that is never developed. The object may have been through many different processes. It may have been designed, packaged, marketed, displayed and bought or bartered or given or exchanged, before it even entered the domestic environment. After that it may have been sold in a house sale, given in a will or thrown out of the window and rescued by a passer-by. Some of these histories are retrievable but some can never be uncovered. All history is partial, but it is preferable to use objects with considerable history attached, if not intact. In this way objects can give pupils some sense of completion and allow them to gain the enjoyment and satisfaction from their investigations that will give them a taste for more.

Making objects work within the history curriculum

How can this area of the history curriculum be improved? How can we make objects work within the history curriculum?

The first step forward has already been taken by many museums. Choose objects with a known provenance which mean something to their owner, be it teacher, child, family, visitor or museum. This effectively means that you now have two sources that can work together: the object and the owner, the material and the oral histories. Both the object and the person can speak of each other. This not only enriches the enquiry with an oral history, it also provides children with the necessary material for a wider, fuller account than the object alone. Figure 10.1 shows what an object's owner can tell you.

An object can have many different meanings and sometimes only the owner can reveal these. The personal and the wider social significance of an object are both important. A particular piece of jewellery may reveal something about a woman's wealth or class but it may also signify an attachment to the person who gave it to them. An object may set off of a whole train of memories. Memories tend, as Gaynor Kavanagh has suggested, to be 'context dependent' (Kavanagh 1996), and so the handling of an object from a person's past life can set off a much deeper and wider reminiscence.

The next step is crucial. Give sufficient time to the research period of your project. Once the child has drawn and described an object, it is important to move on to support the child in actively retrieving information about the wider context in which this object functioned.

- Where the object came from
- How it was obtained
- How it was used
- How it was maintained
- How it was stored or displayed
- How it was valued
- What significance it had and has

Figure 10.1   What an object's owner can tell you

This means moving beyond primary-school resources on the Victorian kitchen, for example. It requires the teacher to find out about cultural and material history from more sophisticated sources. This is time consuming but the exclusive use of books intended for primary children must lead to an impoverished understanding.

It is essential that the teacher be absolutely clear about the learning objectives that relate to history and how they are to be achieved. Sometimes, by combining art or English with history, some objectives are never achieved. Often, time sequencing is neglected, or historical investigation is sacrificed in favour of close observational drawing or speaking and listening.

You do not need to start with the object at all. You can begin with the wider social history and use the object to augment it. Home life is a good example. Depending on the object(s), providing a whole context is rarely feasible. Figure 10.2 shows one example of how objects can be used in a partial, cross-curricular context, with due regard to the historical objectives.

The wider context

If you consider all the other aspects of our past lives, objects were often only the means by which we lived and not the substance of our lives. Anybody who lived through the 1980s knows that the personal stereo and the sports shoe were not the essence of the era, but you can be sure that children of the twenty-first century will be poring over these objects in years to come, believing that they encapsulated their age. The personal stereo does have some important messages about the past to convey. It has something to say about developments in design technology, personal taste, lifestyle and music. But it cannot and does not tell you all there is to know about life or even about youth culture in Britain since the 1930s.

So how do you provide a wider context for an object? You could take your pupils to a museum to see a room setting comprising 1980s objects, including a personal stereo. This will help them to understand the wider visual context of material culture in that decade. It will not help them to understand the social history of the consumer. Rooms, like lives, usually evolve in style and content. The 1960s television and the 1950s radiogram co-existed in many households and need not be separated into antiseptic settings. A room setting that only contains 1950s objects has more to say about the history of design and designers than about the ordinary consumers or citizens of that period.

The children can be taken to a Victorian house that has been conserved in its original form. Brodsworth Hall in Doncaster is a good example of a house that has been preserved but not improved, so the children will gain as accurate an impression as possible of the lives of the occupants from 1860 onwards. This English Heritage property has a special education room in which the children can discuss their findings. They can learn about the various kinds of maid that actually worked in the house and trace their personal histories using the house's written records and photographs. They can learn about the many jobs each servant was expected to perform. In the kitchen the two ranges (regularly maintained by Farr & Sons of Doncaster) required constant attention from the kitchen maid whose jobs included raking out the ashes, cleaning the flues, black-leading the ironwork and keeping the fire going so that the cook could prepare the meals. In the butler's pantry, at the end of the corridor, the butler cleaned and stored all the silver plate, cutlery and glasswear. The large collection of pewter and copper moulds and other utensils, on display in the kitchen, were all washed in the scullery by the scullery maid.

The laundry maid or washer-woman was dependent on fire to heat water and wash the linen. The objects she used (dolly tubs, pegs, possers, ponches) are available from museum stores or loan collections and can be used to examine the difference between past and present practices. Washing soda and soap can be brought into the classroom to compare with modern-day detergents. Children can also investigate clothes and fabric from the nineteenth century and find out how they respond to modern and traditional techniques.

This activity teaches children the social and scientific history of washing and can help attain learning objectives in both history and science (DfEE 1999). However, the learning objectives must be set down, understood and reviewed in order to be clear about what has been achieved.

Figure 10.2   The Victorian kitchen: a successful cross-curricular approach

There are other problems associated with school visits to museums. Museums are struggling to make their collections as accessible as possible. Some good examples are provided in *Building Bridges* (Museum and Galleries Commission 1998), but many children are still not getting as much as they could out of their school visit. Working closely with museum staff in preparation for the visit must be the key. The museum must be an integral part of a wider investigation.

Figure 10.4 shows some other positive steps that can be taken to maximize the benefits of learning from objects.

Figure 10.3 Children using Victorian washing equipment

- Matching objects with photographs of objects in real rooms gives a broader context.
- Looking at an object both in and out of context will stimulate discussion.
- Maintaining coherence in the collection of objects for school displays will maximize their potential.
- Setting up and gradually evolving a school museum over the years is a surer way of building on the potential historical meaning each object can reveal. Each class can add their own contributions each year, and explain the significance of their choices. Clearly this poses some problems in terms of storage space but the dividends are considerable.
- Ensuring that personal histories are displayed alongside each object further exploits the potential for learning.

Figure 10.4 Maximizing the benefits of learning from objects

If a teacher decides to use replicas, they must make it clear to the children that such objects are not genuine. They may not be the same weight, colour or shape as the original. More than this, the replica represents the maker's idea about an object from the past. It can be, in itself, a hypothesis; children must be aware of this when they weigh it as historical evidence. The reconstructions of Roman interiors at the Museum of London give clear indications of what is original content and what is replica. Of course, the idea that one can construct a concrete hypothesis is an important discovery.

Conclusion

What will the future hold ? Historians know that the understanding of history involves an ongoing series of reviews and revisions. Some of these are made because of new knowledge or evidence about a period or a person. Some of them are made because our new culture gives us an entirely new perspective on a particular event. So we know, or at least we suspect, that by the year 2050 our view of any number of past events (e.g. the Irish famine, the Industrial Revolution, the cold war) will have changed. Our whole view of history and the relative significance of each part is also likely to have shifted.

The relative significance of objects is also likely to shift. It is impossible to imagine exactly what these changes will be but we can speculate. Perhaps developments in technology in the twenty-first century will persuade us that the twentieth century was a dark age of sorts, and we will view its objects accordingly. Perhaps we will turn against high technology completely, and only revere examples of alternative or low technology from our past. Or maybe something we now perceive as relatively insignificant, like the Rubic cube, will be seen as seminal, and children will be taken to museums to marvel at it. Who knows?

References

Andrettiti, K. (1993) *Teaching History from Primary Evidence*. London: David Fulton.
DfEE (Department for Education and Employment) (1999) *The National Curriculum: Handbook for Primary Teachers in England*. London: QCA.
Durbin, G., Morris, S. and Wilkinson, S. (1990) *Learning from Objects*. London: English Heritage.
Kavanagh, G. (ed.) (1996) *Making Histories in Museums*. London: Lancaster University Press.
Lomas, T. (1999) *Standards in History in Lincolnshire Primary Schools*. Lincoln: Lincolnshire Education Authority.
Museums and Galleries Commission (1998) *Building Bridges*. London: Museums and Galleries Commission.
Nulty, P. (1998) Talking about artefacts at KS1, in P. Hoodless (ed.) *History and English in the Primary School: Exploiting the Links*. London: Routledge.

11

Geographical enquiry

John Halocha

Of course the first thing to do was to make a
grand survey of the country she was going to travel
through. 'It's something very like learning
geography,' thought Alice, as she stood on tiptoe
in hopes of being able to see a little further.

(Carroll [1892] 1989: 31)

Introduction

The aim of this chapter is to help you reflect on how the learning and
teaching of geography takes place in your classroom and how you might
be able to help your pupils, rather like Alice, to see a little further into
understanding how our world works. There are 11 sections, each of which
focus on an issue in geographical education. Each has important implications for the development of the subject in the twenty-first century. The
sections discuss the extent to which your role as a teacher, the experiences your pupils bring with them to school and the interactive nature
of learning can enable innovative curriculum change to occur, based on
your critical reflection and expertise as a professional decision maker.

Geographical enquiry

*Strategies are sought that will make it possible for teachers and students to work
with and as enquirers to confront their own notions and ideas about the way the
world works and about the meaning of teaching and learning as a process rather
than mere knowledge acquisition.*

(Hart and Nolan 1999: 41)

The enquiry process has been a central part of the primary geography
curriculum since the 1991 version of the National Curriculum. The

2000 curriculum (DfEE 1999) reinforces the interactive nature of geography, requiring teachers to plan activities which enable pupils to:

- ask geographical questions;
- collect and record evidence;
- analyse evidence and draw conclusions;
- identify and explain different views that people, including themselves, hold about topical geographical issues;
- communicate in ways appropriate to the task and audience.

Enquiry takes us far beyond the acquisition of geographical knowledge into learning processes which assist pupils to ask questions in order to help them understand how the world works. It can mean that pupils develop lines of research to which the teacher does not necessarily know the answer. An example of this might be the study of rivers. It is easy for a teacher to give pupils a photocopied sheet of a river and tell them to mark on it the names of the main features. It takes a little more time to set up a river model as described by Lewis (1998) and ask pupils to observe how a trickle of water cuts a channel in the sand and how the river changes over time. They can be asked to predict changes and put on their own settlements where they think the river may not destroy them. Of course, fieldwork experiences will greatly add to these studies, but the model has the advantage of being able to show pupils how time affects change and provides ways for them to interact with an environmental simulation, to ask questions, predict and explain their observations. They can become personally involved and if they are working in small groups, revise their understanding of the world through social interaction.

Enquiry styles can vary and the reflective teacher is able to choose one appropriate for their pupils and learning objectives. *Closed enquiry* is more teacher directed and helps pupils focus on a particular question. For instance, they may open up a web page for a small group of pupils and give them clear questions to research from the site. *Framed enquiry* has specific questions but requires pupils to ask them. An example might be where they are given access to two websites on an environmental issue and asked to collect information and interpret what they find. *Negotiated enquiry* takes place where pupils plan their investigation with support from the teacher. For instance, they have been studying the environmental quality of their local river and now wish to extend their understanding to the wider world by interrogating a number of river-related websites with questions arising from the study of their river, thus building on existing knowledge and understanding.

Geographical enquiry is frequently based on five questions:

1 What do I already know about this place?
2 Where is it?
3 Why is it like this?
4 How is it changing?
5 What would it feel like to be there?

Carter (1997) offers examples of practical activities related to each of these. Asking what pupils already know about a particular place draws upon their previous direct and indirect experience and enables the teacher to assess current understanding. It can also encourage them to use their imagination – for example, when starting to examine photographs of a distant place.

The question 'Where is it?' can be the starting point for helping pupils find, describe, collect and sort information from maps, photographs, local guides, people and the many other geographical resources discussed in a later section (see p. 171).

'Why is it like this?' encourages pupils to explain connections, cause and effect, make comparisions and develop a wide range of relational understanding skills. They learn to compare and not to take the world for granted: some people have one point of view but others may see things differently. A practical example of this might be asking the question, 'Why are there plans to build a bypass to our town?' Children will learn why transport and roads are as they are and how various local people will have different ideas about such plans.

'How is it changing?' presents activities to compare sources of evidence – for example, old and new maps of the school locality. Computer simulations allow pupils to study cause, effect and change. Pupils can also use creativity and imagination to predict how the world may be in the future.

Finally, Carter suggests that by asking pupils what it may feel like to be at a particular place, whether one they know well or one only experienced at second-hand, encourages imaginative work, curiosity and empathy, and thinking about how different people might feel about a place or event. It also helps children to think about values. For instance, what do they think about the loss of local open fields if the bypass is built?

If you intend to plan, teach and assess geographical enquiries, Martin (1999: 4) sums up the advantages of this creative learning and teaching approach by suggesting:

One of the prime benefits of the enquiry approach is that it focusses on learning rather than teaching: learning as an individual enterprise and as a social activity; learning under the control of the learner, learners learning from each other and thereby learning how to learn. In other words, the benefits of the enquiry approach reside in the process as much as in the outcomes of any enquiry.

With so much time in primary schools now taken up with teacher-controlled teaching, you may wish to reflect on how and why the geography enquiry approach could help your pupils develop approaches to learning as the foundations of a lifelong interest in the world around them.

Skills, knowledge and understanding

These form another key building block in the creation of an effective geography curriculum. Geographical enquiries and lessons will contain a balance of all three. One lesson may draw heavily upon skills, while another may emphasize understanding, but never any one in isolation.

This has important implications for the role of the teacher. The way in which you provide a balance of these can have a real effect on the type of curriculum you create. It can say much about the philosophy underpinning your planning. It also raises some fundamental questions about the nature of primary geography. Is it really a content-based subject or are you trying to develop an enquiry-based approach to learning? Is the world really black and white? There are parallels with science education. The Office for Standards in Education (Ofsted) considers that quality in science education may be seen when pupils begin to understand 'the powerful but provisional nature of scientific explanation' (Ashley and Hughes 1999: 213). In just the same way, pupils in geography can also start to appreciate that geographical explanations can change over time and that knowledge is not fixed. For instance, the theory of continental drift was not widely accepted until the 1960s; there are currently various opinions and theories on the long-term effects of global warming. Of course, some areas of knowledge are more fixed than others: the location of the River Thames is fixed, but even that will change over long periods. Children do need to know where places are, but the best geography teaching will also build processes onto the facts and ensure they have the more generic skills to access information. Place names appear to be fixed, but a study of maps of Europe from the last 50 years will show that perhaps it is not geographical facts which are the key to good geography, but the ability to find up to date information, see changes and seek explanations for them.

The place of geographical skills in the curriculum may be compared with current political views that literacy and numeracy have to be taught before they may be applied to other areas of the curriculum. In the same way, if we plan geography lessons which attempt only to teach skills in isolation, we lose valuable opportunities for pupils to see why they are necessary. For instance, it is easy to plan a class lesson where the teacher is dominant and aims to teach grid references. Alternatively, if the teacher provides initial input and examples and then asks pupils to work in pairs to code and decode messages, pictures or routes using grid references, pupils will not only learn the relevant skills, but also begin to understand the reason for the rules of grid referencing and the constant need for accuracy. This example also shows how understanding may be planned into geographical work if the aims are carefully considered and the philosophy behind the lesson sees pupils as active learners rather than passive receivers of knowledge.

Having considered issues surrounding the broad concepts of geographical enquiry, knowledge, skills and understanding we now move on to discuss some more specific issues in current geographical thinking.

Scale

The concept of scale is normally related to maps in geography. While it is important for pupils to use and make maps and plans, and view aerial photographs and satellite images at a range of scales, this section will consider the implications of scale from other perspectives.

'Geographers deal with a local–global dialectic, where local events constitute global structures which then impinge on local events in an iterative continuum' (Taylor *et al*. 1995: 9). Effective planning will give pupils the opportunity to study their own local world, thus placing value on their own experiences. They should also study places and events further afield, right up to the global scale. Within this study of scale it may be worth asking if your current curriculum tends to view this process as one where children study more distant places as they get older. This suggests a rather limited model of what pupils might be able to understand and also fails to make use of any global experiences they may already have had. Graham and Lynn (1989) researched pupils' knowledge and understanding of the wider world and discovered both greater knowledge than expected but also many misconceptions and prejudices: 'Teachers need to be aware of these predispositions so that they can provide classroom activities which will broaden children's thinking' (Scoffham 1998: 26).

Studying the world at a range of scales raises the issue of geographic distance. This may be seen in two ways. The first is the widely experienced one where the effect of distance is studied: for example when pupils decide on the best forms of transport or how long a journey might take at different times of day in a busy town. The second is where we plan activites which begin to introduce pupils to the idea that if we view people, places and events from a distance we see a broad picture, but looking at the world more locally we discover more detail. This is an interesting concept today with increased access to the world wide web. Some pupils think that electronic links actually provide the detail we need to understand faraway places, while the reality may be rather different (Halocha 2000).

Scale can encourage pupils to think creatively about the world. What might it be like to travel huge distances round the planet? Where would they want to go? It can also develop values and spirituality by studying the wide range of cultural beliefs and lifestyles we see spread across our planet.

Relationships

Studying places at the various scales discussed in the last section is an opportunity to plan learning which will help pupils understand cause and effect and develop relational understanding. For instance, if the older children play hectic ball games all over the playground, it can affect the safety of younger pupils. Can a solution be found in getting children to use different parts for different activities? Can our buying habits change the effects of global fishing if people are more aware of the way some types of tuna fishing can affect dolphins? Again, these examples show how enquiry can be done at a range of scales from local to global. Cause and effect are important concepts in helping pupils understand how our planet works: heavy rain up in the hills can cause flooding where the children live.

Thinking skills

Leat (1998) has worked with geography teachers to devise a wide range of strategies to actively develop thinking skills in geography so that pupils are asking questions and challenging our own ideas and views of the world. They do this by working in small groups to solve mysteries that encourage them to develop relational understanding and cause and effect. For example, in one mystery they are given information about a farm and its locality and told of a mysterious event that has occured. They study the evidence and as a group have to offer a solution using a wide range of geographical skills.

Patterns and processes

Geographers look for patterns and processes in the world to help explain what they see. 'Pattern refers to the way in which physical and human features occur or are arranged . . . for example, layout of hedgerows in a landscape . . . Process refers to a series of events that cause change in a place or environment . . . for example, river flow eroding the banks of a river' (DfEE 1999: 19).

If you see your role as needing to provide experiences of patterns and processes, you will be helping pupils to think carefully about what is happening in the world and why. For example, in one school, pupils were plotting their routes from home to school on a large map. They had talked about the idea of shortest routes but actually found that many classmates took a detour. Their enquiries found that by taking a longer route these pupils visited an old hedgerow which contained many aspects of wildlife which they were watching during the year. The pattern they found did not entirely match the idea that people always take the shortest route. This activity valued the pupils' experiences and deepened the teacher's understanding of how they saw their world.

The time dimension

The time dimension offers two main opportunities to develop children's understanding of the world. The first is the development of the concept of change over long or short timescales. An earthquake can change a community's life in minutes while it takes millions of years for oil to be formed: again it is a developing sense of scale we are providing for pupils.

The second concept, which is attracting much growing interest, is futures education: 'In urging that we teach a geography of the future, I do not mean to say that we should give up teaching the geography of the past: but we should make that past the servant of the future. If the future is unavoidable, let us at least not walk backwards into it' (Walford 1984: 207).

Futures education encourages pupils to consider what the future may be like from a personal scale through to a global one. It encourages them to look at patterns and processes to make informed predictions, but also introduces them to the great difficulty we have in predicting anything. It does, however, encourage them to think about the things they may have some control over in the future and those which they may not. It revolves around a proactive approach and can be planned effectively into work on citizenship and values. Hicks and Holden (1995) have researched extensively with this approach and suggest a wide range of interactive classroom activities and research findings.

Citizenship, personal, social and health education and values

'Geography can be creative with Curriculum 2000's "new agenda", to the benefit of the curriculum as a whole' (Grimwade *et al.* 2000: 5). The relative flexibility of the geography orders and their content requiring that pupils investigate their own locality and the wider world, provide an excellent foundation for teachers to develop a creative role in planning the curriculum. Citizenship education revolves around the exploration of values and attitudes. Children should engage in real contexts, with time for reflection built in, to develop values and attitudes (Jackson 2000). It links well with the concepts of scale and relationships discussed earlier, in that activities looking at local issues can be compared with events in the wider world, looking for causes and effects.

Many issues arising in citizenship work have close geographical links. For example, in the study of a local lake, issues may arise about the various demands placed on it by bird-watchers, fishing enthusiasts and a water-skiing club. How might they reconcile their needs in a sustainable way? Are there relationships between the activities? For example, does the noise and water disruption of the skiing have a greater effect on wildlife than the fishing activites? The good thing about such an enquiry, which you can base in your locality, is that so many things are going on that differentiation is easy to find, enabling all pupils to experience an inclusive curriculum. For some pupils, who rarely explore their locality with their families, the chance to visit the lake, enjoy the environment and see what it is used for would be an appropriate objective in order to widen their experience of the local environment. Perhaps even walking round together and sharing a picnic might be an important learning experience in terms of citizenship education. For others, the preparation of detailed questionaires and land-use maps may enable them to develop higher order thinking skills as they work on finding their solution to the conflicting needs of the community. If it was appropriate to extend the scale of the enquiry, pupils could investigate a sea- or lakeside holiday destination abroad, where they could see how tourists such as themselves can affect the lives of local people in positive and negative ways.

Hopefully, this example will help you to begin to think of issues which start with the experiences and needs of the child and how they may be carefully planned to incorporate appropriate parts of the geography and citizenship curriculum.

Environmental change and sustainability

'Geography is a focus within the curriculum for understanding and resolving issues about the environment and sustainable development' (DfEE 1999: 108). The present National Curriculum requires that pupils actively investigate decision making about the environment. It also expects them to examine the quality of life on our planet. These are real advances in content and it is now up to teachers to develop their role in devising active learning experiences which will help pupils to achieve these advances. Slater's (1994) research suggests that simply giving pupils the facts about environmental issues has little effect either on their understanding or later action. The latest guidelines provide a real opportunity for the curriculum to both reflect and contribute to the philosophy and ethos of the school. Clearly, this is not something you can tackle on your own. It requires a whole school approach, but you may wish to think of ways of facilitating discussions on ways forward.

Various teaching strategies may be used to develop learning in this area. Fieldwork can be conducted in many ways. On the one hand it can be entirely teacher led, such as a local walk. For some of your aims this may be very suitable – for example, where you wish to focus pupils' observation very carefully to develop their knowledge of the locality, by walking a route and following it on a map. Another approach is to allow pupils to discover aspects of the locality themselves. For instance, in safely supervised groups they could map the litter and pollution they find around the school and suggest why it is there and what could be done to reduce it. Sensory fieldwork encourages pupils to heighten the use of their senses in the environment. It also gives them time to consider values and emotions: would the locality look better for them if the graffiti and litter were gone? How do they feel when vandals pull up the new trees on the school field? Clearly there are close links here with citizenship education.

Smith and Reid (2000) offer an interesting way of developing progression and continuity in active fieldwork for sustainability and environmental education. Begin by heightening pupils' awareness and spatial understanding of the environment by using discovery and sensory methods. Move on to focused enquiries which will extend their knowledge and understanding by using the geography enquiry methods discussed earlier. Finally, provide opportunities for them to develop a personal value system of concern and action by actually doing something to promote sustainability – for example, by mounting a school litter prevention campaign or planning to improve the local environment.

Information and communication technology

Geographical enquiries can be enhanced by using information and communication technology (ICT), especially if we take time to think about what makes this a powerful tool. This section offers some examples to help you begin to make your own list of how you could use ICT to support active learning in geography.

While the web does have its limitations (Halocha 2000), it gives pupils the chance to collect and analyse information from around the world. With careful planning, it can help them consider issues from various points of view. For example, the BBC News website includes easy to read reports and photographs of natural disasters around the world. As well as providing factual information, the site takes us into the lives of the people who lived through those events through first-hand reports written by them.

Cassette recorders, video cameras and digital cameras allow pupils to record events in their environment and gain geographical data. For instance, when studying transport they can set up a video camera on a busy road outside the school and record traffic and pedestrian movement for, say, four hours. If they view this in fast-forward mode, they will very effectively see how patterns and flow change throughout the day. They can then suggest reasons for this and perhaps predict what might happen on other days – for example, a Sunday.

Computer-controlled buggies (e.g. Roamers, Turtles, Pips, Pixies) can help pupils to develop spatial awareness, vocabulary and key geographic concepts. For example, young children can create a fantasy ride going through caves (cardboard boxes), past spooky creatures (tape recorders hidden in disguises), for a teddy bear and programme the buggy to take it on a journey of adventure. This would allow them to explore the need to plan carefully, develop locational language and think about the feelings the bear may have as it travels around.

Portable data loggers help pupils to easily monitor and record events in the classroom in a spatial context. For example, if they have some plants they wish to put in the school garden which have particular needs, they can record light and temperature levels in different locations and at different times of day. These can be plotted onto a plan and then decisions made about the best locations for the plants.

An apparently isolated school in the North Pennines has strong links around the world. When their headteacher exchanged jobs in New

Zealand for a year, extensive use was made of email to learn about the country first-hand from the pupils there. The English pupils relayed their end of year concert to their new friends in New Zealand using a web camera on a computer. Planning the live broadcast taught them a lot about time zones around the world!

I have seen excellent use made of software not initially designed for educational school use. One example was a garden design programme for adults. A student teacher used the excellent mapping facilities with Year 5/6 pupils to develop a wide range of geographic concepts. This programme helped pupils consider location, scale, climate, change over time, design and values, site conditions, orientation and perspective, and many other ideas.

This final example is perhaps appropriate to end on as it illustrates how a student teacher used her knowledge of geographical skills and understanding and looked for software which actively allowed pupils to engage in learning which helped them to think, offer ideas and justify their actions.

Geographical resources

Interactive and creative teaching needs a range of appropriate resources to support it. Halocha (1998) and Bowles (1999) suggest a wide variety of geographical resources and sources and advise where they may be obtained. Here are some suggestions:

- Use resources which help pupils to gain first-hand experience. Most localities are rich in people, artefacts, buildings, various land use, change and events. Find local contacts for photographs, maps, visitors to the school and physical items.
- Build contacts in other parts of the country and around the world. Exchange real objects as well as using ICT facilities: we cannot learn everything electronically.
- Encourage pupils to find their own geographic resources. What can we learn from dolls and toys brought home from around the world? What is the view like from the bedroom window: what do they like and what would they change?
- Keep a range of items to see how places change. Photographs of the locality make excellent historical and geographical resources five years after they were taken. It is amazing just how much around us does change and many pupils will be able to understand this timescale.

Resources also help to develop a growing media literacy as part of citizenship education. Who took this photograph? Why did they take it?

What is missing? One very effective way of doing this is by having a link with a school either in England or another country. You then actually create the geography resources which the other school will use and they do the same for you. When children have to decide what to photograph, what items to select, which maps to choose, they begin to understand that we only receive very selective information about other places, people and events. This is crucial knowledge in a world of increasing communication and interaction.

Conclusion

Geographical understanding requires that pupils learn to observe, analyse and suggest explanations for what they see happening in the world. As Catling (1998) has said, encouraging children to provide explanations helps to develop higher-order thinking skills. As teachers we have to decide whether we want our pupils to become passive citizens with few skills to understand the increasingly complex events taking place on our planet and how they interact with them. The alternative is to create a rich learning environment where pupils are encouraged to think, question and develop values which will promote understanding (Haggett 1990). Hopefully, that understanding will be of themselves as human beings and thinking individuals.

References

Ashley, M. and Hughes, M. (1999) Towards uncertain futures?, in M. Ashley (ed.) *Improving Teaching and Learning in the Humanities*. London: Falmer Press.

Bowles, R. (1999) *Resources for Key Stages 1 & 2*. Sheffield: Geographical Association.

Carroll, L. ([1892] 1989) *Alice Through the Looking Glass*. London: Dragon Works.

Carter, R. (1997) Geography in the whole primary curriculum. Paper presented to the Geographical Association Annual Conference, London, 2–4 April.

Catling, S. (1998) Geography in the National Curriculum and beyond, in R. Carter (ed.) *Handbook of Primary Geography*. Sheffield: Geographical Association.

DfEE (Department for Education and Employment) (1999) *The National Curriculum: Handbook for Primary Teachers in England*. London: QCA.

Graham, J. and Lynn, S. (1989) Mud huts and flints: children's images of the Third World, *Education 3–13*: June: 29–32.

Grimwade, K., Jackson, E., Reid, A. and Smith, M. (eds) (2000) *Geography and the New Agenda: Citizenship, PSHE and Sustainable Development in the Primary Curriculum*. Sheffield: Geographical Association.

Haggett, P. (1990) *The Geographer's Art*. Oxford: Blackwell.

Halocha, J. (1998) *Coordinating Geography Across the Primary School*. London: Falmer Press.

Halocha, J. (2000) Rags to riches, *Primary Geographer*, 42: 28–9.

Hart, P. and Nolan, K. (1999) A critical analysis of research in environmental education, *Studies in Science Education*, 34: 1–69.

Hicks, D. and Holden, C. (1995) *Educating for the Future: A Practical Classroom Guide*. Godalming: World Wide Fund for Nature, UK.

Jackson, E. (2000) Citizenship, in K. Grimwade, E. Jackson, A. Reid and M. Smith (eds) *Geography and the New Agenda: Citizenship, PSHE and Sustainable Development in the Primary Curriculum*. Sheffield: Geographical Association.

Leat, D. (ed.) (1998) *Thinking Through Geography*. Cambridge: Chris Kington Publishing.

Lewis, L. (1998) Rivers, in R. Carter (ed.) *Handbook of Primary Geography*. Sheffield: Geographical Association.

Martin, F. (1999) The enquiry approach: what, why and how?, *Primary Geographer*, 38: 4–8.

Scoffham, S. (1998) Young geographers, in R. Carter (ed.) *Handbook of Primary Geography*. Sheffield: Geographical Association.

Slater, F. (1994) Education through geography: knowledge, understanding, values and culture, *Geography*, 79(2): 147–63.

Smith, M. and Reid, A. (2000) Environmental change and sustainable development, in K. Grimwade, E. Jackson, A. Reid and M. Smith (eds) *Geography and the New Agenda: Citizenship, PSHE and Sustainable Development in the Primary Curriculum*. Sheffield: Geographical Association.

Taylor, P., Watts, M. and Johnson, R. (1995) Global change at the end of the twentieth century, in R. Johnson, P. Taylor and M. Watts (eds) *Geographies of Global Change: Remapping the World in the Late Twentieth Century*. Oxford: Blackwell.

Walford, R. (1984) Geography of the future, *Geography*, 69(3): 193–208.

12

What is design and technology?

David Banks

Introduction

Human use and development of technology separates us from all other members of the animal kingdom and defines our position in time and space. As the hole in the ozone layer grows, we can see that none of us on the earth's surface can escape the effects of technology. If you drive down any country road and look over the landscape you will most likely be moving along a strip of asphalt with a hedge-row and fields. These reflect human activity that has changed the soil, created the vegetation and altered the chemical composition of the atmosphere. The road will be dotted with signs of human habitation and strung with pylons or cables; more signs of human activity and technology.

So what is technology? The first National Curriculum working group on technology, a part of the Science Working Party, defined it thus: 'Technology is a creative human activity which brings about change through design and the application of knowledge and resources . . . It is a means whereby mankind makes progress and society develops' (DES 1988, para. 2.4: 7).

There was a famous advertisement that talked about technology as 'the appliance of science'. In reality, technology uses all our know-ledge in an attempt to enhance human experience and activity whether it be the appliance of mathematics, art, language, science or any other subject.

In many ways, technology defines us as humans and is the mechanism whereby society progresses and develops. However, this does not mean that all technology is either appropriate or desirable. Using technology can have catastrophic consequences and effects beyond our imagining. This was witnessed when the first atomic bomb was dropped on Hiroshima. Yet these negative effects of using technology involve choices. We can, and should, always make choices about which technologies we use and how we use them. There is a wonderful story in the Old Testament that tells of a high-tech Goliath being defeated by the low-tech sling and stones of the boy David. He chose a technology appropriate to his needs and abilities, rejecting the armour and weapons provided by King Saul. The children of the twenty-first century will face many choices about the technologies they use and they need to be 'informed users'. As Tina Jarvis (1993: 3) says:

> Pupils should learn that technological change cannot easily be reversed. Ideally they will understand its great power and start to appreciate their responsibilities in its process. If children are able to understand the process of technological change they will not just unquestioningly accept it but feel that they can challenge and alter it.

This is endorsed by the National Curriculum for the year 2000 which claims that 'through design and technology, all pupils can become discriminating and informed users of products, and become innovators' (DfEE 1999: 15).

The creative conflict

While technological activity can be a very creative process it is not an activity that can be undertaken for its own sake. Music and art can allow free expression to reign, regardless of the opinions or desires of others. Technology can not. Technology is there to satisfy, or create, a need. It exists to solve problems and to generate wealth and economic activity. It is often about function and form and about the economical use of resources. Cost matters. The design process is about achieving fiscal and economic ends and the aesthetics are the icing on the cake. If the cake is stale and unappetizing it does not sell. Technology is about making a better cake, or a better mousetrap, or a better can-opener, more cheaply and efficiently. One of our most famous current designers is James Dyson, who revolutionized the humble vacuum cleaner by making a more efficient and effective dirt and dust remover. This is not to deny the importance of creative design, as seen in the Dyson design or in the design of the Apple imac computer (a product of a British designer, Jonathan Ive).

The National Curriculum

We are unique in having design and technology as a compulsory element of our curriculum and in many ways this reflects the concerns of the nation with regard to our role in a modern industrial society. It is vital that our children be both technologically aware and technologically competent, and these two vital issues are part of our National Curriculum and will be discussed later in this chapter.

The introduction and development of the National Curriculum for design and technology was a rough and rocky path. Many mistakes were made and teachers were baffled by the constant changes made within a relatively short timespan. Before the introduction of the National Curriculum, primary technology existed mainly as craft activities. It was often based on skills such as the needlework of the Victorian sampler or the gingham skirt, or provided opportunities for creative play. At secondary school it was formalized into materials-related activities, with woodwork working with wood, needlework with fabric, home economics with food and metalwork with metal. At the very start of the process of defining a National Curriculum, design and technology was part of the remit of the Science Working Party. This was a primary-focused body who met and reported in 1988. Later, design and technology was considered by a separate group but with no specific primary representation. The formalized structure of design and technology that emerged in the early National Curriculum caused enormous problems within the primary sector, and before long changes were made. Even so, the demands made on primary teachers with regard to the use of tools and materials, and engagement with the design process, led to much criticism of practice in schools by inspectors. Technology is still regarded as one of the most poorly taught subjects in primary schools: 'Design and technology (at Key Stage 2) remains weaker than most other subjects in all aspects of provision and response, mainly because of teachers' weaker subject knowledge and experience' (Ofsted 2000, para. 19: 26). The current version of the National Curriculum, which took effect in September 2000, is a much slimmer and more helpful document. Along with the guidance from the Qualifications and Curriculum Authority (QCA) and from organizations such as the Design and Technology Association (DATA 1996) we have a more manageable and understandable subject. National Curriculum changes and government guidance, together with the in-service education undertaken during the 1990s has done much to raise teacher awareness and to provide the skills and understanding needed. However, despite all this work, difficulties still exist and problems related to pupil underachievement continue to be raised. Thus there is a continued need to enhance classroom practice.

Issues for classroom practice

In order for effective design and technology teaching to take place there needs to be an understanding of the two major aims of design and technology:

• to raise the technological awareness of the pupils;
• to develop pupils' technological competence.

Developing technological awareness

The first set of questions we need to ask is: what do we mean by raising technological awareness, and how might this be achieved?

Considering the process of developing pupils' technological awareness can help us to answer both these questions. The process is one that has links with many other curriculum areas and emphasizes the cross-curricular nature of technology. At the beginning of the process we need to give children a structure that enables them to observe specific artefacts, to observe the features that reflect the 'design and make' process. We start by drawing attention to the key physical features of the object (e.g. shape, size, colour, texture). In particular we can draw attention to those features related to the way the materials are used and the ways in which the materials have been cut, shaped and joined. Children should investigate how the artefact functions and performs, analysing the structures and mechanisms employed to enhance efficiency of operation.

The materials chosen are a key feature of any artefact because they will have been chosen to match their properties to the intended use. Paper is often chosen as a material because it is cheap, easy to cut and shape and can be attractively printed. The properties of the paper can even be changed, such as when we seek to make it waterproof. Children can learn the story of two brothers who became multi-millionaires as a result of their ability to put liquids into what might be called 'paper bags'. Children can look for the label 'Tetrapac' for evidence of the brothers' influence on modern packaging. Fabrics are chosen for their warmth, flexibility and ability to take colour. Some repel water while others soak it up, and we use some of them to dry ourselves, some to keep us warm, others to keep us cool. The invention of new fabrics or fabric combinations can have an important effect on social life. For example, the introduction of 'Lycra' as a fabric has revolutionized sportswear. If you want an object to cut – that is, to have an edge – then you pick metal. So effective has metal been in terms of its hard-wearing and cutting properties that it has defined ages within our history, such as the Iron Age and Bronze Age. Some materials are easier to cut, shape and join than others, and this is important in making choices as to which materials to use in the primary classroom. The way things are cut and shaped provide an interesting insight into the tools and techniques used. Many metal objects show how they have been pressed so that what sticks out on one side goes in on the other, while others show signs of having been moulded.

Getting children to investigate the way things are joined provides a fascinating exploration of the way technologies are employed to solve simple everyday problems. Velcro fastenings have made a significant difference to the ability of young children to fasten their shoes. Zip fasteners are an amazing invention and one which not only revolutionized fastenings but probably made a fortune for the inventor. Cardboard boxes have flaps that help you close the lid and many have tiny slits on the edge of the lid to stop it falling open. Even the glues we use depend on the objects we seek to join, and this makes the correct choice of glue for joining things important. Children might explore just some of the range of stitches that have been devised to join pieces of material together and investigate how these have been extended to provide decoration.

The way things work determines the effectiveness of the product. Children should be encouraged to explore how the structure employed gives the object strength without making it too heavy. They should notice how strong triangular structures are, and observe them in action within the environment – for example, on the gate to a field or on electricity pylons. Children can also be encouraged to observe how we use mechanisms such as wheels, inclined planes or levers to make work easier. The power of the inclined plane revolutionized farming with the invention of the plough and helped raise monuments such as the pyramids. When that inclined plane was wrapped around itself, it led to the invention of the screw and allowed Archimedes to raise water from the Nile. Today it helps us jack up our car. With a lever, ancient philosophers claimed they could move the world. We might simply use a lever to open a door. With the invention of the wheel, something the Incas with all their skills never invented, we could move at incredible speeds. We could join wheels together with bands and turn them into pulleys to speed up or slow down motion, and even change the direction of that motion. We could add teeth to these wheels and set up gear systems and use them on our bicycles to help us to pedal our way uphill.

Children can also be encouraged to discover whether their artefact has any mechanism for storing energy. We might store energy in a coil of metal, or a rubber band, or in any other material that wishes to return to its original shape and form. We may store it as chemical energy in a battery. We may ask how the energy is transmitted and how that makes the object of use to us. Children can read about the fascinating world of machines in books such as *The Way Things Work* by David Macaulay (1989).

Children's exploration of objects might continue with issues of design. This can include exploring how well the object does the job, how durable it is and what the designers have done to attract you to purchase that item. Finally, the children should discuss issues related to the cultural context in which the artefact is found. We can do this by exploring what the artefact tells us about the society that made it:

- What does the artefact tell us of the technologies in use at the time?
- What does the artefact tell us about the values within society?
- What does the artefact tell us about the lifestyle of the people within the society?
- How does the object reflect change over time?

You cannot really undertake any historical research without exploring the artefacts of the age you are studying. The whole field of archaeology is about exploring past technologies and trying to find out what they tell us about peoples' lives, organizations and values. English Heritage produced a fascinating teacher's guide entitled *A Teacher's Guide to Learning from Objects* (Durbin *et al.* 1990) which highlights the ways in which an exploration of past technologies can inform our understanding of history. When we study geography we can reflect upon the relationships between civilizations and their environments. For example, is the savanna grassland the result of human activity or is it a piece of natural vegetation?

This exploration of artefacts should set the whole of technological activity in context and help children to understand their role in society:

> At primary level the role of Design Technology is particularly to develop technological awareness and to begin to build an understanding and capability; an understanding and acceptance that problems do not have a single solution and that we are able to respond to our environment in many ways and at many levels. The future quality of our man made environment is our responsibility.
>
> (Williams and Jinks 1985: 23)

Developing technological competence

The second set of questions we need to ask is: how do we develop technological competence, and what are the key elements that will enable us to be successful in developing such competence in children?

Children need to develop skills in the use of tools and materials and, where possible, these should be set in the contexts of clearly defined activities. The National Curriculum calls these 'focused practical tasks' (DfEE 1999: 17, 19). In the early days of the National Curriculum the whole emphasis was on 'designing and making' and this led to much frustration as children struggled to overcome the problems they faced due to lack of skills. In the world of work the long tradition of 'apprenticeship' was aimed at giving the craft worker the skills needed to tackle new and innovative activities. When working with children we need to remember that design and technology is more than just skills. Children also need to develop knowledge about the properties of materials, knowledge to enable them to pick the appropriate tool for the job and knowledge of how to use such tools safely. They should start with materials that do not offer too much resistance such as paper and fabric before moving on to those that offer more resistance, especially materials such as metal and plastic. We need to restrict the range of materials offered to children in order to focus them on the properties of those materials while developing skills in their use. As long ago as 1978, Her Majesty's Inspectorate of Schools (HMI) were delivering this message: 'More discrimination in the selection of materials by teachers . . . would have contributed to better standards of work. The emphasis which has been placed on children using a wide variety of materials has in some cases resulted in children working in a superficial way' (DES 1978, Sections: 5.89, 5.94).

When people talk about making choices they often mean making a random selection. Choice requires knowledge, information and experience. If children are truly to make choices about the materials and tools they use to complete a task, we need to help them to develop the knowledge, collect the information and gain the experience. There are three basic skills that children need to acquire when dealing with materials,

- cutting and shaping;
- joining and combining;
- finishing.

These three skills do not proceed in a linear order. For example, finishing might well come at the start of the process, such as when adding a design to a piece of fabric or card. The National Curriculum for Design and Technology at Key Stage 1 sums up these issues through the following requirements (DfEE 1999: 16):

Working with tools, equipment, materials and components to make quality products

2. Pupils should be taught to:
(a) select tools, techniques and materials for making their product from a range suggested by the teacher
(b) explore the sensory qualities of materials

(c) measure, mark out, cut and shape a range of materials
(d) assemble, join and combine materials and components
(e) use simple finishing techniques to improve the appearance of their product, using a range of equipment
(f) follow safe procedures for food safety and hygiene.

As well as considering how to use tools and materials effectively, children need to develop an understanding of structures and how they might be created and strengthened. They also need to develop an understanding of simple mechanisms, how they work and how they might be powered. Their understanding of mechanisms will begin with issues such as how wheels require an axle to achieve movement and how levers require a pivot, again to achieve movement. This might involve adding wheels and an axle to a box to achieve movement or providing moving arms for a cardboard teddy bear with the use of paper fasteners. Looking at wheels can lead to an exploration of pulleys which could be powered by a simple motor, and this leads to exploration of simple electric circuits.

Children as designers

In the initial stages of the development of design and technology in schools there was an assumption that designing meant drawing. I have seen many cases where children drew their designs and then made something that bore little resemblance to the original drawings. There has been an increased recognition that designing can take many forms and we only have to look at design in the real world to see this. It must be remembered that good design does not start in a vacuum. It usually begins with an investigation of what already exists and often this requires some form of market research – that is, ensuring that there is a match between context and need. If children are going to design a picnic lunch for their classmates they need to know what food preferences they have. Market research is followed by a discussion of a range of possible solutions and some decision making. This is usually followed by the making of a prototype that allows for testing to take place. When children design a pop-up card for someone's birthday it is a good idea to test out their ideas in paper first. When making structures or designing simple machines there are a whole range of construction kits that can help you model your ideas – Lego in particular is an excellent tool for modelling. There might be an assumption that this is 'play' and not 'learning' but designing, testing and evaluating are highly creative activities that stimulate and inspire.

When it comes to making a specific design for the end product then there are many examples in industry we can copy. In the area of food technology the traditional recipe with its list of ingredients, its record of the processes involved and its illustration of the outcome, is an excellent and precise example of how design can be moved to product. The paper pattern in textiles is a clear example of how items might be replicated. There is no better way of transferring design to cloth than through the use of chalk, the marks of which can be easily removed. The computer is also an excellent tool for design, especially when creating cards or posters.

So design involves research, discussion, planning, modelling and finally communicating. Children need to tell others how they have achieved or intend to achieve their outcome. This helps to develop the skills and knowledge and express the expertise gained through experience.

Progression

As pupils become more confident and competent so they will begin to show a capability, and an awareness, related to the products they produce and those they evaluate. They will show a greater understanding of materials and their properties and be able to make real choices about which material is most appropriate for specific tasks. The children's developing manual dexterity will express itself in more accurate measurement and in more precise cutting, shaping and joining. They will be able to tackle more resistant materials and show a better match of design to customer needs. They will show greater depth to their research and a more focused approach to their designing. They will begin to make more effective use of their knowledge, skills and understanding. In order to test and extend these developing skills and knowledge, we need to present children with design and make tasks that are appropriate to their age and ability. The QCA offers an excellent selection of 'design and make' tasks (QCA/DfEE 2000). These are linked to the initial evaluation of relevant artefacts and to focused practical tasks that ensure children have the necessary skills.

Conclusion

As the present National Curriculum (DfEE 1999) says, design and technology enables pupils to respond to and take part in our rapidly changing technologies, to think creatively, to solve problems and to build up teamwork skills. Technology is not new. What is new is the rapid pace of technological change. If children are to become discriminating users of technology they need to be aware of the processes involved. Too often we see children being manipulated into wanting the latest fashion item or piece of technology. They need to be aware of the process behind the pressure. It is also through technology that we can apply the knowledge and skills of other disciplines. The principles of mathematics are used to decide on optimum shapes and sizes. For example, a cylinder holds more for the material used than an equivalent cuboid. If you want to look at the appliance of science ask the simple question of why tea towels are made from cotton and not from wool? There is also great virtue in a subject that helps children develop their observation skills in a focused manner, enhances their fine motor skills and relates education to the world around them. There is much to be valued in a subject that encourages teamwork and gets children to reflect critically upon their own actions. Technology defines. The education system must reflect its power as we study its consequences.

References

DATA (Design and Technology Association) (1996) *The Design and Technology Coordinators' File*. Wellesbourne: DATA.

DES (Department of Education and Science) (1978) *Primary Education in England*. London: HMSO.

DES (Department of Education and Science) (1988) *National Curriculum Report: Science for Ages 5–16*. London: DES.

DfEE (Department for Education and Employment) (1999) *The National Curriculum: Handbook for Primary Teachers in England*. London: QCA.

Durbin, G., Morris, S. and Wilkinson, S. (1990) *A Teacher's Guide to Learning from Objects*. London: English Heritage.

Jarvis, T. (1993) *Teaching Design and Technology in the Primary Classroom*. London: Routledge.

Macaulay, D. (1989) *The Way Things Work*. London: Dorling Kindersley (also available as a CD-ROM).

Ofsted (Office for Standards in Education) (2000) *Annual Report of Her Majesty's Chief Inspector of Schools*. London: The Stationery Office.

QCA/DfEE (Qualifications and Curriculum Authority/Department for Education and Employment) (2000) *A Scheme of Work for Key Stages 1 & 2, Design and Technology*. London: QCA.

Williams, P. and Jinks, D. (1985) *Design and Technology 5–12*. London: Falmer Press.

13

The significance of art in the primary school

Kathleen Taylor

Introduction

When Robin Tanner addressed teachers at Bishop Grosseteste College at the opening of the Arts Centre in 1985 (Tanner 1985), he talked about his belief that education should be delivered primarily through the arts. His belief was that through art we develop respect for words, sounds and the great craft materials of the world; we learn to handle materials sensitively.

For the purpose of this chapter I will be discussing the significance of art to the primary child mainly through the medium of paint. However, much of what will be discussed can be applied to a variety of media, especially clay. I believe paint and clay to hold unique qualities, which support the whole education of the child. Learning through materials that can be moulded and changed supports communication and also allows the child to create and develop ideas. In other words, in paint and clay ideas are born. The whole essence of this ideology lies in the notion that art is a tool for learning. Unlike literacy and numeracy it is not bound by a set of configurations – on the contrary, it has no bounds. Children live in a world that has a vast number of visual ideas to understand, rearrange and add to (Barnes 1987).

Art and perception

Historically, many of our most creative figures (for example, Einstein and Sibelius) have not utilized the written or spoken word in creative thought. It is likely that many children use other means for creative thinking. It may follow therefore, as Arnheim (1965) suggests, that by forcing young people to use verbal and numerical signs we may be causing intellectual damage to their reasoning abilities. Arnheim's thought-provoking comments lead us to question the education of our children:

• Are we forcing children to think too much in the verbal and numerical sense?
• How are we providing opportunities in the classroom for pupils to play with images?

It is probable that painting will feature significantly in the development and use of visual images, as it is in this activity that the child's perception of the world can be clarified and developed further. For example, a young child may not be able to verbally articulate what anger means, and would certainly not be able to write about it; but painting enables them to express, in marks and colour, a representation of their anger. This idea of painting for expression is different to therapeutic exercise, whereby the emotions can be relieved. In education, it is through sensitive direction on the part of the teacher that the idea of anger can be explored and represented. Through the medium of painting the child is able to capture what can be visualized in the mind and the tangible result enables the child to make comparisons between what was visualized and what ended up on the paper. The entire painting process is one which allows the child to modify and change ideas and to visualize fresh ideas which can then be tried out. If thinking is, as Arnheim (1965) suggests, a procedural operation, then it would seem essential for the teacher to find some means of liberating this perception – especially in the primary years, when so much of human development takes place.

The process of painting would seem to particularly complement perceptual operations. We know that very young children use pictures of the world to make sense of it. Early comprehension of story is derived, at first, through the accompanying pictures rather than the words. In effect, the child is engaging in comprehension through pictures. It *sees* what is frightening or funny, happy or sad. As children develop they can use painting and drawing to articulate perceived abstract images. For this reason art should be considered an essential element of the curriculum, on a par with core subjects.

The artistic process

Creating art is a process which can complement perceptual operations. This is particularly so with the painting process. Probably the most valuable quality of paint lies in its fluid nature. This allows the child to push colour and shape around the paper at will. It is an unpredictable medium and so it affects the child's perceptions. It may be that the child has to modify, or adapt, or change what they are thinking. The flexibility within the thought process that the child experiences while painting makes the whole process creative and inventive. Of course, the finished results may not always be what one was looking for, but within any activity that is creative there will always be uncertainty. Thus, in effect, the process allows not only for experimentation and perceptual development but also for the child to experience and cope with uncertainty. Indeed, Barnes (1987), in reference to children's art, says that art teaching is made worthwhile when teachers value the individual statements made by children.

It should be the teacher's aim to enable the child to experiment in this way with a variety of artistic materials. However, this will not happen unless the materials are suitable, the child is taught how to use them, and is then allowed to practise using them as often as possible. Teachers are instrumental in providing suitable materials for painting, clay work and other artistic work. For example, when painting, unmixed powder paint provides for greater opportunity for the child to experiment with colour than do ready-mixed paints (Barnes 1987; Gentle 1993). Teachers also support the development of an artistic environment where children can develop skills and become more at ease with the materials used. Children who develop an ease with the materials they use are more likely to reach the stage of feeling confident enough to play with their thoughts on paper.

Children mixing powder paints at an early age will have the opportunity to practise the true process of painting and support the development of perceptual powers. This develops further through ample opportunities for familiarization with the process through practice throughout primary education. The ideal range of powder paint to provide for painting is as follows:

- Crimson red
- Vermilion
- Ultramarine
- Prussian blue
- Chrome yellow
- Ochre yellow
- White
- Black.

To mix the paints the child will need a palette and water pot. The child will need to be shown how to pick up the paint on a damp brush, place it on the palette and then pick up another colour and combine the two. Alongside the value of seeing the colour changes that take place there is also the value of experimenting with the consistency of the mixture.

It is not always ideal to use the same brush that has mixed the paints to apply the paint to the paper. Children should be supplied with a variety of brushes so that they may build up knowledge of what each brush can do. We cannot expect children to interpret the delicacy of, say, a flower if the brushes provided are thick, stubbly and hard. Many children recognize the frequent inappropriateness of the materials provided but do not know what the alternatives are. It is the teacher's role to enable children to determine for themselves the appropriateness of the materials by providing a range. This enables the children to appreciate the properties and uses of different materials.

Introducing different materials to children is a long process which should not be rushed. We should not present children with the vast array of materials and resources that are possible all at once. It is far better to build up an awareness of the materials by gradually introducing more until the full range is available. For instance, in the beginning, painting and printing with a restricted range of colour is worthwhile, as is providing the child with a range of projects. These might include such things as the mixing of blue and yellow to explore the creation of a wide range of greens, or finding out what two different reds and a blue can make. Similarly, limiting the child to white, yellow and vermilion may be a good starting point to talk about light colours.

In this way the teacher can help the child to develop skills and prepare to accept and enjoy using colour as a medium for expression. From experimenting with light and dark or hot and cold, the idea of colour being associated with abstract concepts (e.g. beauty, sadness, fear, etc.) can be easily and naturally introduced. Just as colour can be associated with abstract concepts, so can the choice of brush and movement – i.e. the action of the brush on the paper. In this way children can learn to use the brush as a tool which affects the painting and allows thoughts and feelings to be expressed.

Planning and discussing

The careful planning and organizing of resources for art work is a crucial aspect of the environment provided by the teacher. It is not appropriate to go into too much detail regarding the quality of resources, but an organizational feature of the teacher's plans should allow for time and care to be spent ensuring that the resources are maintained in pristine condition. Children need just as much practice in looking after their resources as they do in the artistic activity. A clean and well organized workspace is especially needed for printing, painting and collage. When painting, its absence will result in disappointing, muddy paintings because of dirty pots, brushes and palettes. The result will be an inevitable loss of interest by the children.

Another important feature of the artistic environment should be the opportunity for children to talk about what they are doing, preferably to an adult. Painting and other artistic pursuits are often seen as self-running activities that need little intervention. If artistic activities are set alongside other curricular activities, many teachers feel pressurized to devote themselves to the seemingly more academic activities such as reading, writing and number, while leaving the children to engage in craft-like activities by themselves. If art is taught as a subject and undertaken by the whole class there may be few opportunities to develop skills effectively, unless careful planning is involved to ensure effective use of time and a focus on specific skills and knowledge.

If we are to take on board the educational value of art then it must be upgraded from the role of a filler activity that it often occupies. Children are aware of which activities have high and low status and it is up to the teacher to redress the generally low status of art. The teacher is an important role model here, just as they are in reading and mathematics. A teacher who reads is likely to support the engagement of reading in children within their class. A teacher who engages in artistic pursuits will encourage the children to do likewise. If the teacher spends little or no time personally engaged in children's art activities then it is obvious that the child will assume painting to be less important than those other activities on which the teacher does spend time.

Talking about art, like talking about anything, enables children to take on board other people's ideas and thereby to confirm, reassess, refine or possibly change their original ideas. In this way, discussion can be thought provoking. Developing the children's language of art enables them to extend their ideas through other media, especially if they have been given opportunities to work with a variety of artistic materials. Surely it should be the aim of the teacher to encourage children to be inquisitive of the materials they use and develop an appropriate vocabulary that allows them to pursue an idea in art. It is quite disheartening to see the valuable time given to children for observation and discussion lost in the, often silent, process of painting. So much could be gained by talking about, for instance, whether the lines and colours are capturing what the child wished to convey, questioning the suitability of the brushes, colours, etc., taking delight in what is emerging and discussing modifications and developments.

'Pre-painting'

Teachers seem to be able to respond enthusiastically to the demands of pre-painting. This is often reflected in the way that many teachers inspire children by alerting them to the wonders within the environment rather than to the painting process itself. Perhaps if the painting process was linked more closely, as it should be, to higher-order abstract thinking then art might take on a more prestigious status in the curriculum. The reason that teachers devote so much time to observational activities prior to the child engaging in either drawing or painting is in order to directly increase the child's visual awareness or sensitivity. The teacher knows that if the child is to try and capture, through painting, what it sees in the environment, then the child must be alerted to features previously unnoticed. Looking, but not really seeing, is part of our human condition. We are surrounded by a wealth of visual detail and events, most of which pass us by. Joicey and Bennetto (1986) point out that we do not notice the real dramas within our lives and communities because we are too busy looking at fictional dramas within the media.

Children are naturally inquisitive and most have an exploratory, adventurous spirit. However, the teacher can still inspire and encourage by pointing out the finer detail that sometimes eludes the child. Most teachers will have a wealth of personal experience that confirms a child's fascination for detail. A child will run through a field, roll in it, jump in it, etc., but once alerted to the tiny creatures that lurk in the flower heads, or on the stems and leaves, may become absorbed and fascinated. In effect, through adopting a different view, one that reveals a finer detail, the child becomes more in touch with the environment. Things are seen that would otherwise be missed and once the child is aware of the secrets and fascinations within the greater environment, that awareness will remain and can have a profound effect on the way the child views the world and relates to it. Undoubtedly, artists must try to look at things as though for the first time and thereby respond in an original and unique way. As De Bono (1972) says, creative people often wish they could perceive as a child without the constraints imposed upon them by being adult. Many teachers believe that children draw artistic inspiration from their surroundings and this may be why so many teachers use the environment for inspiration, thereby nourishing the internal vision the child has of the world. Undoubtedly, by its very nature, art is a means of expressing the inner self (Eisner 1972).

Art's capacity to provide a means of expression must never be underestimated. Its very lack of limitations and boundaries frees the child to express what they are able to perceive but may not otherwise be able to articulate. Art can be a means of capturing the child's fascination, excitement, fear and wonder of the environment that it experiences.

Conclusion

All the issues discussed so far are of value to children but they are not the sort of benefits that are actually tangible or that children can recognize. For example, children do not know that being involved in creative work seems to have a beneficial effect on academic development. However, the artistic process and the resulting products do offer them certain special values that are recognizable. It is an area where success and quality can be attained very early in development. When other areas may prove frustrating, or lack the quality children wish, art often provides them with a sense of fulfillment and pride because they can recognize that what has been produced is pleasing both to themselves and to others.

Quality pictures will, however, only result from the process that the teacher provides. Children are often the best judges of quality, and even at an early age they will pass opinion on what they think is good or bad. For a child to produce something that is considered a 'work of art' is a tremendous achievement. Just as 'child art' is recognized by adults, children, too, can see that their own work can be truly considered 'art'. Without question, the sort of fulfilment and recognition that the child experiences throughout the production of a painting can only serve to raise their self-esteem, and this is instantly tangible to them.

References

Arnheim, R. (1965) Visual thinking, in G. Kepes (ed.) *Education of Vision*. London: Studio Vista.
Barnes, R. (1987) *Teaching Art to Young Children 4–9*. London: Allen & Unwin.
De Bono, E. (1972) *Children Solve Problems*. Harmondsworth: Penguin.
Eisner, E.W. (1972) *Educating Artistic Vision*. London: Macmillan.
Gentle, K. (1993) *Teaching Painting in the Primary School*. London: Cassell.
Joicey, H.B. and Bennetto, H. (1986) *An Eye on the Environment*. London: Unwin & Hyman.
Tanner, R. (1985) The way we have come. Unpublished address on the opening of the Arts Centre at Bishop Grosseteste College, Lincoln.

14

Creative music

Ashley Compton

Introduction

'Creativity is a commodity in short supply. It is and should be valued by all segments of society' (Weinberger 1998b). Music has often had to defend its position in the curriculum, especially in times of increased emphasis on the three Rs. Weinberger (1999) postulates that music education has a second-class status because it involves emotions and is therefore seen as antithetical to reason and logic. However, Weinberger then counters this idea with the many cognitive processes involved in music and its value in developing emotional intelligence.

Music is an important part of the world around us. Its uses range from ceremonial to entertainment, from stirring national fervour to providing a background to an elevator ride. Songs form part of our culture and provide a way of learning about other cultures. For some, this is sufficient reason to include music in schools. According to Gardner's theory of multiple intelligences (1991) music is one of the ways that people learn about and come to know the world. Several research studies have been carried out about the positive effect music teaching can have on pupils' understanding of mathematics and language (Lamb and Gregory 1993; Rauscher and Shaw 1997; Overy 1998) and this is also put forward as a defence for music education. Yet another rationale for music education is creativity. Creativity is generally perceived as a desirable goal in western education and music is generally perceived as a subject that develops it.

Weinberger (1998a) reports that several researchers have found correlations between the study of music and increased creativity, in studies ranging from preschool children to university students. Another group of researchers performed a study with 2046 pupils in 12 schools in the USA (Weinberger 2000) and found that pupils in schools which emphasized the arts were more successful in creative thinking tests, had more self-confidence, were better able to express themselves, were more willing to take risks and were better at cooperating with peers and teachers.

Setting the scene

It's the week before opening night and there's a buzz of excitement throughout the classroom as each group puts the finishing touches to its work. Two parallel Year 5 and 6 classes have been taking part in a major undertaking, that of writing, producing and performing their own original opera, following the Royal Opera House's *Write an Opera* project. This has covered many areas of the curriculum, but especially English, art, technology, mathematics, and of course music.

Before the project started the children had considerable experience in composing, performing, listening and appraising, built up progressively over many years. In composing they had started with simple sound effects, then moved on to sound pictures and sound journeys. They had composed simple melodies using a pentatonic scale and had created accompaniments and ostinati (simple repeated patterns) for familiar songs. At each stage they started by working in groups or as a whole class with the teacher, exploring the sounds together. The pupils were used to the idea that compositions did not appear instantly in their finished form but required rehearsal, appraisal, refinements and then more rehearsal.

The project began many months previously with the classes working together with their teachers to devise a theme, create character descriptions, establish a setting and chart out a plot full of crises and resolutions, all things demanded by the Literacy Hour but they were being done with a real purpose and a real audience in view.

The children are in charge of everything except directing and worrying – these activities have been reserved for the class teachers! Nevertheless, the two teachers and occasionally an ancillary assistant have been vital through their interventions, questioning, challenging, working alongside and encouraging the children. On a regular basis the working groups report back to the whole company to share their accomplishments. These are then discussed critically, sometimes with suggestions for

Figure 14.1   The music project: the children are in charge of everything except directing and worrying

improvement but always with praise from their peers. The children particularly like singing the songs that the composers have created and are able to provide vital feedback.

Now it's nearly time for the dress rehearsal. The actors are rehearsing with the librettists serving as prompters. The composers have swelled the ranks of the musicians and are going over the dynamics and the balance among the instruments. The set designers are having a technical rehearsal with the backstage and lighting crews, occasionally checking cues with one of the prompters. The wardrobe and make-up teams are setting up the 'dressing rooms' and double checking that they have everything. The front of house group have just sent out some press releases to local radio stations and newspapers, are checking ticket sales and seating plans and suddenly have the idea of having a raffle, as well as refreshments, during the interval. This results in a renewed flurry of activity and planning.

Defining creativity

According to Prentice (2000), a precise, universal definition of creativity does not exist and Duffy (1998) warns that attempting to define creativity can limit it. However, many definitions do exist and there are several common factors among them, perhaps the most important being that although creativity is central to the arts, it is not exclusive to them (Prentice 2000).

De Bono, well known for his work on creativity, especially in the realms of creative thinking and problem solving, describes the simplest level of creativity as 'bringing into being something that was not there before' (De Bono 1992: 3). However, for artistic creativity he requires another condition, that of having *value*. Craft (2000) associates creativity with questioning, change and exploring possibilities. However, she echoes De Bono in saying that creativity involves making something out of nothing. This definition of creativity can be applied to composing and improvising.

Policastro and Gardner (1999) describe a variety of creative behaviours rather than trying to define creativity itself. These range from problem solving to 'high-stake performances' such as Ghandi's hunger strikes. Two of the behaviours listed apply particularly to music: creating permanent work in a symbolic system (i.e. composing), and performance of a ritualized work (i.e. performing). Craft (2000: 65) describes 'being in relationship' as an important aspect of creativity. This is when the pupils explore how to perform another composer's work. This can be developed further by considering how the composer would have reacted to various interpretations. In some cases this can be checked with the actual composer but frequently would involve imagination and conjecture.

Beetlestone (1998) proposes six strands in her definition of creativity: creativity as a form of learning, representation, productivity, originality, thinking creatively/problem solving and universe/creation-nature. These strands involve a variety of skills, emotional responses, imagination, making connections and taking risks. Duffy (1998) also views making connections as an important aspect of creativity. In music, the making connections aspect of creativity is well represented in listening and appraising.

According to Webster (1996) creativity in music requires a combination of imagination, creative thinking and musical skills which results in a musical product. However, he does not limit this creativity to composition but applies it equally to performance, improvisation and listening and appraising. There is a creative cycle in music with the participants as creators, interpreters and appreciators. The pupils can enter into this cycle at any point and at a variety of levels, either starting with their own work or starting with someone else's composition or performance.

With the breadth of definitions available, each of the National Curriculum music strands can be seen as an opportunity for developing an aspect of creativity. Is creativity therefore an inevitable part of music education?

Music education in Britain

Creativity has not always been a major focus of music education in Britain. In the 1920s primary music consisted mainly of singing but in the next decade the introduction of radios and gramophones to schools and homes changed the main focus of music lessons from singing to listening, or 'appreciation of music' (Rainbow 1996: 11, 12). This was supplemented by instrumental work – the school orchestra, piano lessons, pipe-playing and percussion bands (Cox 1998). The emphasis in performing was playing together, following the teacher's interpretation, and the emphasis in listening was learning about 'good' music. There was little scope for creativity, as defined above. During this period provision for music was patchy, depending very much on the skills and interests of individual teachers.

In the late 1960s the Plowden Report (CACE 1967) condemned the current state of music education for its domination by the teacher and its lack of opportunity for individual expression and progression. Instead it recommended a more creative approach with more opportunity for individual work and exploration. This emphasis on creativity coincided with a period of great musical experiments in both the pop and classical worlds. Experimentation in schools was aided by the introduction of graphic notation, used at that time by avant-garde composers, which allowed the pupils to record their compositions without being limited by their knowledge of standard western notation. The success of these experiments with musical creativity depended largely on the ability of the teacher to intervene appropriately to guide and encourage the pupils. Unfortunately, many teachers did not have the knowledge, skills or confidence to accomplish this (Rainbow 1996).

Although vestiges of graphic notation remained, the experimental improvisations and compositions of the 1970s gradually faded away through the 1980s. An analysis of music lessons in the mid-1980s found that the emphasis was on developing aural and performance skills. This involved listening games, identifying metre, recognizing changes in dynamics, imitating rhythms and learning rhythmic patterns by rote (Swanwick 1996).

The situation changed again in the 1990s with the introduction of the music National Curriculum. Although the balance has altered in the various versions of the National Curriculum there has been a consistent emphasis on the elements of music and the strands of performing, composing, listening and appraising. Individual creativity and progression are encouraged, in addition to pupils working in small and large groups. The music experienced should represent a range of times and cultures. Performing, composing, listening and appraising are now seen as interrelated activities which pupils should participate in actively (DfEE 1999). Spruce (1996: 1) comments that:

> Music education has undergone a remarkable transformation in recent years. Lessons which were once dominated by passive listening and the didactic imparting of information, are now characterized by the involvement of children in performing, composing and related listening and appraising. Children now learn about music through actively engaging with it.

Many people, though not creativity researchers, believe that creativity is a special gift that cannot be taught and which only a few people possess (Prentice 2000). De Bono (1992) feels that this idea is merely a convenient excuse that relieves teachers of the responsibility of developing creativity. Duffy (1998) claims that all children are capable of creativity and need to be given the opportunity and environment to allow them to develop it further.

Although an environment which values and encourages creativity is important, it is not enough to provide the opportunity to be creative. It is important also to develop the skills to enable the pupils to realize their creative urges: 'it is frustrating to have a burning desire to create a sound but to lack the technical skills necessary to achieve it' (Duffy 1998: 27). Webster (1996) and Collins (1992) also emphasize the need for musical skills to enable the creative process. These skills not only relate to composing and performing but also to listening and appraising. It is very important to develop a discerning ear through close observation of musical material. This starts with identifying large contrasts such as loud and quiet and develops to subtle distinctions among several sounds. It also includes being able to recognize and discuss how and why sounds have been put together.

Therefore, teachers need to plan music programmes which develop skills progressively while allowing for structured, progressive opportunities for creative activities. Anyone who has been told to sit down and write a story knows that this is much easier to achieve if some guidelines have been provided.

Sternberg (1997) claims that the only way to encourage any sort of creativity is to model it. This can be very frightening for teachers because it is usually very different from their own experiences of music lessons and they are worried about exposing themselves. Most adults take part in music through listening and occasionally through singing along to the radio or a recording, though they are often self-conscious about singing in front of other people. Very few have any experience of composing and improvisation and do not know where to start to model or develop these skills.

In research with teacher training students, Hennessy (2000) discovered that many of her students were very worried about teaching music. A significant factor in this fear was the belief that music required special skills or 'gifts' that are possessed by only a select few, which did not include themselves. They were afraid of having to perform in front of the children and were concerned that they did not have enough knowledge to be able to assess the children and provide feedback. Fortunately, Hennessy discovered that the students gained in confidence considerably once they had had a successful experience teaching music with a supportive teacher-mentor. However, she found a mixed picture of music provision in schools and not all of her teacher training students had positive experiences. Some schools hired specialist teachers for music, often taking classes throughout the school, while others relied on generalist teachers with their own classes. Although some generalist teachers were able to model good practice, others avoided music or depended entirely on structured music programmes such as BBC's *Time and Tune* tapes.

Rainbow (1996) describes the difficulties inherent in the generalist and specialist music teachers. The generalist teacher may lack sufficient knowledge, skills and confidence to teach music effectively. This problem is likely to be compounded by the current trends in teacher training which concentrate on the core curriculum, often with little or no coverage of music. The problem with specialist teachers relates to the attitudes that may develop in the children. Because specialist teaching is not the norm for primary schools, having a specialist music teacher may encourage the belief that music is only attainable by a select few or that music is not viewed as important by their own class teacher. Use of a specialist teacher also confines music to specific timetabled sessions, disassociating it from the rest of the curriculum.

Miss Northway, the Reception teacher, does not feel very confident about music and says she does very little music teaching. Yet observing her in the classroom contradicts her claim. Singing is a regular part of her teaching across the curriculum: nursery rhymes and chants in English and mathematics, familiar tunes with topical words in science and simple religious songs in religious education. The children move to instruments or taped music in physical education and play rhythm games at spare moments during the day. Usually there is a music corner set up with a few instruments for the children to use. This half-term it has an electric keyboard where the children experiment and play accompaniments to their own singing. However, Miss Northway does not feel that any of this counts as music because it's not part of her scheduled music time.

During music lessons the children experiment with a variety of instruments, imitate and invent rhythms, play listening games and occasionally learn a new song. They compose and perform accompaniments to familiar stories like 'The Three Little Pigs' or add percussion parts to well-known songs like 'Hickory Dickory Dock'. Miss Northway does not really consider this to be composing because they're just 'making up sounds to go with the story' and it's not recorded as the traditional 'dots with tails'.

One way to increase the teacher's confidence and ensure better music provision is through careful planning. This helps guarantee that the technical skills are developed progressively while providing opportunities to develop creativity. In music, a considerable proportion of time is spent on process rather than product. Beetlestone (1998: 74) warns that we must consider both process and product when planning:

> The process provides the learning experience, but it is the product which gives pleasure to others and is the shared outcome of the artist's work. As teachers we have a difficult role to play in balancing these two needs. On the one hand, we need to foster the process as part of each individual child's personal experience. On the other hand, we have to decide when a product may be needed.

It is necessary as teachers for us to plan for both process and product and to find ways of valuing each.

Confidence is key to all this. A group of infant teachers was taking part in a samba-style improvisation as part of a music course. This had started with the teachers copying the leader's rhythm. Then they were instructed to leave out one of the notes in the pattern. Then they added an extra note to the rhythm. They experimented with other variations, such as playing only a single note, doubling one of the notes or playing in the gaps. At the end of these experiments each teacher had to choose a rhythmic pattern to fit in with the leader's original rhythm. Finally, they played their individual patterns together as an ostinato, which was interspersed by short breaks for individual or small group improvisations. At the end the teachers were all very pleased with the learning process they had just experienced but several stated that they wished we had recorded it because it sounded so good. Just like real music!

Another way to increase confidence is to learn more about music. This could be through courses with your local education authority or via organizations such as the Schools Music Association (SMA). It could involve instrumental lessons on the piano, guitar or recorder. It may also come from joining a local singing or dance group. You might even try inventing simple tunes while humming in the bath. Just as you would research the ancient Greeks if you were unfamiliar with them, you need to experience areas of the music curriculum that are unfamiliar to you.

The benefits of studying music go beyond the music classroom. Music develops creativity, confidence and cooperation. Pupils learn more about themselves and the world around them. Music enriches the whole person.

Getting started

- Develop listening skills – for example, 'Odd One Out'. Make a tape with three musical excerpts. These can be based on a common theme or may be completely different. The pupils have to identify which piece of music is the odd one out, explaining the reasons behind their selection. You can focus the pupils on specific elements such as pitch, rhythm, tempo, dynamics, timbre or structure by your choice of music. However, it's more useful to choose three pieces of music randomly where there is no preselected odd one out and where correct answers rely entirely on the pupils' reasons for their choice.
- Develop performing skills – for example, 'How Many Ways?' Choose an instrument or an object such as a biscuit tin with a beater. This is passed around the circle and each pupil must play the instrument in a different way from everyone else. If the first pass is successful try going around a second time. This is much harder with some instruments (e.g. maracas) than others (e.g. guiro).
- Develop composing skills – for example, 'Music from Words'. With the whole class make a list of words related to a category (e.g. animals, football teams). Practise saying the words with an exaggerated rhythm. Then consider the pitch, tempo, timbre and dynamics appropriate for each word. Once you have settled on a way of saying each word, assign words to different groups of pupils. Try saying the words in turn and then in combinations. Decide on an order (structure) for your words, and perform. Appraise the performance and discuss what aspects were most successful and how it could be improved. Now move on to group composing. Start with a short text. This could be a poem, a passage from a novel or a headline from a newspaper. In groups the children have to decide how to say the words to create music. They can repeat words, omit words, change the order or anything else they can think of. They need to think about pitch, rhythm, tempo, timbre and dynamics. Then they need to construct a structure for their piece with a definite beginning,

middle and end. After some rehearsal time the groups perform for each other and appraise the performances. The groups are then given more rehearsal time and an opportunity to refine their compositions in light of the appraisals, before a final performance.

References

Beetlestone, F. (1998) *Creative Children, Imaginative Teaching*. Buckingham: Open University Press.

CACE (Central Advisory Council for Education) (1967) *Children and their Primary Schools* (the Plowden Report). London: HMSO.

Collins, D. (1992) Creativity and special needs, in G. Spruce (ed.) *Teaching Music*. London: Routledge.

Cox, G. (1998) Musical education of the under-twelves (MEUT) 1949–1983: some aspects of the history of post-war primary music education, *British Journal of Music Education*, 15(3): 239–53.

Craft, A. (2000) *Creativity Across the Primary Curriculum*. London: Routledge.

De Bono, E. (1992) *Serious Creativity*. London: HarperCollins.

DfEE (Department for Education and Employment) (1999) *The National Curriculum for England: Music*. London: DFEE/QCA.

Duffy, B. (1998) *Supporting Creativity and Imagination in the Early Years*. Buckingham: Open University Press.

Gardner, H. (1991) *The Unschooled Mind*. London: Fontana Press.

Hennessy, S. (2000) Overcoming the red-feeling: the development of confidence to teach music in primary school amongst student teachers, *British Journal of Music Education*, 17(2): 183–96.

Lamb, S. and Gregory, A. (1993) The relationship between music and reading in beginning readers, *Psychology of Music*, 13(1): 19–27.

Overy, K. (1998) Can music really improve the mind?, *Psychology of Music*, 26(1): 97–9.

Policastro, E. and Gardner, H. (1999) From case studies to robust generalizations: an approach to the study of creativity, in R.J. Sternberg (ed.) *Handbook of Creativity*. Cambridge: Cambridge University Press.

Prentice, R. (2000) Creativity: a reaffirmation of its place in early childhood education, *The Curriculum Journal*, 11(2): 145–58.

Rainbow, B. (1996) Onward from Butler – school music 1945–1985, in G. Spruce (ed.) *Teaching Music*. London: Routledge.

Rauscher, F.H. and Shaw, G. (1997) Music training causes long-term enhancement of pre-school children's spatial-temporal reasoning, *Neurological Research*, 19: 2–8.

Spruce, G. (ed.) (1996) *Teaching Music*. London: Routledge.

Sternberg, R.J. (1997) *Thinking Styles*. Cambridge: Cambridge University Press.

Swanwick, K. (1996) Music education before the National Curriculum, in G. Spruce (ed.) *Teaching Music*. London: Routledge.

Webster, P. (1996) Creativity as creative thinking, in G. Spruce (ed.) *Teaching Music*. London: Routledge.

Weinberger, N.M. (1998a) Creating creativity with music, *Musica*, 6(2) (Spring), http://musica.uci.edu/mm/V5I2S98.html#creating (accessed 13 July 2000).

Weinberger, N.M. (1998b) Musical compositions by schoolchildren, *Musica*, 5(3) (Fall), http://musica.uci.edu/mm/V5I3F98.html#compositions (accessed 13 July 2000).

Weinberger, N.M. (1999) The second class status of music education, *Musica*, 6(3) (Fall), http://musica.uci.edu/mm/V6I3F99.html#second (accessed 13 July 2000).

Weinberger, N.M. (2000) The impact of the arts on learning, *Musica*, 7(2) (Spring), http://musica.uci.edu/mm/V7I2S00.html#impact (accessed 13 July 2000).

Teaching physical education

Sally Newton

Introduction

Physical education (PE) in the primary school is a very technical subject involving six types of activity: games, gymnastics, dance, swimming and water safety, athletics and 'outdoor and adventurous activities' (DfEE 1999). However, technical ability is affected by other issues. It is the aim of this chapter to consider how to address the essential issues surrounding the teaching of PE. Each issue is important to the development of PE for the future. PE is a statutory foundation subject within the National Curriculum (DfEE 1999) and is invaluable in the education of the whole child. It is important as a way of improving the quality of life – in terms of health and fitness, culturally, competitively and for pure enjoyment, both now and as a baseline for the future. Although we can justify the inclusion of PE in the curriculum, it struggles, as do other subjects, to be allocated sufficient time within the primary timetable. The amount of time available to the subject needs to be considered and be reflected in whole school policy and in long- and medium-term planning.

The requirements in the National Curriculum are encouragingly broad, providing for a wide range of learning experiences for children. In order for all of these areas to be delivered well, as quality experiences for all children, we need time, expertise and planning. Well thought-out planning and organization is crucial to the quality of delivery in PE. Another important feature of good practice in PE is a safety awareness strategy. It is the basis of all good PE lessons and should include reference to good equipment and resources, and a well organized curriculum plan within the school.

Cross-curricular links with other subjects may help with time allocation problems within the timetable. For example, spiritual, moral, social and cultural development (SMSCD) can be achieved through PE. Indeed, PE has been said to play an important role in the development of children's personal skills (Grey *et al.* 2000). This is also stressed by the National Curriculum which emphasizes the importance of inclusion, providing effective learning opportunities for all pupils. This is essential, whether they have special educational needs, disabilities or cultural differences. In order to do this effectively, barriers have to be overcome. So what are the practical implications in a class setting?

Inclusion

Inclusion in Education involves the processes of increasing the participation of students in, and reducing their exclusion from, the cultures, curricula and communities of local schools.

(Booth *et al.* 2000: 12)

Inclusive practices are concerned with ensuring that classroom and extra-curricular activities encourage the participation of all students. In the primary school the main areas of concern regarding inclusion in PE are gender, ethnic groups, disabled pupils and issues concerning low and high ability pupils: 'A concern with overcoming barriers to the access and participation of particular students may reveal gaps in the attempts by the school to respond to diversity more generally' (Booth *et al.* 2000: 12). Schools need to question whether, in implementing the National Curriculum, they employ restrictive practices. For example:

- Are the activities provided for girls perceived as having a lower status than those for the boys?
- Do school policies allow for the full integration of all ethnic groups?
- Are the activities designed so that they can be adapted and modified to allow all pupils to make progress and succeed?
- Is there sufficient support available for those pupils who need it, and are the specific medical conditions of pupils sufficiently managed?

Gender

The main gender issue in the primary school is concerned with ensuring that classroom and extracurricular activities encourage the participation of boys *and* girls. In the primary school there are no real physical size and strength differences between boys and girls, and so all the children can work in mixed-sex groups with no real concerns over physical safety. But as with any careful teaching, if mixed-ability groupings and children of varying physiques are working together you should ensure that learning games, skills and tactics does not entail any kind of risk. Many PE specialists believe that games teaching in the primary school situation should never include a full game, but rather that small-sided games and 'mini-sports' should be encouraged. These ensure maximum participation and a greater emphasis on building the movement vocabulary, through skills which are inherent to all sports.

There can be a tendency towards stereotyping within the PE context, as Green and Scraton (1998: 272–90) concluded from research carried out in 1993. Boys are often seen to be daring, enthusiastic and fast, whereas girls are seen to be graceful, controlled and poised. Boys may therefore dominate lessons, particularly in games, as they can be more competitive and aggressive, and overall it would appear that in many mixed-group situations, boys control the learning environment. It would be prudent for any teacher to plan and organize their lessons so that this situation does not occur and so that every child has an opportunity to develop their potential. A conducive environment for boys and girls will be developed by:

- working on a wide range of skills;
- using a wide variety of different shaped and sized equipment;
- providing an environment that encourages cooperation;
- encouraging all children to explore their ideas and skills.

All pupils need encouragement to develop their abilities in different areas. This means moving away from fixed, stereotyped ideas (unconscious or otherwise) which may have the effect of limiting pupils to certain kinds of activity or behaviour. For instance, many schools are now following the international trend of having women's football and rugby teams. Others are forging ahead of international practice by offering netball (traditionally a women's game) to boys as well as girls. This is an exciting development which should be more widely disseminated.

It is also crucial that there is not an overemphasis on competitive team sports as this tends to alienate girls. Hence, a balanced curriculum across the three areas in Key Stage 1 (dance, games and gymnastics) and across the six areas in Key Stage 2 (games, gymnastics, dance, swimming and water safety, athletics and outdoor and adventurous activities) is essential. With young children, it is important to provide a broad base of experiences and a variety of experiences. Teachers should:

- plan carefully the groups that children work in;
- organize cooperative activities;
- provide fun, full participation games, competitions and activities.

This should encourage both genders to participate fully.

Cultural diversity

The school needs to provide a secure, accepting, collaborating, stimulating community in which everyone is valued.

(Booth *et al.* 2000: 9)

The National Curriculum must be delivered appropriately for all pupils in British society. Schools must therefore take the reality of cultural diversity into account in their planning and provision of facilities. The teacher of PE needs to be knowledgeable about, and sensitive to, these cultural differences. There is a popular misconception that Islam is associated with low participation in sports and various leisure activities. However, the reality is that Islam encourages PE as long as religious requirements are adhered to (Parker-Jenkins 1995). Islam has a concern for health, exercise and a balanced education. After puberty, there is a requirement to dress modestly and since primary children may be moving into puberty this is an issue that schools need to address. Islam requires that a girl's body, arms and legs are completely covered while a boy should be covered from the navel to the knee, although many boys also like their bodies to be fully covered. In PE there is often a school dress code and this needs to be reviewed and revised if it excludes Muslim pupils from participating. Many younger pupils also feel distressed if they do not feel they are modestly dressed. Girls and boys should be allowed to wear long-sleeved tops and tracksuit trousers if they wish. Muslim children should also be allowed to wear swimsuits that cover their whole body during swimming lessons. If girls are required to wear a veil this needs to be securely fastened for safety reasons.

Another cause for anxiety is mixed-sex changing environments, which are common in primary schools. It must be recognized that Muslim children may prefer privacy when showering and changing, and this is particularly important if the children are getting changed for swimming, as public nudity is forbidden in Islam, even in single-sex situations. The public visibility of PE is also a concern to Muslim communities. If PE is held outside in the playground, on playing fields or in halls that have thoroughfares, the children *must* be modestly dressed.

The teaching of dance has to be in an educational context which is sensitive in its selection of themes, music and performance. After the age of puberty, classes necessitating mixed dance are not appropriate for

Muslim students. It is therefore desirable to give Muslim students the choice to opt out, or to participate in an alternative activity if they so choose.

Another feature of Islam is the month of Ramadan, during which Muslims are required to abstain from food and drink from dawn to sunset. (This requirement does not apply to the sick or the very young, but some primary age pupils do choose to join the fast.) It is appropriate at this time to allow any fasting children to do low-energy activities or to opt out, as they will tire easily and will dehydrate quickly.

The issues discussed above are of concern to Muslim parents and children, and do not usually apply with other groups. A useful wider discussion of multi-cultural issues in PE may be found in Carroll (1998: 314–32). If teachers consider these inclusive factors within the context of whole school planning, all children will be able to participate in and enjoy PE.

Adapted activities and inclusion of those with special needs

There has to be a recognition that inclusion needs to be planned and acted upon. The whole concept of physical education relies on the fact that children work together in groups, with partners or on their own. The way the groups are organized will make a considerable difference to the way the child with a disability participates. The group a child works with should give them support and encouragement. Therefore, the group needs careful organizing and structuring. They need to be taught to be responsible, responsive and considerate – for instance, in their level of physical contact. The support children receive will give them confidence and will enable them to develop good teamwork skills. Some children with disabilities may also have adult help, and that adult needs to work in conjunction with the teacher to deliver the aims and objectives of the lesson.

It is important not to underestimate the intelligence or ability of young disabled people. Teachers should explore ways of including rather than excluding them. 'Adaptation' is the term used to modify the activity, task or game so that all the children can participate and achieve. Adaptations should be planned and only used if necessary. Lessons can be adapted by considering the following:

- who the child works with;
- what equipment is appropriate for the child and the activity set (e.g. consider the size and weight of the ball, the size of goal, the bat, or any other implements used);

- whether the rules have to be adapted;
- whether the size of the pitch needs to be altered, so making the task achievable by all.

Once the barriers have been considered they are increasingly easy to overcome and this will greatly enhance children's chances of achieving their full potential. This approach is one which is sensitive to special needs and the interests of individuals through personalized instruction. PE teachers need to develop a way of creating positive body images and self-concepts, and promoting appropriate levels of independence, so that all children may become motivated (Jowsey 1992).

The PE curriculum aims for children to learn from experience. Through experiences children develop skills, improve their motor ability and work better together with their peers. A child with a disability may well take longer to achieve learning objectives, so this aspect should be taken into account when planning. The teacher must assess each individual child's needs and may seek advice from parents or specialists as to how certain aspects of the disability will impair movement. This of course must include talking to the pupil involved. Once those needs are identified, children with movement difficulties will have the opportunity to achieve the learning objectives if, as in any good classroom teaching situation, the teacher works to create a variety of fun and inclusive ways of working.

Differentiating for all pupils

All children need to work at a level, and use skills, appropriate to their abilities. Teachers need to differentiate activities to ensure work is appropriate to age and individual needs. Without differentiation, many pupils will not reach their full potential in PE. Any of the six areas of physical education at Key Stage 2 can be made more or less challenging, but it is important for the teacher to have considered any adaptive ideas beforehand. Elements can be changed or altered to make the task more challenging or easier depending upon need and ability. Space, distance, equipment, direction, level, speed, force, body parts, partners, groups, introducing an opposition, the linking of skills and static or moving practices are all areas in which an activity or task can be changed to make it easier or harder. The teacher should be constantly aware of the activities planned and encourage progression and achievement by increasing the skill level gradually. When the lesson is being planned, and progressions and follow-on activities are being incorporated into schemes, the main points to consider are:

- How are the children grouped?
- Is the range of tasks set challenging to all pupils?
- Is there differentiation by task (setting a variety of tasks and working on a challenge that is appropriate to ability), or differentiation by outcome (setting open-ended tasks which can be 'achieved' at many levels)?
- Have resources, equipment and apparatus been considered for a range of abilities and experience, so that everyone can achieve?
- Have children who are physically more mature been set an extended challenge?
- Have less able children an achievable task and the means by which to progress?

The reason for setting a particular task must be considered by the teacher. Is it, for example, a practice task for consolidation of something already learned? Is it to introduce new work or does it build upon existing skills? Or does it develop skills already learned and put them into a variety of new contexts? The pace of the lesson also needs to be considered, as this is important to meet the variety of needs found within the classroom.

The quality of performance is a crucial consideration when planning. Progression is not just about the ability to perform a skill, but the ability to do it well. Time should therefore be built in for reinforcement, positive feedback, repetition and revision. Analysis of performance by both the teacher and the children is important in appreciating quality. Having the ability to evaluate good quality performance is a learned skill which needs to be incorporated into the lesson, so that the children can analyse, improve and assess their work.

Safe practice in PE

Many primary-school teachers are anxious and lack confidence about teaching PE because of the implied dangers of the subject. Accidents do happen. There is now an increased awareness of negligence avoidance throughout the curriculum, but by its very nature PE has an element of risk and challenge. Even at the simplest level of children moving in a confined space, PE could be deemed hazardous. How can this fear be overcome? The main strategy is to realize that the risk can and should be managed. Again this comes back to the recurring theme within this chapter that planning is crucial to all good practice in teaching PE. The lesson must be conducted in a safe working environment, without constricting the development of the activities taking place. It must be shown in the planning that safety aspects have been considered for each lesson, and that there are opportunities for the children to be taught about hazards, risks and risk control. The children, as well as the teacher, must be able to manage the environment to ensure the health and safety of themselves and others. Elements that need to be considered are the environment, the group, the individual and the tasks set.

Primary schools are not usually purpose built for PE, so an awareness of the environment is essential, and in particular an awareness of hazards in the teaching space. Within many schools these include:

- stacked chairs;
- a piano;
- protruding features (e.g. door handles and radiators);
- unsafe floor areas due to dirt, spillages, etc.

Outside, the hazards include:

- loose gravel;
- broken glass;
- unsafe boundary fences.

The children should be encouraged to consider the environment and report anything amiss. All equipment needs to be well maintained and this usually involves a yearly inspection by an outside agency, which should be built into the school health and safety policy. Teachers who notice a problem with equipment should report it immediately. The layout of the equipment and the spacing of activities also require pre-planning as does the way the children utilize and move around the space. A calm, disciplined working atmosphere is required. There is inevitably going to be noise as the children commence the activities, but it needs to be a 'working noise' that is acceptable. Children also need to be aware of starting and stopping signals and should be able to respond to them quickly. Young children in particular need tight control, as they will not realize the implications of their actions. Each individual's safety is paramount and the first aspect to consider is that the children are appropriately attired – laces done up and jewellery removed. If for cultural reasons jewellery cannot be removed, it should be covered with surgical tape, or wrist bands. Special needs pupils and their requirements must also be considered, as discussed earlier.

The tasks set must take into account the age group, maturity and ability levels of the children. There should be maximum participation with the correct degree of excitement and challenge, without the risk of injury. The planning should be such that there is a reduction in the level of danger while still maintaining enjoyment, challenge and individual expression. The term 'risk assessment' conjures up all sorts of images and teachers are required to consider this in their planning. But what goes into a risk assessment and how do we go about considering it? Risk assessment is seen as the fundamental process by which good health and safety measures should be developed. First, it requires the hazard to be identified, along with who may be harmed by it and what risk it poses. For example, water could be the hazard and the risk may be immersion. The next stage is to evaluate the risk and decide how it can be adequately controlled. This done, is there still a risk, and if so is it acceptable and has every possible step been taken to make the activity as safe as possible? The way risk is managed needs to be recorded in the planning or schemes of work. Most PE activities need to be considered and obviously some activities are more hazardous than others. If there is an accident, the teacher should follow the school's accident procedure. This will mean stopping the class, never leaving it unattended, dealing with the incident, sending two sensible children to get help, knowing where the first-aid station is and making the injured child comfortable. The accident needs to be reported and recorded using the school reporting system: who, where, what, why, when, the action taken and who was informed.

Partnerships and using outside agencies

Extracurricular activities are an important part of a school's programme. They can be envisaged as one aspect of differentiation, giving children an opportunity to participate at a higher level, or they may provide opportunities to try a new activity that is not normally incorporated within the curriculum – for instance, line dancing or 'Olympic' gymnastics. Effective partnerships which provide extracurricular opportunities can help to improve the quality of PE (Macfadyen and O'Keeffe 2000) and an extended curriculum of this sort is an important way of promoting active lifestyles. The Youth Sport Trust have developed resources to aid in the delivery of PE, and have also encouraged important links with sports development officers and the national governing bodies. These bodies are available to run schemes at lunchtime or after school, and even to develop curriculum links. Other bodies that can enhance the delivery of PE in the curriculum and as an extracurricular activity are further education colleges, which may provide students completing the Community Sports Leader Award and Higher Leader Award (administered by the British Sports Trust).

Partnership within education is also important. Both primary and secondary schools should have knowledge of the full curriculum at different stages of learning, and strong links between the two types of school can develop better understanding. PE is an ideal medium to develop such links, which can also involve partnership with outside agencies.

At the very least, schools should be aware of what is being delivered at each stage of development and ensure that their input is at an appropriate level for the children and that progression is possible. Extracurricular activities should not be exclusively for the élite, but activities for all, promoting full, fun participation.

Citizenship and spiritual, moral, social and cultural development

PE's contribution to the spiritual, moral, social and cultural development (SMSCD) of children is wide and far-reaching. Children have the opportunities to develop skills of observation, planning and evaluation as well as skills that promote citizenship, such as responsibility and leadership (Grey *et al.* 2000). PE provides many opportunities for personal and social development, way beyond the initial elements of fair play. To plan for good sporting behaviour requires forethought. The ability to give the children a wide range of experiences to practise and learn this behaviour is also important.

The children need to be given an environment where they can work cooperatively and respect others. Due to the teamwork that PE encourages, children can learn with and from others. A feeling of trust and respect can be built upon. Games in particular can bring together a sense of belonging and teamwork, especially if the environment is thought about carefully by the teacher and does not alienate some members of the class. Outdoor and adventurous activities is unlike the other areas of the physical education curriculum, in that it offers a large number of opportunities for personal and social education. Its team building nature enables responsibility, respect, care, consideration and trust to be developed from a well-planned lesson. The outdoor and adventurous activities curriculum should ideally begin in the school grounds. With access to these opportunities, children will learn cooperation, leadership and the ability to interact, hopefully with sensitivity and tolerance. Such opportunities need to be extended both within the school and beyond (for instance, through trips) as much as possible.

PE enables children to learn the initial strategies of coping with success, failure and disappointment, in a controlled environment with a teacher to guide their reactions and hopefully an opportunity to explore their feelings further in a classroom situation. Children need the means to be fair and to discuss the issues surrounding fair play, good conduct, self-discipline, aggression, individual differences and knowing your limitations. A well planned PE curriculum can help address these issues. The PE curriculum can also complement other subjects via a cross-curricular planning strategy. For example, the link between outdoor education and the geography curriculum: outdoor and adventurous activities raises issues of the environment and introduces children to the practical application of mapping skills through the medium of orienteering. In fact, all areas of the curriculum can be enhanced by or integrated into a collaborative scheme of work. There are links with language, mathematics, science, humanities, music and art. PE, therefore, should not be seen as a separate part of the curriculum, but integral to the education of the whole child.

Figure 15.1 offers you a practical example of the planning of PE. In this example, an invasion game is planned with warm-up and cool-down activities. In the heart of the plan, key skills are identified. You could use this lesson as it is, or adapt the activities for other objectives.

Lesson plan for Year 3: Introduction to invasion games

Key learning objectives

- To develop sending and receiving skills;
- To start developing strategies to score points.

Rationale of activity	Activity instructions and skills
The warm-up activity should prepare the body for what is to come later and leave the children warm, motivated and slightly out of breath. This part of the lesson should be fun and active. It should also be a preparation for what is to come later in the lesson.	Warm-up 'Bean Game'. Act out the instructions. • Runner bean – run • Chilli bean – shiver and shake • French bean – cancan • Broad bean – move in a large shape • String bean – move in a tall thin shape • Baked bean – lie spread-eagled on the floor • Jelly bean – wobble • Jumping bean – jump around Warm-up 'Ball Tag'. Every child carries a ball in two hands. The object is to 'tag' as many players as possible in one minute, while avoiding being 'tagged' by others. To 'tag' a player, touch the ball onto the middle of the player's shoulders.
Development of individual skills	
The development of individual skills should provide the children with time to practise and improve their skills in a more complex game or on apparatus. The equipment and the activities need to be appropriate to the age and	'Speed Ball'. Pass the ball as quickly as possible between children. Concentrate on accuracy of throw. Repeat activity with different throws. 'Moving Throwing and Catching'. In pairs, throw the ball just in front of a moving player so that the ball is easily received.

Figure 15.1 Planning with PE considerations in mind

maturity of the children. Having enough appropriate equipment for all children to participate and succeed is crucial. This may mean that not all the children are using the same sized ball. It may also mean that the tasks set are open-ended so that all children can achieve at their own level.

'Square Ball'. In pairs, one child runs around a small square while their partner stands in the centre and throws the ball. There should be one throw along each side of the square.

'Hoop Ball'. Two players versus two players, in a small grid area with two hoops at each end. Players pass the ball to their partner but do not run with the ball. The object of the game is to bounce the ball in either of the two hoops in the opponents' half. Players must defend without making contact. Consider making the activity easier by having a smaller area, more hoops or a lighter, larger ball. Consider making the activity harder by having a larger area, moving hoops away from the end lines, introducing a three-second passing rule or playing the game using basketball dribbling.

Development of the small game apparatus/dance

This development should enable the children to utilize the skills learned and to work in pairs, threes or fours to develop the personal, social and health education skills which are essential elements of PE. Differentiation may involve adaptation of the rules or equipment to include all children.

'Chair Ball'. In teams of 4 (4 vs. 4) or 3 (3 vs. 3), one child from each team sits on a chair and the others have to pass the ball at least four times before they can score – by throwing at the seated child who has to catch the ball sitting down. Pupils must think about tactics to beat their opponents. Start the children thinking about rules such as how the game is started or restarted.

Concluding activity

The 'cool-down' activity should be of two to three minutes' duration. It brings the class together in a short plenary/calming activity.

Light jog, shake, slow walk, relax.

Figure 15.1 (*Cont'd*)

Conclusion

PE can provide an arena for children to improve their physical competence and develop their personal and social skills. It can promote a positive attitude towards an active and healthy lifestyle. Through well planned and organized teaching, primary teachers are able to give an enriching experience to all pupils and allow them to discover their aptitudes and develop a lifelong involvement in, and enjoyment of, physical activity.

Bibliography

Armstrong, N. (1996) *New Directions in Physical Education*. London: Cassell.

Armstrong, N. and Sparks, A. (1991) *Issues in Physical Education*. London: Cassell.

Booth, T., Ainscow, M., Black-Hawkins, K., Vaughan, M. and Shaw, L. (eds) (2000) *Index for Inclusion: Developing Learning and Participation in Schools*. Bristol: Centre for Studies on Inclusive Education.

Carroll, B. (1998) Multi-cultural education and equal opportunities in physical education: conflicts and dilemmas, in K. Green and K. Hardman (eds) (1998) *Physical Education: A Reader*. Aachen: Meyer & Meyer.

DfEE (Department for Education and Employment) (1999) *The National Curriculum: Handbook for Primary Teachers in England*. London: QCA.

Evans, J. (ed.) (1993) *Equality, Education and Physical Education*. London: Falmer Press.

Green, K. and Hardman, K. (eds) (1998) *Physical Education: A Reader*. Aachen: Meyer & Meyer.

Green, K. and Scraton, S. (1998) Gender, coeducation and secondary physical education: a brief review, in K. Green and K. Hardman (eds) (1998) *Physical Education: A Reader*. Aachen: Meyer & Meyer.

Grey, T., Hopper, B. and Maude, T. (2000) *Teaching Physical Education in the Primary School*. London: Routledge.

Jowsey, S. (1992) *Can I play Too? Physical Education for Physically Disabled Children in Mainstream Schools*. London: David Fulton.

Laker, A. (2000) *Beyond the Boundaries of Physical Education*. London: Routledge.

Macfadyen, T. and O'Keeffe, J. (2000) Co-ordinating primary physical education, in R. Bayley and T. Macfadyen, T. (eds) *Teaching Physical Education 5–11*. London: Continuum.

Parker-Jenkins, M. (1995) *Children of Islam: A Teacher's Guide to Meeting the Needs of Muslim Pupils*. Stoke-on-Trent: Trentham Books.

Williams, A. (ed.) (2000) *Primary School Physical Education*. London: Routledge.

16

Finding a place for drama in the primary school

Ruth Sayers

Introduction

This chapter reflects the wide range of activities which are labelled 'drama' in the primary school, and offers an example of drama teaching which uses the strategy of the teacher working 'in role' alongside the children. Even very young children are able to identify moments within a lesson which are remembered because of a real tension in the room. Teachers can build productive tension into their work in order to hold a group's interest. When the teacher does this through a character, and offers the children decision making powers, a wide range of learning areas can be addressed.

Drama is important to children. This fact was reinforced recently by my 6-year-old daughter, Esther. She arrived home from school brimming with excitement, and announced, 'I'm going to be the noorator in the play.' She was unbearably overexcited for about the next 24 hours. The next day she was a little more subdued. 'I'm not the noorator any more. I'm a giraffe. But it's a *very* important part.' The giraffe costume was duly prepared and giraffe-walking was practised at length. The day of the event arrived, and Esther returned from school inconsolably upset: 'The noorator forgot to say the bit about the giraffe, so I had to stand at the side instead of coming onto the stage.' The disappointment was deep-rooted and she could not be won round for a couple of days. This taught me that children care a great deal about performance, and that their perception of the importance of a play is out of proportion to the length and significance of the event.

Children find the idea of acting out events and stories very natural and enjoyable. They have the chance to enter a world of adult decision making as they play the characters. They have control. Their 'acting out' experiences are formalized at school, most often through assemblies or the 'school play'. These opportunities are usually very exciting, and the preparation for performance is taken very seriously, with attention to detail and recognition of the tension which performance creates. However, this kind of dramatic event is one which has the potential to leave children elated or bitterly disappointed. They are acutely aware, even at the age of 5 or 6, of 'acting out' in front of others, and of the possibilities for embarrassment and self-consciousness. It is at this age that some children decide whether they are 'good' or 'not good' at acting. If their experience of drama at school is always about acting in front of others, this experience may be negative, and there are likely to be 'stars' emerging within the class. The school assembly and school production have an important place within the variety of drama opportunities for children in schools, but they form only a small proportion of the range of possibilities. The rest of this chapter will consider some other possibilities, and the likely learning outcomes. In particular, it will describe a lesson which uses 'teacher in role' as a mode of teaching, and which may be a helpful example for anyone who is not familiar with this strategy.

The purpose of drama in the primary school

If drama is viewed as an activity which can enhance the individual's growth in confidence, and this is the prime aim, then the music and movement type activity, in which children grow from seeds to flowers on their own in the space, might be considered successful. If the aim is to develop and practise language skills, then a paired activity in which children improvise and perform a short, structured argument, might also be considered successful. If the aim is to encourage productive group dynamics, then dividing the class into six groups, and asking each to work out a short sketch to perform to the others at the end of the activity will also probably meet all its aims.

Each activity contains valuable learning experiences for children, and the quality of each will be very different. Individual confidence, language development and physical control should be enhanced by all. Interpersonal skills and social interaction will probably be improved by some. However, unless the learning potential is deepened in some way, and if the activity is not rooted in reality for the children, they will not invest enough commitment in the work to take it beyond a superficial level.

So, for example, if the teacher introduces the children to a stimulus, and then sends them straight into groups to improvise ideas and shape them into theatre form for presentation, there should be positive elements such as:

- teamwork;
- negotiation;
- interpersonal skills;
- sharing.

But there could also be negative aspects:

- they may not take it seriously;
- they may not want to watch other groups;
- their own work will occupy their thoughts while others are performing, and they will continue to talk about it;
- they may ridicule others who perform.

One way of trying to lessen the negative possibilities and increase the learning potential is to use drama strategies as a tool to learn about other areas of the curriculum, so that children's group work relates to something that they have already been studying, and in which they have hopefully invested some interest.

Perhaps the best way of increasing children's commitment to the drama situation is to use whole group activities with the teacher working 'in role'. The example which follows describes both a sample lesson and also gives a commentary on the teacher's planning and actions.

Teacher in role

When the teacher is within the action, the spectator is removed. All those present can be within a fiction, and the 'acting' element is lessened. The teacher responds to the individuals within the class 'as if' they were their character, and this allows an obliqueness which is usually not possible. The teacher engages earnestly with Tom in his role as butcher, discussing the price of beef, rather than saying, 'Well done, Tom, you really sound like a butcher.' This is the best way to try to encourage children to 'suspend their disbelief' as they can become involved in the action at a deep level, while always knowing it is a fiction. There is never the attempt to persuade them that it is real. Indeed, reflection on the action will be frequent and will interrupt the natural flow in a deliberate way. The teacher's involvement will give the action greater integrity, and this in turn will allow the children to become immersed in the 'story'. The teacher will also respect the information which the children offer, and can assume less knowledge than they have. In other words, the whole class play the 'game' of the teacher being informed by the class – and it is a game which children *love* to play.

Let us imagine how this teacher in role strategy might work in practice. A Year 6 class are to find out about the plague village of Eyam in Derbyshire. The teacher is aware that as well as supporting the history curriculum, her drama lesson might also address issues within citizenship. She especially hopes to encourage the children to consider how societies operate and how a community reacts when one of its members behaves in an unacceptable way. Individual need will conflict with the 'greater good' in this example.

Sometimes drama will open a new area of the curriculum for children, and sometimes it will develop and reinforce existing knowledge. In this case the children do not know anything about the plague village.

The teacher wants to:

- involve all the children actively;
- keep them together as a community facing a potential challenge (if the group is divided into factions, it is likely that conflict will develop rather than productive tension);
- give the group ownership of the direction the drama follows, to encourage decision making skills and language development; this can be promoted through the use of what Gavin Bolton (1992) has described as 'immediate time' – 'I am making it happen, it is happening to me' – because a sense that it is happening *now* will make any decision more urgent;
- promote the children's self-esteem through the drama.

There will be a very basic use of Dorothy Heathcote's 'mantle of the expert' approach (Heathcote and Bolton 1995), in which children assume the craft and knowledge of an adult worker.

The *contract* which the teacher establishes with the children for drama work is important, even though she knows them well. The teacher and class need to understand that they are working together as 'artists': 'The effective drama teacher, like the theatre artist, is working with live material that is constantly shaping and reshaping itself, in response to the environment, individual intentionalities, communal needs and narratives' (Morgan *et al.* 2000: 9).

In order to maintain the creative energy of the work, there must be cooperation between the group members. The teacher needs to effectively relinquish her responsibility for managing behaviour during the drama, and hand that responsibility over to the group. As long as the content of the work is powerful enough to hold the children's interest, they should be willing to manage their own behaviour. A simple control mechanism can be established during the contract stage. For example, if the class feel that the action is not believable they can shout 'stop!' and the participants will stop the work. The teacher will then ask why they have stopped the lesson, and as a group they will try to find a solution. This is significantly different from the situation in which the teacher interrupts the work. For example, Fiona stops the role-play and declares 'It's far too noisy, miss. The people in the market wouldn't make that much noise.' The teacher responds, 'Oh, then perhaps we need to do it differently. Does anyone else agree with Fiona that it was too noisy?' Of course the teacher knew it was too noisy, but rather than stop it herself, she wants the children to take responsibility for the action. This approach allows the usual classroom relationship to be suspended and promotes a creative atmosphere. During the drama lesson the teacher as spectator is removed.

There are several 'steps' within the lesson through which the children pass as they become involved in the work. Morgan and Saxton (1987) refer to 'a taxonomy of personal engagement', and classify the steps as:

- becoming interested in the task;
- engaging: being involved in the task;
- committing: the development of a sense of responsibility towards the task;
- internalizing: the recognition of the relationship of the task to the self, revealed as a 'change of understanding';
- evaluating: the willingness to put that understanding to the test.

Setting the context

There are two clear ways in which the background information which the children need before they can engage in the activities can be given. This corresponds to the 'becoming interested in the task' step, above:

- through class discussion;
- through the teacher using a role to speak to the children.

The teacher wants to let the children imagine what it was like in a small village in the sixteenth century and has decided that they need specific tasks in the drama so that they can be busy, and not *too* concerned with talking, which is hard to do in a historical context. In addition, the pressure to talk is likely to inhibit them in role. They will all be 'adults', as this will help them to adopt a more responsible attitude and will help with social interaction. They will all be able to be involved with decision making.

In this case there is a discussion. The teacher begins: 'We're going to tell a story together today. Our story happens a long time ago, before any machines [elaborate here, giving as much help as the children need] and it happens in a small village. Let's try to imagine the jobs that people would need to do in the village.' The children volunteer suggestions, and the teacher reinforces the fact that everyone in the village has at least one job. The teacher may choose to state that in drama anyone can take a male or female role because there are dangers that the girls will be far less active in the role-play than the boys if they think they are not allowed to do an outdoor job. The importance which the teacher places on correct historical knowledge will depend to a large extent on the expected learning outcomes, and whether this is primarily a history or citizenship lesson. Each teacher will have a different tolerance level, and given that no reconstruction of history can be totally authentic, some inaccuracy is inevitable. Firming up the roles for children with cards of written information, video, drawings, etc. can be a great help in building their confidence. Each child selects a job that they will do, on an individual basis, or the teacher may allocate jobs based on the cards, mentioned above.

Defining the space

The teacher suggests, 'Let's pretend that this room is our village. We need to decide where some of the places in the village are going to be.' In order to retain the whole group feeling, only communal spaces will be decided. No one will have an individual 'home' as this could become divisive. There are several ways of organizing the space:

- through 'paper location' – where children write the name or description of a place, or draw a small picture of it, and put it down on the floor in the agreed place;
- through simple agreement – 'This area near the tables will be the wood'.

Fabrics or objects can be used (e.g. a long strip of blue fabric for a stream or river). There is little point in letting the children spend a long time making these decisions, as there will be many more important ones to take later. At this stage the teacher is still firmly in charge, and closes down unproductive discussion and argument. It is a good idea to have a space which will be 'out of the story' where the progress of the work can be discussed – usually a small corner where everyone can sit on the floor to talk.

Keying the children into role: 'the game'

In order to take part in the role-play the children need to have some sense of the role they will play, but they do not need to know all the characteristics and history of that person. They just need to know enough to help them understand the dilemma which the teacher will offer later. The role should be strong enough for them to engage with the issues of the story. This can happen through:

- discussion;
- task-related action;
- introducing appropriate ideas about language.

Playing with the role is the way to begin engagement. The children need to understand that everyone will be either 'in' or 'out' of the drama at any given moment, and the signal for starting and stopping will be clear. 'Freeze' or other suitable words can be used. A good, clear way of starting the action is essential. This could be done initially through mimed action, with everyone working on their own. The teacher should also be doing the mimed action, and not acting as a spectator/judge of the children's work. After 'playing' with the mime for a while, the children may wish to introduce language and interact with each other. At this stage there may need to be discussion to decide how the people of the village talk. The space can be used which was identified as the reflection, 'out of the story', place. The children should not be encouraged to use silly accents but the content of their conversations could be considered. This is likely to be task related. When the teacher speaks to the children she could elevate the level of the language slightly by making it more formal or poetic, and by introducing the use of second names (e.g. 'Fine weather for the time of year, Mr Jones'). This will help to remind the children that the context is historical.

The 'playing' continues as the children proceed with their tasks, but now use language and engage with others in the group. Sometimes children find a simple hand-prop or tool very helpful in giving them a focus, but cloths/tools/props can also get in the way a good deal. Teachers will need to make their own decisions. If costume is available some children will wrap themselves in all kinds of layers, and they are not necessarily being disruptive – they feel more secure if they are dressed up.

The tasks are now being undertaken in a more purposeful way. The children are enjoying themselves because this is similar to the home corner play that they enjoyed as infants. However, while this activity is fun because it is happening 'here and now' their investment will be limited because there is no tension within the activity, and nothing to deepen their belief in the community. The sense of responsibility suggested by Morgan and Saxton (1987) (for 'committing' to take place) is still missing.

Committing

To pull the children into the community and give them a sense of shared interest, the teacher can introduce information about the plague, via a role. In this example the teacher takes a role as the children sit in the space for reflection and watch. This makes use of *theatre form*, which is very valuable within a drama lesson. Some teachers may worry that asking the children to watch them 'acting out' is rather indulgent, but actually the children are used to watching and listening to the teacher. This is just a different way of giving the information. The role is the tailor of Eyam, a nearby village. To introduce the role, the teacher could use *narration*: 'In a nearby village, the tailor received a parcel from London . . .' A piece of clothing, wrapped in a parcel, can be used to denote the tailor. The parcel is carried carefully onto the floor in front of the children and unwrapped. As the parcel is unwrapped the tailor talks about his expectations of the fine cloth, etc.

There is a real tension in the opening of a box or unwrapping of a parcel, if it is done slowly. The teacher is not taking on a set of characteristics here – the role is simply presenting an attitude or mood. There is no change in the pitch of the voice. It is more like telling a story than acting. As themselves, the children are invited to ask the tailor some questions. This is called *hotseating*. The teacher can come out of role to introduce this convention, or it could have been introduced before the tailor unwrapped the cloth. The tailor talks about the cloth and who it is for, and what Eyam is like. Leaving the tailor's package at the side of the room as a visible symbol of sickness nearby, the teacher narrates the class back into their tasks: 'And so they returned to work the next day, but now they knew that the sickness which had arrived with the cloth had killed not just the tailor, but many other villagers, too. They spoke of the rumours of sickness as they worked.' This is the cue for the children to continue with their village tasks, but to also discuss the nearby plague village. The situation is like the 'game' at the start of the practical work, but there should be commitment as well as engagement with the task.

Opportunities for reflection should be built in at several points from now on, so that the children are forced to consider their opinions as the story unfolds. The simplest way is to freeze the work and ask the characters how they feel about events that have happened (alternatively, small group discussions can be overheard by the whole class). The bundle of cloth is present at the side of the room as a tangible reminder of the sickness. The children could be offered the opportunity to approach the bundle and speak their thoughts about the events in the next village. How close they choose to go could reflect their curiosity, fear or empathy with the villagers of Eyam. This is an example of the importance of *symbolic objects* in a drama lesson.

In a central place, a *village meeting* is held to decide how the community should respond to the news of the sickness. The potential threat should unite the villagers, but there could be very different views about how to respond. A message could be read out which describes the fact that the people of Eyam have decided to remain within the village. Views about this can be shared.

At the end of the meeting the teacher, in role as one of the villagers, declares that she intends to go to Eyam to see if her sister is well. This is the point at which the teacher is putting much more pressure on the group. They cannot remain neutral to this declaration. This is when the teacher hands over responsibility for the action to the class.

The next part of the lesson is hard to describe, because the villagers could respond in a number of ways, and the teacher needs to have strategies ready to challenge them in their decision. It is likely that the class will say that she cannot go. This is the most important part of the lesson, and it is the point at which the teacher hopes the children will 'internalize' the dilemma, and recognize the real human issues within a historical story.

The teacher in this example wants to push the children to the point where they have to decide whether or not to accept the community member back after she has been to Eyam. She also wants to calm down the situation and break up the group for a while. She can then narrate the next part of the story, as the villagers prepare for bed. A darker atmosphere will support this. The teacher can move in and out of role as she narrates the falling darkness, and suggest that the tired villagers lie down to sleep. The teacher continues to narrate that it is morning, and that the woman has gone to see her sister. The villagers then meet together to discuss what they should do when she returns. This is the first point at which the group have continued with the action while the teacher stands outside it, supposedly away at the next village. It is likely that the class will ignore the teacher, as she has made it clear through the narration that she is no longer in the village. The teacher should not interfere with their meeting, as she would then hear their plans for the woman's return. This may be an opportunity to take the class away from the drama for some reflection, or it may be appropriate to continue with the moment when the woman returns.

This is a difficult moment to control within the drama, and it is useful to remember that there are many strategies available for slowing down or stopping the action, and crystallizing the events and feelings of the moment. The return of the woman to the village is one such moment when it might be advantageous to make a *still picture* of her arrival and allow the children to show their role's reaction to her. A still picture takes an instant out of the drama and freezes it so that the children can examine the actions/reactions and expressions. This can then form the basis for discussion. When the scene is brought to life there should be a productive debate about the woman's actions and whether or not she is to be allowed to come back and live among them. Many different moral standpoints could be taken. A lot will be revealed about the group's ability to make a decision, and about how they function on a political and social level.

Provided the children are engaged with the material, the outcome is not as important as the discussions which are going on. It may be necessary to stop the work and allow them to 'regroup' their ideas about what would happen before returning to the village. It may be that they need to take time out to decide on the leadership structures within the village before returning to the action. If they decide that village communities need structures for making difficult decisions, they can be encouraged to relate this to the classroom community in reflection later on.

Resolution may be desirable for the children, but the most valuable learning will have taken place during the discussion. Rather than letting the work continue until a decision has been reached, it may be more appropriate to close the work with some group images which show different possible outcomes. The essential element of resolution is to prompt reflection on the story and its wider implications. The children can be asked, at the conclusion of this work, 'What was that story about?' and they may be able to see universal links between one small community and the way people treat each other in many other situations.

Conclusion

The lesson described in this chapter is simply a different way of allowing natural 'acting out' to take place. It hopefully brings children a little closer to the events than some other forms of dramatic activity, and shields those with less confidence from the embarrassment of being 'watched' by everyone else. It can comfortably form part of a journey, which leads to scriptwriting and public performance, and can be seen as an improvisational part of a more familiar process.

References

Bolton, G. (1992) *New Perspectives on Classroom Drama*. London: Simon & Schuster.

Heathcote, D. and Bolton, G. (1995) *Drama for Learning*. Portsmouth, NH: Heinemann.

Morgan, N. and Saxton, J. (1987) *Teaching Drama*. London: Hutchinson.

Morgan, N., Saxton, J. and Miller, C. (2000) Being present at the rendezvous: the teacher as artist. Unpublished paper presented at the National Drama Conference, York, 13–16 April.

17

Coordinating the whole curriculum

Derek Bell

Introduction

The curriculum is more than a series of individual subjects. It should be a coherent series of effective learning experiences which enable the learner to develop skills, knowledge and understanding in a range of disciplines which have relevance to the learner. While the National Curriculum (DfEE 1999), which can be described as the *official* curriculum, sets out what must be taught in schools, it is by no means the *whole* curriculum. Kerr (1968: 16), for example, defined the curriculum as 'all the learning which is planned and guided by the school, whether it is carried on in groups or individually, inside or outside the school'. Other writers (e.g. Pollard and Tann 1987) have used the term 'hidden curriculum' to highlight the fact that children do not learn simply from what is planned, nor do they learn everything that is planned. Furthermore, what is planned (the 'intended curriculum') is not necessarily what is taught (the 'actual curriculum'). One of the many challenges for us as teachers, whatever phase of education we work in, is to try to ensure that what is planned to be taught is appropriate for those being taught, and, in turn, to close the gap between the intended curriculum and the actual curriculum as experienced by each individual learner.

Although it might be argued that the National Curriculum, and initiatives such as those on literacy and numeracy, have removed many of the grounds for debate about the nature of the primary curriculum, this is not the case, as the contributions to this book demonstrate. There is,

in fact, a greater need to understand and agree the aims and purposes o
the primary curriculum nationally. This is also the case in each schoo
where the overall approach to the curriculum should be reflected by th
work in individual subjects. This is not to say that every area of th
curriculum will be taught in the same way. On the contrary, it is essen
tial that the teaching approaches used and the learning opportunitie
provided take account of the many factors that influence the learnin;
environment, including the subject matter being taught. What is import
ant is that we are able to 'readily articulate [our] teaching – to explai
why [we] are utilising particular approaches, materials, types of clas
room organisation etc. and how these relate to the needs of [our] pupil;
(Porter 1996: 262). This chapter aims to explore how a coordinate
approach to teaching the primary curriculum might be developed. I
particular it will highlight the importance of the roles taken by curriculu
leaders in working towards this goal and providing effective learnin
opportunities for all pupils.

The roles of curriculum leaders

Curriculum leaders have a key position in the organization, developme
and management of the curriculum in primary schools and come in ;
shapes, sizes and guises. It is beyond the scope of this chapter to co
sider the complexities and subtleties of the terminology used to defi
their roles and responsibilities. This has been done elsewhere (e.g. B
and Ritchie 1999). However, it is necessary to define how the ter
'curriculum leader' is used in this chapter where it will refer to a
individual in a school who has responsibility for some aspect of t
curriculum. As such it includes, among others, those teachers w
oversee work in a particular subject (often referred to as subject c
ordinators), year leaders, key stage coordinators, deputy headteach
and headteachers. Whatever their title or the exact definition of th
responsibilities, curriculum leaders aim to provide the best possible lear
ing opportunities for the children in their school at any given time. T
roles which they take on are complex (see, for example, TTA 199:
rapidly evolving and require a more proactive stance than has be
recognized previously. The use of the term 'leader' is in recognition
the need for curriculum leaders to move things on and bring about t
desired improvements in quality and standards. As such, curriculu
leaders are agents of change involved in development and maintenan
planning and implementation; organization and delivery; and monitori
and evaluation. Thus they will need to initiate, facilitate, coordina
monitor and evaluate the development of teaching and learning in th

area of the curriculum and to educate others (including teachers, class-room assistants and parents) in order to help them contribute to such development in their school.

In working towards effective coordination of the whole curriculum it is appropriate that curriculum leaders should see themselves as part of a learning organization. Southworth (1994: 53), for example, suggested that a 'learning school' has five interrelated characteristics:

- the focus is on the pupils and their learning;
- individual teachers are encouraged to be continuous learners themselves;
- teachers and others who constitute 'staff' are encouraged to collaborate by learning with and from one another;
- the school as an organization is a 'learning system';
- the headteacher is the leading learner.

Schools are also teaching organizations, providing appropriate opportunities for learning that are crucially dependent on the interactions between individuals, groups, materials and events, all of which contribute to the total learning environment. Effective coordination of the whole curriculum depends on developing a shared view of the curriculum and how it is to be implemented.

Making an impact on teaching and learning

Curriculum leaders need to work at a number of levels in their efforts to coordinate the curriculum and bring about coherence and consistency in the overall approach to the teaching and learning that is planned and implemented. At the whole school level, curriculum leaders have made a significant impact on their schools through the production of policies, schemes of work and more focused resource provision. While this has enabled many schools to produce the necessary documentation to meet external requirements for inspection purposes, few curriculum leaders 'felt they exerted considerable influence on the general teaching of the curriculum area for which they had direct responsibility' (Whiteside 1996: 39).

In order to address this issue curriculum leaders need to focus more attention on what happens in individual classrooms and on working with colleagues to explore ways of improving the interactions between teachers and children, inside and outside the classroom. It is interesting to note that recent shifts in emphasis during Office for Standards in Education (Ofsted) inspections and in the Literacy and Numeracy Strategies have raised the profile of the teaching process itself. This provides an opportunity for curriculum leaders to open up a dialogue with their

colleagues on the nature of the curriculum that is being taught in order to establish a common view of the overall outcomes and ways of achieving them. O'Neill (1996: 220) however, points out that:

> Moving towards an informed overview of the curriculum which is rooted in classroom practice is indeed a significant and potentially very threatening undertaking. It is one which rejects the notion of [curriculum leaders] providing necessary but anodyne arm's-length support for colleagues by merely digesting documentation on their behalf and organising a suitable repository for shared resources.

The dialogue needs to start by developing a shared language and understanding of meaning across different subjects and elements of the curriculum. What, for example, are the similarities and differences in the collection and interpretation of evidence in history, as opposed to, say, science? How and when are common activities (e.g. the use and construction of graphs) introduced to meet the needs of different subjects? What opportunities are there for skills developed in one subject to be used to enhance the learning in another area of the curriculum? One of the strengths of the primary curriculum and its teaching has been the opportunity to find answers to such questions and to put them into practice. The best teachers have always made such links in an appropriate and effective way. The challenge now is to ensure that all teachers and schools do it in a manner which is explicit, so that nothing is left to mere chance. A subject-based curriculum always has the potential to fragment so that the benefits of the whole curriculum are significantly reduced or even lost altogether. It is essential, however, that the efforts to coordinate the curriculum are not superficial, as O'Neill (1996: 221) again points out:

> The likelihood of arriving at a close understanding of the difficulties of teaching and learning essential concepts in, say, music, or art or PE is remote if the dialogue is limited simply to a discussion of the content of the National Curriculum documentation or the formal language often adopted in school based policy documents.

A policy for teaching and learning

One step towards bringing about a common approach to the curriculum is to consider the development of a policy for teaching and learning (see West 1995). This should be one of the first policies that are put in place. It can provide the basis for other curriculum policies that are required. Instead of making additional work, preparation of a generic policy for teaching and learning should help to:

- reduce the potential for overlap in other policies yet strengthen the core principles on which the curriculum and the school's approach to it are based;
- provide a sound underpinning for all subject areas, thus ensuring continuity and consistency in approach and planning without producing uniformity;
- highlight the core of the school's activity as a teaching and learning organization;
- ensure that the central issues, values and principles of teaching and learning which are at the heart of education are debated from time to time, rather than being marginalized by the inevitable day-to-day consideration of matters relating to implementation and practical organization.

In reaching agreement on such a policy, a school should be able to make a clear statement about: what the policy is intended to achieve; what are considered to be the key characteristics of teaching and learning; what is expected of teachers; what are the opportunities and expectations for children's learning; and the features of a quality learning environment. Once agreement on such fundamental issues has been reached, such a policy will form the basis for auditing, monitoring and evaluating the teaching and learning across the whole curriculum throughout the school. Curriculum leaders can support their colleagues in applying the principles to particular areas of the curriculum.

Enhancing teaching and learning

Curriculum policies are important and when developed with the involvement of all colleagues can have a significant impact on overall school improvement. To bring about change in the classroom, however, requires teachers with inside knowledge of the children, the locality, the school culture and the environment. With this information, and by working together in teams, teachers can translate the demands of the *official* curriculum in such a way as to meet the needs of the children in their school. Although the curriculum content can be defined, the process of learning and the effectiveness of the teaching which supports it are influenced by several factors which are summarized in Figure 17.1 and that need to be taken into consideration by curriculum leaders as they try to coordinate what takes place in the classroom. By working with colleagues to find ways of addressing the questions raised by such factors, curriculum leaders can move towards coordinating the curriculum in a meaningful manner.

Prior learning Age, stage and conceptual level of pupil's thinking; have these been effectively diagnosed?	**Thinking** Are processes such as interpreting, generalizing, hypothesizing envisaged? Do you expect practice or transfer?	**Sequencing** Does the area have clear delineation and articulation within it? What elements of discovery/guided learning are envisaged?
Differential access Are individual differences catered for?		**Independence/ responsibility** Are these encouraged?
Motivation Are you exploiting known motivation? Can you plan to sustain it?	**Teaching and learning**	**Self-esteem** Is the work designed to enhance this?
Evaluation What types are involved? Do they include self-evaluative and diagnostic procedures?	**Teacher knowledge/ enthusiasm** Is it an area easily analysed by the teacher? Is it enjoyed? What help is necessary?	**Classroom climate/ grouping** What is the optimum form of grouping for this topic? Is interdependence an integrated part?

Figure 17.1 Factors affecting teaching and learning
Source: Day *et al.* (1993: 91).

Similarly the identification of cross-curricular issues followed by an audit of how, where and when they are addressed in the different curriculum areas will lead to increased coordination of the curriculum. Citizenship, personal, social and health education (PSHE), equal opportunities and provision for special educational needs (which have all been discussed in earlier chapters of this book) are particularly important elements of the curriculum that need to be considered explicitly in order to develop a coherent and consistent approach to them.

Coordinating the curriculum must not be a paper exercise; curriculum leaders in consultation with their headteachers must find ways of increasing their influence on enhancing classroom practice. It is not easy to find the time nor to make appropriate arrangements for cover, but it can be done. The key is to ensure that the arrangement has a clear purpose and is planned, monitored and evaluated. The activity might involve work with individual colleagues to address particular concerns they have in one area of the curriculum, or it might result in opportunities to disseminate good practice through the exchange and discussion of ideas on how to approach a particular topic. Over a period of time consideration might be given to different aspects of teaching, such as:

- the reasons for and the appropriateness of particular forms of class organization (whole class, group or individual) which might be extended to consider, for example, the quality of the group work that takes place;
- the suitability of particular activities to achieve the stated aims of the lesson or sequence of lessons;
- the types of pupil–teacher interaction that are taking place, especially the nature and quality of the questions being asked by both teacher and children;
- the diversity of ways in which children present the outcomes of their activities so that they are given opportunities to demonstrate a wide range of communication skills;
- matters relating to differentiation, progression and continuity.

Day-to-day pressures often prevent discussions about such issues but there are opportunities, which arise out of other tasks, that can be used to raise some of these fundamental matters. For example, the moderation of children's work and monitoring of their progress quite rightly focuses on the children in order to be as fair as possible to them as individuals, and to ensure that standards are being applied appropriately. It is also an opportunity to ask questions which have a bearing on the teaching process. Is there any evidence that children are interpreting particular activities in a way that was not foreseen? What responses have children made to questions that have been surprising? Looking at questions such as these across the whole school helps to provide a basis for discussions which focus on the teaching and its effectiveness.

In a similar way, the selection and use of resources requires decisions ranging from the number of an item needed to the selection of a newly-published scheme. Each choice is influenced, either implicitly or explicitly, by a preferred teaching approach. Hence it is possible to ask some fundamental questions about why particular choices have been made and what are the implications, if any, for what happens in the classroom. For example, a decision to buy enough magnets so that every child can have one to explore/play with in a science lesson suggests that the idea of 'hands on' activity is felt to be important. The curriculum leader might ask whether or not this is the most effective approach and whether it is something that everyone agrees with.

Each school has to find its own mechanisms for dealing with the many issues that influence the enhancement of the teaching and learning that takes place. Southworth (1996) distinguished three groups of activities for teachers aiming to bring about improvements in the quality of teaching and learning in their school:

- activities addressing issues at year group or school level (e.g. joint planning, writing policies, leading staff workshops, mentoring students and new teachers, pairing subject leaders, curriculum reviews and joint work: visits, concerts, parental events, school assemblies);
- activities drawing attention to the teaching process and classroom interactions (e.g. classroom action research, visiting and observing classrooms, team teaching, explaining and/or demonstrating classroom and teaching practices to colleagues, teacher appraisal, touring the school and 'showing' assemblies);
- activities focusing on pupils' achievements (e.g. analysis of pupil outcome data, review of pupils' reports, shadowing pupils, monitoring pupils' work, assessment trialing agreements and staff conferences on individual pupils).

Coordinating the curriculum: a shared responsibility

Successful coordination of the curriculum depends in part on individuals but it also requires everyone to accept a share of the responsibility for the leadership, management, development and delivery of the curriculum. Figure 17.2 summarizes the different contributions that the headteacher, curriculum leader and individual teachers might make. It is by working together that colleagues can learn from and teach each other in such a way that professional development is not about going on courses (although these can be very useful) but is part of the school's culture. By accepting such shared responsibility it is possible for schools to improve as they become part of what might be called 'the learning movement' (Day *et al.* 1998), in which learning takes place at both the individual and the organizational level. In other words, the school itself becomes more effective in bringing about improvements in the quality of education it offers.

Conclusion

To say that effective coordination of the primary curriculum simply requires the development of appropriate policies and the implementation of agreed schemes of work is to take a mechanistic view not only of management but also of the curriculum and what it stands for. In bringing together the contributions of this book the authors have tried

Headteachers should:

- encourage a shared ownership of the curriculum as an important element in children's learning and teaching in the school;
- encourage an overall sense of responsibility for the curriculum within which roles and specific responsibilities are clear;
- encourage the development of links with other schools and support agencies;
- show a positive attitude towards all areas of the curriculum;
- support the curriculum leaders and enable them to provide clear leadership in their area of responsibility.

Curriculum leaders should:

- provide clear leadership in their curriculum area;
- promote their area as an important element of the curriculum ensuring that all the requirements of the National Curriculum are met;
- work with colleagues to maintain links across the curriculum as a whole to ensure continuity and coherence of children's learning;
- support and encourage colleagues in their teaching;
- manage the provision and deployment of resources;
- monitor and evaluate the teaching, learning and development of their area of the curriculum.

Individual teachers should:

(a) As curriculum leaders
- identify links with other areas of the curriculum and work to strengthen them, establishing continuity and coherence in children's learning;
- be aware of ways in which different curriculum areas complement theirs and vice versa.

(b) As class teachers
- contribute to the development of a policy and scheme of work for the different curriculum areas and use these as the basis for their own short-term plans;
- provide the best possible opportunities for children's learning in each curriculum area and work towards improving their teaching and approach to the work;
- work with the curriculum leader to monitor, record and evaluate children's progress and achievements;
- provide feedback to the curriculum leader on topics, teaching approaches and resources for the subject;
- share successes and failures in order to encourage and support colleagues, helping to develop a shared responsibility for learning, teaching, management and leadership in all areas of the curriculum.

Figure 17.2 Contributions to the leadership, management, development and delivery of the curriculum
Source: Underwood (1996).

to show that the spirit of the curriculum and approaches to teaching and learning are crucial elements in the process. Each of the authors in their own way has addressed the different factors which contribute to the creation of a learning environment. More importantly, the authors have a shared view of teaching and learning which emphasizes that: the quality of learning depends on the quality of the interactions between those involved in the process (teacher, child, parents and others); a variety of teaching styles is essential to support effective learning; and, most importantly, the child should be at the centre of the teaching and learning process. It is only through developing such shared values that the curriculum can be truly coordinated.

References

Bell, D. and Ritchie, R. (1999) *Towards Effective Subject Leadership in the Primary School*. Buckingham: Open University Press.

Day, C., Hall, C., Gammage, P. and Coles, M. (1993) *Leadership and Curriculum in the Primary School*. London: Paul Chapman.

Day, C., Hall, C. and Whitaker, P. (1998) *Developing Leadership in Primary Schools*. London: Paul Chapman.

DfEE (Department for Education and Employment) (1999) *The National Curriculum: Handbook for Primary Teachers in England*. London: QCA.

Kerr, J.F. (ed.) (1968) *Changing the Curriculum*. London: University of London Press.

O'Neill, J. (1996) Conclusion: co-ordinating teaching or learning?, in J. O'Neill and N. Kitson (eds) *Effective Curriculum Management: Co-ordinating Learning in the Primary School*. London: Routledge.

Pollard, A. and Tann, S. (1987) *Reflective Teaching in the Primary School*. London: Cassell Education.

Porter, J. (1996) Issues in teacher training, in B. Carpenter, R. Ashdown, and K. Bovair (eds) *Enabling Access: Effective Teaching and Learning for Pupils with Learning Difficulties*. London: David Fulton.

Southworth, G. (1994) The learning school, in P. Ribbins and E. Burridge (eds) *Improving Education: Promoting Quality in Schools*. London: Cassell.

Southworth, G. (1996) Improving primary schools: shifting the emphasis and clarifying the focus, *School Organisation*, 16(3): 263–80.

TTA (Teacher Training Agency) (1998) *National Standards for Subject Leaders*. London: TTA.

Underwood, J. (1996) Co-ordinating information technology in the primary school, in J. O'Neill and N. Kitson (eds) *Effective Curriculum Management: Co-ordinating Learning in the Primary School*. London: Routledge.

West, N. (1995) *Middle Management in the Primary School*. London: David Fulton.

Whiteside, T. (1996) The role of the co-ordinator auditing for development, in J. O'Neill and N. Kitson (eds) *Effective Curriculum Management: Co-ordinating Learning in the Primary School*. London: Routledge.

Index